ESCAPE

How We Can Fix Everything by Fixing Our Money

SAM GOLD

ISBN: 979-8-89316-764-1 - Paperback
ISBN: 979-8-89316-765-8 - Hardcover
ISBN: 979-8-89316-763-4 - eBook

Cover design: *Wandering Words Media*
Illustrations: *Gold*
Interior Design: based on the LODE template https://www.lode.de/template.

Libertinus © 2003-2022 SIL Open Font License, Version 1.1.
http://www.sil.org/

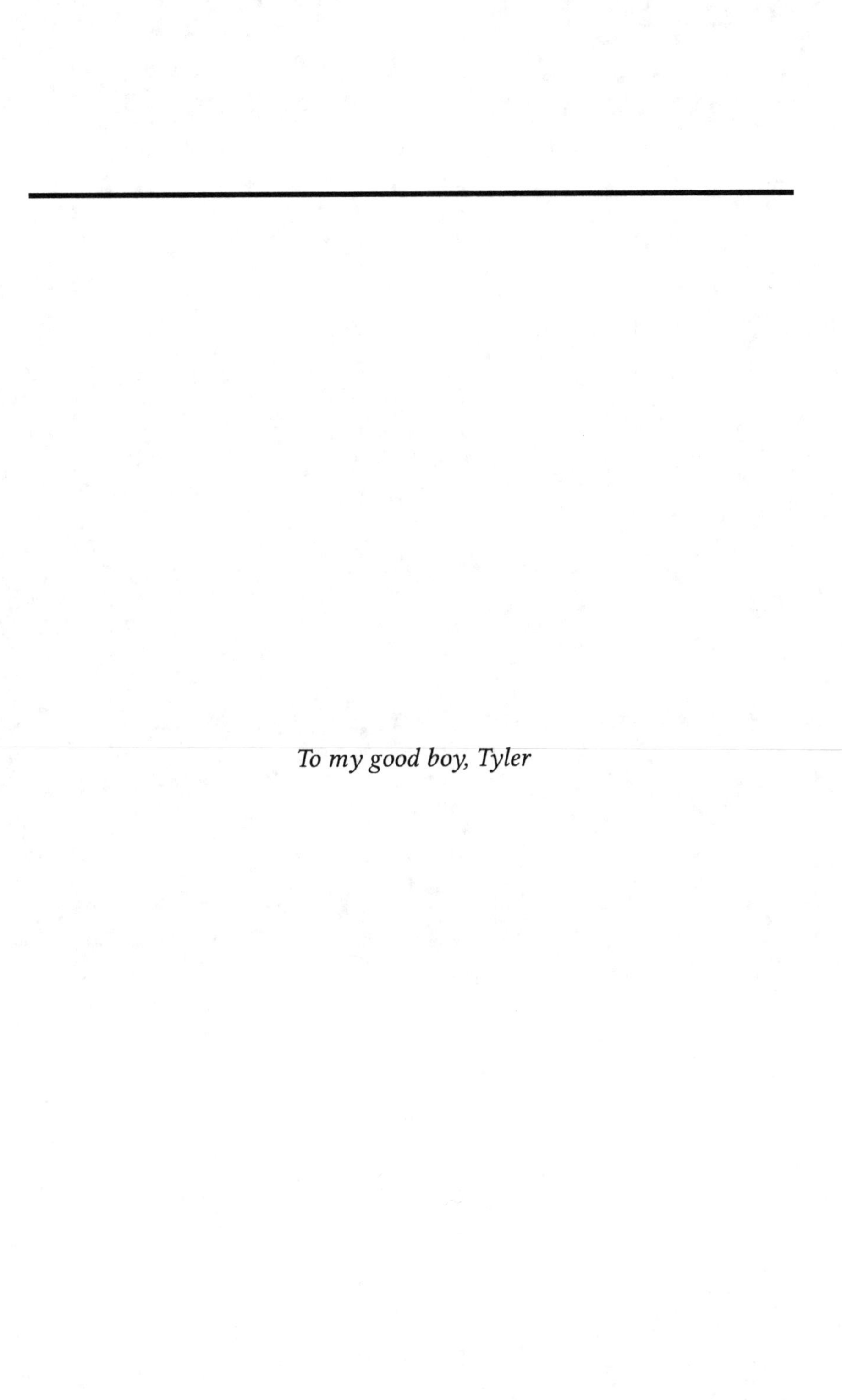

To my good boy, Tyler

ACKNOWLEDGMENTS

Our escape is possible thanks to the giants among us: those clear-headedly analyzing our situation here on the earth—Ludwig von Mises, Friedrich August von Hayek, Murray Rothbard, Jörg G. Hülsmann, Thomas Sowell, Tom Woods, Jr., Gertrude Margaret Coogan, Hans-Hermann Hoppe, Walter Block, Walter Williams, Leonard E. Read, Rudolph J. Rummel, David Bohm, and, of course, too many more to list here; the brilliant engineers and scientists finding ways to achieve scarcity in the inherently non-scarce world of computers, e.g., the designers of bitcoin and other cryptocurrencies—Satoshi Nakamoto, Evan Duffield, Daniel Diaz, Vitalik Buterin, and many more; the brilliant engineers and scientists discovering how to regrow human limbs—Ken Muneoka, Manjong Han, David M. Gardiner, and more; and those discovering how to measure plant respiration rates remotely—Gina H. Mohammed, Pablo J. Zarco-Tejada, John R. Miller, and again many more. Because of their contributions, we can finally escape to our science-fiction future (*Jetsons*, not *Bladerunner*).

This work was made possible thanks to excellent editing. Special thanks must be given here for the high-quality editorial feedback received from Shawn Wright and Joseph Montana. Kindly making time in their busy schedules, they caught copy, content, and development mistakes and provided valuable, correction-aiding feedback. Any mistakes remaining are the author's, and to the extent he got anything right it is substantially thanks to them.

CONTENTS

Part VI. Appendices — 213

PREFACE

Dear Political Peer here in one of these fifty united[1] States of America:

I'm reaching out to you because we need to talk about money. And more than just talk about it, we need to do something about it. As you may know, our federal government is bankrupt, meaning we, as a group, are bankrupt. This crisis is far graver than it may first appear, fueling widespread poverty, crime, and environmental degradation. Compounding the problem, our U.S. dollars' status as the de facto reserve money of the world exports these issues globally, affecting all of humanity. Our situation is intolerable, yet, as you will soon discover, escape from those plagues is within reach. In the chapters ahead, we will learn our group has the power to transform our national money in such a way our situation becomes not just tolerable, but excellent. In this work, the claim is made, and defended, that our group has the power to fix everything, without any one of us knowing how. We'll show how a simple modification to our money will cause our high division of labor price discovery machine to produce wealth not poverty, morality not crime, and health not environmental degradation.

I'm a retired aerospace engineer who spent his career designing and testing automatic control systems. Thanks to this background, and some extra-curricular reading, it has become obvious to me we can use our US dollars as a feedback mechanism in an automatic control system that solves humanity's big problems. In my work, I used optimization techniques to search for the best possible control systems. Here, I believe we can use our federal government to implement an optimizer that automatically searches for the best version of this new control system.

---

[1] A small u is used in deference to the title of the Declaration of Independence, which reads: "The unanimous Declaration of the thirteen united States of America." In this work, a capital U is used when conceptualizing our political group in a unitary fashion; e.g., "The United States warned Russia not to mess with NATO." A small u is used when conceptualizing our political group as a group of 50 political peers; e.g., "The thirteen states united to bring into existence a government to serve at their pleasure, eventually referred to as the federal government."

Ranger Rick from the National Wildlife Federation gets the credit for starting me down this path. He taught me the people from the big city were hurting the woods critters and made me want to help. Later, other authors taught me some of the people in the big city were hurting others in the big city, too, and much of the harm the city dwellers were causing was the unintended result of complex factors. Eventually, I discovered money was involved. As I learned more, the pieces of information began fitting together like the pieces of a jigsaw puzzle, forming a stunningly gorgeous picture. In this work, I'll paint the picture in words, holding it up for you to see, saying "Look! We can escape, right now! We have everything we need!"

In essence, I'm proposing the way we save the world is we don't. Instead, we build a machine to do it for us. After learning the details presented here, I sincerely hope you come to the same conclusion, and help us all escape to a new and greatly improved Spaceship Earth.[2]

In love and peace,
Sam Gold
13 December, 2025

---

[2] R. Buckminster Fuller popularized the term "Spaceship Earth" to describe our planet. He felt we're all passengers on Spaceship Earth, and should work together to keep our world healthy [1]. The term was used at least as early as 1879 by Henry George, while George Orwell, Adlai Stevenson, Barbara Ward, and Fuller developed the concept further over the next century [2].

INTRODUCTION: FIXING IT ALL WITH MONEY

There's something each of us does every day without being aware of it: we earn and spend gold. We think we're earning and spending US dollars, and we are. However, as will be detailed throughout this work, dealing with dollars means dealing with gold. A US dollar is a fixed weight of gold, by statute, treaty, and custom, and is officially referred to as a gold US dollar, or gold dollar. This language is used in official federal government documents such as, for one example, the text of the 1934 Gold Reserve Act, which states in part: "Nor shall the weight of the gold dollar be fixed in any event at more than 60 per centum of its present weight" [SEC. 12 of 3]. Our US dollars are known as gold dollars partly because they each consist of a fixed weight of gold, and partly because they could consist of a fixed weight of something other than gold. For example, a US dollar could be a fixed weight of silver, as it was in the past, and could be called a silver US dollar if that were true today. A dollar is an unambiguous, fixed amount of something, but it doesn't have to be any particular thing, like gold or silver. It can be whatever We, the People, in our capacity as a collective, say it is. We're used to thinking of earning or spending US dollars, and few of us stop to think about what we're using as money. For good reasons, we tend to focus exclusively on how many of them we have or need rather than what they are.

There's something else we all do that rarely or never enters our consciousness: we spend and earn dollar *bills*[1] in our financial dealings, not dollars. We think we're dealing with dollars, which is true, but at the same time not true. When we spend or earn a dollar *bill*, we've spent or earned a *bill*, not a dollar. Each dollar *bill* is an IOU for a dollar, by the full faith and credit of We, the People, but the bank has closed. Dollars and dollar *bills* are no longer equivalent, and it is an important difference.

---

[1]*Bill* is emphasized as a memory aid in the present work because the difference between a dollar and a dollar *bill* is central to our escape.

Our lack of awareness of these subtle and seemingly trivial details about our national money is a deep blind spot exploitable for our escape, from our present problem-filled world to a paradise planet. What we use as money has consequences, and this fact can be manipulated to our advantage.

We, the People, have the power to design and adopt new and improved US dollars, changing *what* we use as money and, therefore, changing its consequences. We also have the power to continue to use US dollar *bills*, making changes to our US dollars effectively invisible to their users, and to make those *bills* naturally electronic in form. Here, a business proposal is made to We, the People, of the United States of America, to exercise our powers and change our US dollars so they bring us the consequences we want. It is a business proposal because herein we'll defer to the "Official Story"[2] in which, through our federal government agents, We, the People, come together to take actions as if we were one. This Official Story is memorialized in the traditional motto of the United States: *E pluribus unum*—Latin for "Out of many, one." In an example relevant to this business proposal, when our U.S. Department of the Treasury borrows money, we are acting as one and borrowing money. In another relevant example, we're in the banking business together, banking our gold US dollars in our vault at Fort Knox.

Thinking of us as a collective, or perhaps more usefully as a fifty-strong committee of giant committees (one for each state), this proposal can be considered a motion to be put forward for a vote by the committee. Because this committee controls the production of the world reserve money, our US dollars, and because of the material reality of currently available data and software, this proposal will, if accepted, change our US dollars so they cause the lives of everyone on the planet to improve dramatically.

We have the power to make this happen due to how the committee fits into our worldwide systems of production. If we divide those systems into owners, managers, and workers, we are presented with the opportunity to keep focused on which group we are, and behave

---

[2]It is understood the actual story isn't necessarily the same as the Official Story. The Official Story is used here as a way of exercising our kung fu, bending like the willow and using the Story to our advantage. If we're told we're in business together, electing represenatives and "voluntarily" paying taxes for them to spend, then so be it. "We" are in business together, and "we" will be making the decisions from now on. "We" will be the "deciders," as one of us reputedly said.

that way. Specifically, this fifty-strong committee of committees owns the right to produce US dollars and dollar *bills*. It guards that right jealously, requiring its agents to deal swiftly and violently with individuals who manufacture their own. Owners hire managers, who hire workers. Workers do the work, and managers do the work of getting the work done by hiring workers. The committee is presented with an opportunity to make a decision about the production of our US dollars, and rely on its management team at the US Department of the Treasury to implement that decision by hiring the job out to the appropriate workers. Making this decision and thereby causing the desired change to our US dollars is something the committee really can accomplish—as is made clear in this work, the proposed decision is one we committee members all want it to make. As we'll demonstrate, miracles can happen, and We, the People, can make them happen by thinking and acting like the owners we are.

To persuade us to make the proposed decision, we'll follow the money in Part I to determine what *has happened*, and engineer the money in Part II to determine what *will happen*. Following the money, we'll discover our US dollars have serious negative consequences, and those negative consequences can't be eliminated without design changes either to human nature or the dollars themselves. Choosing design changes to the money rather than human nature, we'll find those negative consequences can be transformed into positive by 1) designing a new kind of US dollars that inverts our current US dollars' energy flow, implementing an automatic control system, 2) sizing the control system loop gain appropriately, freeing us from our federal government revenuers, and 3) setting the money free, implementing an optimizer that searches for improved versions of the control system. Then, to change this from a theoretical to a real-world exercise, in Part III we'll learn an easy administrative action we can take to manufacture and adopt the new and improved money, and in Part IV we'll learn what each of us can do to make it happen. We can think of our group as a team for the purpose of creating these new US dollars, each doing his or her part to achieve the goal.

As we're about to discover, We, the People, can engineer and adopt new and improved money that advances us swiftly and surely into our science-fiction future. Curiously, we're also going to discover money can grow on trees, contrary to what our parents told us. So let's follow the money, engineer it, and look forward to meeting up on the outside.

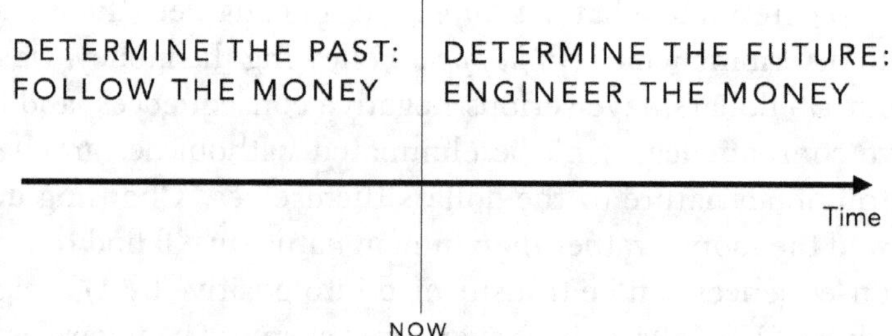
DETERMINE THE PAST:
FOLLOW THE MONEY
DETERMINE THE FUTURE:
ENGINEER THE MONEY
Time
NOW

Part I.

Hell on Earth: Cheated with Money

1. POVERTY, CRIME, ENVIRONMENTAL DEGRADATION

FOLLOWING the money, we all sense we're being cheated as we watch prices run away, making us work harder and harder to pay our bills. Many keep sliding closer to the cliff edge of insolvency, with some falling over it—one of the most disastrous things that can happen to a person [4–20].

As prices rise and rise, then rise more, we watch helplessly, hoping to earn more money in a desperate race to keep up. We anxiously watch the homeless encampments grow, more springing up every month, and feel the chill wind on our necks as we hope we don't join them, or the sickening horror if it already happened. Every day more of us fall off the cliff from solvent to insolvent, and every day the rest of us dig our heels in more, knowing we're getting dragged closer to the edge regardless. We wonder how we'll feed our families as we watch the price of butter go up a little more, and the price of milk a little more. We get our daily mail in dread of the landlord raising our rent beyond what we can afford, or the county raising our property tax beyond what we can pay.

Yours truly recently got an earful from his automobile mechanic about his price woes. He said parts get more expensive every week, and it isn't feasible to simply pass the price increases on to customers—he has to eat part of them since he knows his customers, too, are suffering from general price increases. Every year his property taxes go up, and he's one of the lucky ones who owns his property. The mechanics who rent are in even bigger trouble as their rents go up. Every year his taxes increase; this year, he repaired 25 percent more cars than last year, but his net income went down 20 percent. His labor expenses have to increase every year because his employees' rent, grocery, and medical expenses keep going up. The oil recycler used to pay him $1 per gallon for used oil but now charges $1 per gallon, and his costs to recycle other consumables, such as oil filters, air filters, brake fluid, and so on, are also increasing. It wasn't hard to feel the fear behind those words as the trend didn't start just this year or last. The mechanic, and all of us, can see which way prices are headed. We know the only difference between tent-people and roofs-over-their-heads-people is a relentlessly shrinking savings account.

We may even close our eyes and hope to open them in a sane world with sane prices, but we don't. We know this isn't just a bad dream—terrifyingly and implacably, it's really happening [21]. We know from our history books price runaways can and do ruin millions upon millions of people just like ourselves. According to a report from the CATO Institute, seventeen hyperinflationary runaways, each starting just like the price increases we're seeing now [22], happened in countries all around the world in the twentieth century alone [23]. Hyperinflationary price runaways have affected people even in the author's small circle of friends—his friend from the Ukraine got wiped out when she was only twenty five years old, with a new baby, and another friend's parents in Romania got wiped out twice.

A sense of where we're headed, absent a course correction, can be found in an example involving just one individual, from just one of those terrible hyperinflationary runaways. This example took place in the Weimar Republic of Germany after World War I, and remember to multiply it by millions for a real sense of the horror. From Hans Eicholz's discussion[1] of a tragic story from Frederick Taylor's *The Downfall of Money: Germany's Hyperinflation and the Destruction of the Middle Class* [25]:

> One particularly arresting story is that of Maximilian Bern, a man of literary education exemplary of Germany's formerly middle class *Bildungsbürgertum*. In 1923, writes Taylor, he "withdrew all his savings—100,000 marks, formerly sufficient to support a modestly comfortable retirement—and purchased all it would buy by that time: a subway ticket. The old gentleman took a last ride around the city, then went back to his apartment and locked himself in."
>
> If you are like me, you probably assumed the next sentence would conclude with suicide. No. "There he died of hunger."

---

[1]Eicholz described the evil of an inflating money supply in his 2014 essay *The Currency of Destruction* [24].

I had to linger over that sentence to fully grasp the reality: starvation in a society that had recently been among the most technologically and commercially advanced of any on Earth. [24]

This pervasive threat of running out of money, and resulting exposure to the desperate crimes of others also running out of money [19], is bad enough, but unfortunately, there's more. Our money problems incentivize us to harm our living world, upon which we depend completely to live. This threatens our lives as much as going broke, though we may not think much about harm to our living world when we're struggling to pay bills. Upon pausing and pondering the situation, however, the extent of our complete dependence on the fellow living beings with whom we share this small world becomes obvious—we're so dependent we don't even get to breathe without the oxygen produced by our helpful friends the plant people.[2]

The incentive to harm our living world results from the fact that, while a few manage to benefit in this rising price environment, most struggle to make their incomes meet ever-increasing expenditures.[3] One of the means utilized to increase income is of course to produce more, and thus earn more. Because to produce, consumers must participate in supply chains turning raw materials from the agriculture, timber, and mining sectors into retail products,[4] producing more causes us to consume more raw materials, leaving less for our living world. In short, our money problems are incentivizing us to harm our living world by incentivizing us to make our supply chains more productive, to produce more products to sell to get more money to pay our bills.

---

[2]Here we use the animistic worldview held by our ancestors, who called the trees the tree people, the strawberries the strawberry people, and so on (this viewpoint is being adopted by an increasing number of modern biologists [26]). For example, Grandfather Stalking Wolf, an Apache scout who was the subject of the book *Grandfather* [27], by Tom Brown, Jr., spoke of the deer people, the pheasant people, and so on, and even the rock people and the water people. For him, as for many of our ancestors, the entire world is alive and sentient.

[3]Charles Hugh Smith explained that the purchasing power of wages here in the fifty states has declined over time [28]

[4]To earn a living, we all must participate in supply chains in one way or the other. One can participate directly, for instance, if you design integrated circuits for a living, or indirectly, for instance, if you train people at the gym who themselves participate directly. We're all part of the complex web of supply chains turning raw materials into retail products and services, as was brilliantly described by Leonard Read in his 1958 essay *I, Pencil* [29], later extended to interest rates by Tom Mullen in *I, Interest Rate* [30].

Increasing economic inequality, as the few beneficiaries of the rising prices get richer while the rest don't, also results in the wealthier and more powerful imposing environmental degradation costs on the less wealthy and less powerful [31–33]. The general biologically-impactful side effects of production activities and economic inequalities are depleting wildlife, depleting wildlife habitat, and pollution. Additionally, as described further in Chapter 8, our money problems incentivize us to consume rather than save, tending also to increase raw material consumption, wildlife loss, and pollution. Consistent with these dynamics, it looks like our living world is in real trouble [33–131, pp. 365 - 381 of 132]. Worse, it is now unambiguously obvious that in damaging our non-human living world we're hurting sensitive beings who feel pain, care about their children, and don't want to die [133–135].[5] The only silver lining to this cloud is we humans are not born to be, and don't have to be, planet wreckers. The situation instead is we're more or less compelled to harm our world to earn a living [120, 136].[6]

Worldwide, we're caught in a fatal dilemma: we have to work harder to pay our bills, but we have to stop working harder because it's killing our world. Many of us don't even have time to think about how to stop killing our world because we have to spend all our time killing it, so we can pay our bills while prices are running away. Though we don't always connect them, the two parts of the dilemma aren't a secret; many attempts have been made to fix each.

To fix the price runaways, we, through our government agents, have interfered with individuals' economic decisions. We've implemented price ceilings, price floors, subsidies, tariffs, public works, and any other intervention we could dream up [137]. But prices stubbornly continue to rise [138, 139]. Meanwhile, our growing pool of the poorest gets

---

[5]In the Spring 2023 issue of *PETA Global* magazine, Lisa Jones-Engel reported, "The monkey jumped right onto my lap and grabbed my cheeks. I gasped, thinking she might tear off my face. But she just sat there, her face so close to mine, for the longest time. It was as if she were trying to make me *really* see her. . . . Each one of them [monkeys in primate research labs] was an individual with a mind and emotions like the monkey who grabbed my face and helped me see" [135].

[6]The September 27, 2023 proposal by the New York Stock Exchange (NYSE) to the Securities and Exchange Commission (SEC) to list Natural Asset Companies (NACs) states, "Although there is significant demand to deploy financial capital toward sustainability, stewards of natural landscapes have often had little choice other than extractive development to fund their budgets or garner a return on investment" [120].

sicker and poorer [20, 140, 141], more victimized by crime, and even lonelier [142]. Stansberry reported in 2017 the bottom 60 percent of us struggle to raise even a few hundred dollars for an emergency, and have saved less than $20,000 for retirement. Such poor financial situations correspond with deteriorating health, with a 20 percent increase in premature deaths since 2000 [p. 10 of 6]. Whatever the effects of these economic interferences, making the great mass of people healthier and wealthier doesn't appear to be among them.

To spare our living world from harm, various groups have been helping out. Conservation groups such as The Nature Conservancy have been using charitable contributions to buy land and protect it with conservation easements. Government departments, such as the US Forest Service, have been incentivizing some forested parcel owners to keep their land healthy with payments for certain ecosystem services [143]. Some hunting and fishing groups have been providing similar incentives with payments to landowners for the ecosystem services of game to hunt and fish to catch. Groups like the Sierra Club and the Natural Resources Defense Council have been lobbying our elected representatives to enact protective statutes[7] and suing those who violate the statutes. The Savory Institute manages grasslands to facilitate its large-scale regeneration [146, 147], groups like American Forests [148] and the Arbor Day Foundation [149] work to get more trees planted and fewer cut down, and many others are working various aspects of our environmental problems.

If what all these people have been doing is helping, it's not helping enough [121]. Australian journalist Caitlin Johnstone reports:

> We are witnessing a mass extinction the likes of which we
> haven't seen since the end of the dinosaurs 65 million years ago,
> with some 200 species going extinct forever every single day.
> The very ecosystemic context in which we evolved is vanishing

---

[7]Statutes are invented laws imposed on populations by princes, kings, parliaments, legislatures, etc. Statutory laws can be contrasted with discovered laws, such as our Anglo-Saxon customary law traditions, the Catholic Canon law, the Jewish Mosaic law, and the Xeer tradition of Somalia. Discovered laws can come in the form of, for example, the amount of damages awarded by an Anglo-Saxon jury for assault or battery if it finds one of those has occurred. Discovered laws are called discovered because our ancestors used an initially unwritten process of trial and error to discover ways to make their lives better with high quality dispute resolution [144, 145].

underneath us. More than half the world's wildlife has vanished in forty years, and the worldwide insect population has plummeted by as much as 90 percent. Fertile soil is vanishing, and so are forests. The oceans are choking to death, 90 percent of global fish stocks are either fully fished or overfished, the seas are full of microplastics, and phytoplankton, an indispensable foundation of Earth's food chain, have been killed off by 40 percent since 1950. [150]

Worse, some things being done to help may instead be hurting. In one example, many hope solar panels and wind turbines will reduce the chance of catastrophic global warming. However, dimming that hope, they rely heavily on taxpayer subsidies [151], may not be able to meet world economic demand for energy even in theory [152], and wildlife destruction, wildlife habitat destruction, water contamination, colonization, toxic and voluminous waste, slave labor, greenhouse gas emissions, and wars are unintended side effects of their manufacture, operation, and disposal [122, 152–171]. In another example, many of us diligently put our plastic refuse in the recycling bin, hoping to reduce pollution, but we now know much of it "is dumped into rivers, fields or oceans halfway around the Earth" [172]. Corroborating that story, former EPA administrator Judith Enck and Last Beach Cleanup founder Jan Dell have informed us, "Plastic recycling does not work and will never work" [173].

Similar to our poverty reduction attempts, our efforts to eliminate environmental degradation aren't working, and time isn't our friend.

2. THE COLLECTIVE'S PROBLEMATIC GOLD US DOLLARS

PRICES are running away, causing poverty and therefore crime and environmental degradation, but why? Supply and demand changes can and do make prices change, but typically can't make them change too much, and not over substantial periods. This kind of price stability is caused by consumers purchasing lower-cost substitutes when prices rise. For example, they may purchase margarine if butter prices rise, or see medical doctors (MD) if doctors of osteopathy (DO) prices rise. Because of this substitution effect, supply and demand issues generally aren't known to cause the economy-encompassing price increases we've been observing over the years. If supply and demand issues aren't responsible for sustained price increases of seemingly everything, what could it be?

Upon observing all prices include the common numerator of money, such as dollars/apple or dollars/orange, the culprit becomes apparent: the one thing that can make prices of almost everything rise over time is increases in the quantity of money in circulation [174, 175].[1] It is a simple matter of more money chasing the goods and services. More dollars means more dollars/apple and dollars/orange, all other things being equal. The Weimar Republic hyperinflationary runaway of 1923 provides an infamous example of this dynamic; the quantity of money in circulation ran away, and so did prices.

Has the number of US dollars in circulation been increasing? No, but prices have been rising anyway. How could that be? Prices have been rising because we use dollar *bills* to complete transactions, not dollars, and the number of dollar *bills* in circulation has been increasing (Figure 2.1 [177]). But a dollar *bill* is a note worth a dollar, so how can

---

[1]Peter Bernholz found the highest price inflations, including all known cases of hyperinflation, occurred exclusively under fiat paper money regimes, in which governments greatly expanded the money supply [176].

the number of *bills* be increasing but not the number of dollars? The answer is it can't—a dollar *bill* is as good as a dollar, at least according to the Official Story. Unfortunately, however, that story is a fiction.[2]

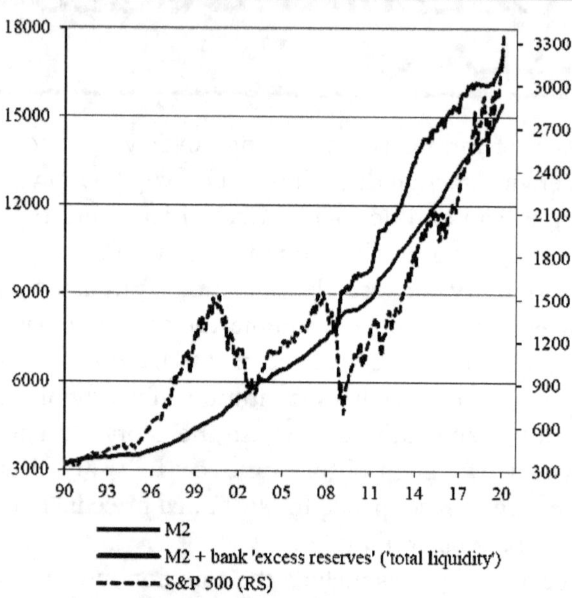

Figure 2.1. *M2 (US dollar bills in circulation; left axis, US$ bn), S&P500 (right axis, S&P500 index) vs. time. (Plot courtesy of Mises Institute, https://www.mises.org.)*

A US dollar is defined as $1/42\frac{2}{9}$ (~1/42.2222) of an ounce of gold[3] [180–184] and a dollar *bill* is a note communicating ownership of a dollar. A

---

[2]M2 in Figure 2.1 is a measure of the number of US dollar *bills* in circulation. It includes currency, coins, savings deposits, and money market funds. S&P500 in the figure is the Standard and Poor's 500 Index, a capitalization-weighted stock market index measuring the performance of 500 large publicly traded companies in these united States.

[3]The Bretton Woods Agreements Act of 1976 [SEC. 6 of 178] repealed section 2 of the 1972 Par Value Modification Act [SEC. 2 of 179], which had defined a gold US dollar as 1/38 of a fine troy ounce of gold. The 1973 reenactment of the 1972 Par Value Modification Act had subsequently defined a dollar as 1/42.2222 of an ounce of gold [180], but it too was effectively repealed by the 1976 Bretton Woods Agreements Act. However, the US Department of the Treasury records $42.22 in

dollar *bill* is to a dollar as the deed to your house is to the house. When we buy and sell dollar *bills*, we are theoretically buying and selling ownership of dollars, each of which is a fixed weight of gold. However, the reality doesn't match the theory as there are more dollar *bills* in circulation than there are dollars in the vault.

This situation has come about due to certain properties of gold, along with the natural desire of any energy-consuming being to get low-cost energy. This desire has led some to take advantage of a societal vulnerability to which the use of gold as money has exposed us. It is the fact our US dollars consist of gold,[4] along with this natural desire to minimize energy expenditures, that is at the root of our runaway prices and, therefore, many of our other problems.

The use of gold as money exposes us to many of our big problems due to a pair of shortcomings. First, it causes environmental degradation problems directly (and, unfortunately, crime problems in some cases [189]) because landowners can get paid by excavating their land and spending any recovered gold into circulation. Second, it exposes its users to price runaways, and therefore environmental degradation indirectly, as a side effect of its weight and bulk. Because it's heavy and bulky it's inconvenient to carry, and worse, dangerous—its bulk can make it visible, making the carrier a target for thieves.

In the long long ago, there was still a lot of healthy land, so the first problem, damaging the earth[5] to mine gold, wasn't considered a problem by the miners and others in their societies. But the second problem was different. Losing your gold and maybe even your life in a robbery was something to be avoided if you could. Possibly for around 3,000 years, starting in Babylon [p. 52 of 191], consumers have taken to solving gold's robbery problem with increasingly negotiable

---

its books for each ounce of our gold [August 31, 2025 report from 181]. While it appears our elected representatives forgot to keep our documents up-to-date, the guardians of our treasure implicitly recognize every forty-two and two-ninths dollar *bills* as a claim on a fine troy ounce of gold.

[4]Starting with the Coinage Act of 1792, there was a bimetallic system in the United States [pp. 130 - 131 of 185, 186]. In this system, a US dollar was officially defined as both a fixed weight of silver and a fraction, 1/15 [p. 130 of 185, **CHAP. XVI**, Sec 9 of 187], and then later, with the US Coin Act of 1834, 1/16 of that weight of gold [p. 131 of 185, **CHAP. XCV**, Sec 1 of 188], and still later abandoned for a gold-only system.

[5]Other than quotations, in this work our world is referred to as "the earth," rather than "Earth," in honor of the fact it is special, our only home, not just one of the nine planets [190].

(can be transferred to a different party) paper instruments. The earliest such instruments could only be redeemed in money by a specific party, as described in the original creation of the paper or papyrus. Later instruments were made out to a specific party but could be signed over to another party who could redeem it instead. At the end of this evolutionary process, the paper notes were inherently bearer assets, with no one's name on them, freely negotiable and payable to the physical bearer of the note [ch. 6 of 192]. In other words, consumers solved the robbery problem by paying a third party to store their gold and carrying paper receipts for it instead of the gold itself. If the third party is known to be trustworthy, always redeeming receipts on demand, users of gold tend to trust the receipts and conduct business directly with them, instead of redeeming first and completing their transactions with gold [p. 38 of 185].

The problem is when users get habituated to the receipts, rarely redeeming them for gold, third parties always[6] end up cheating their customers by surreptitiously spending more paper receipts into circulation than there is gold in the vault [p. 53 of 191, 185, 193].[7] It works for everybody—vault owners can profit by loaning at interest gold they don't have, and vault owners issuing paper claims to gold are providing a legitimate service to society, at least to the extent they don't issue more receipts than they have gold. Paper claims to gold have greater divisibility and portability than gold, with similar durability, giving them important advantages over gold in regional and global commerce [ch. 8 of 192]. These advantages increase the economic demand for paper over gold—in other words, everyone likes easy money [194]. While the divisibility and portability of paper claims to gold have given them competitive advantages over gold, the paper claims are also burdened

---

[6]"Always," not "often" or "sometimes," is indeed the correct term here. Hülsmann [185], Cantelon [191], and Griffin [193] informed us every bank in known history has eventually succumbed to the temptation to practice what is now euphemistically referred to as "fractional reserve" banking. As Hülsmann noted regarding this tendency, "A look at the history of institutions reveals this temptation was virtually impossible to resist. . ." [p. 40 of 185].

[7]When a vault owner promises to return an equal amount of gold on demand, but not necessarily the same gold deposited, the deposit is a *mutuum* [184]. Vault owners did this, and still do it, without notifying their depositors, who believe their gold, or paper claims to gold in the case of modern banks, remains in a situation of *depositum*. In a *depositum*, gold deposits remain the property of the depositor when in the vault, and the vault owner has promised to return not just the same weight of gold, but the same gold [184].

with the competitive disadvantage of being easy to print. This causes the paper to be less scarce than gold, in turn causing monetary system instability [ch. 8 of 192]. Historically, every third party, or bank, that issued fraudulent receipts for its gold was eventually driven out of business [193, p. 212 of 185]. The business would end with an old-school style run in which holders of paper receipts (the gold depositors) realize their receipts might be fraudulent and "run" to the vault at the same time and empty it, with latecomers getting stiffed because the gold is gone.[8] In modern times, the problem has been compounded by the new version of third-party vault owners—banks. Instead of storing gold, banks store paper receipts for gold, also known as dollar *bills*, or "base money" [ch. 15 of 192], in their vaults. In the same way it's easier to carry paper than gold, it is generally easier to carry and transact with a credit card or cell phone than with paper, especially remotely. Therefore, market participants have taken to transacting with electronic claims to paper claims to gold, and unsurprisingly, these modern third-party vault owners have taken advantage of the situation. Old times gold vault owners would issue more paper than there was gold in the vault, and modern banks issue more electronic claims to paper, also known as "broad money" [ch. 15 of 192], than there is paper in the vault. They accomplish this by crediting lenders' accounts when a loan is taken out without debiting the accounts of the bank's other customers [ch. 15 of 192]. This is done with the approval of our federal government banking statutes and rules and regulations, which only require banks to hold a fraction of their book claims in physical paper in the vault.

We the People, with 7,413 tonnes[9] of gold in Our vault at Fort Knox, are in this late-game situation—the collective of us has spent many more receipts into circulation than there is gold in the vault.[10] We've

---

[8]See the movie *It's A Wonderful Life* [195] for an uplifting story revolving around a barely averted bank run. In this story, the customers of Bailey Brothers Building and Loan, fearing for their money after hearing rumors of insolvency, "run" to the bank at the same time in hopes of rescuing their savings [196]. Unfortunately, deposit-destroying bank runs occur regularly here in the real world, ruining many thousands of fractional-reserve banks and their depositors [197].

[9]According to the US Department of the Treasury, our gold treasure consists of 261,498,926.241 troy ounces, or 7,413.37 tonnes [181] (a tonne is a metric ton, which is 1,000 kilograms, or 2,204.6 pounds, as opposed to a US, or short ton, which is 2,000 pounds).

[10]According to some accounts from people in the know, around half our gold is in the vault beneath the New York Federal Reserve building, and encumbered. In his 1973 book *The Day the Dollar Dies*, Cantelon reported there are over a hundred

been cheating our customers by printing excess paper claims on our gold and spending them into circulation. The same as for previous cheating vault owners, our day of reckoning looms.

---

thousand gold bars in that vault, marked with the stamps of the central banks of over seventy foreign countries [p. 44 of 191]. Lips reported in 2002 the US gold reserve has not been audited independently since 1955. In September of 2000, more than 54 million ounces of gold were switched from the "Gold Bullion Reserve" category to the "Custodial Gold Bullion" category in the Treasury Report, with no explanation. Lips said subsequently, in the May 2001 Treasury Report, the "Reserve" and "Custodial" gold categories had been replaced with a "Deep Storage Gold" category, and then-Secretary of the Treasury Paul H. O'Neill had not yet responded to inquiries about the matter [p. 227 of 186]. For the purposes of settling our bankruptcy, as will be described later, the important part is to find out exactly how much gold We, the People, truly own, so We can give Our creditors the correct haircut (how much gold creditors will get in the bankruptcy settlement vs. how much we owe them).

3. THE COLLECTIVE HAS A SPENDING PROBLEM

GOLD enables the price runaways because its weight, bulk, and limited divisibility incentivizes third-party vault storage, with receipts for gold instead of gold in circulation, but doesn't cause them. The vault owner still has to do the surreptitious fraudulent receipt deed. Back in the day, vault owners would do it on their own due to economic incentives—it was profitable, and if they didn't do it their competitors would, attracting gold deposits to the competitors' vaults [ch. 8 of 192]. In our highfalutin modern times, we do it by committee, for the common good, at least that's what we tell ourselves. In reality, we do the surreptitious deed for the less noble reason of attempting to get something for nothing.

Here in the States, the vault owner is the committee[1] known as We, the People, who have been facilitating the common good with our federal government system. In this system, the people of each of the states choose representatives who in turn choose how to spend the national treasure [198]. It sounds innocuous on a surface level, but the devil is in the details.

The dynamics of individuals working to control how the national treasure is spent get the collective caught in a debt trap because the collective has created a commons and, therefore, a tragedy of the commons.[2] The commons, in this case, is the huge pot of money resulting

---

[1]The committee, or the fifty committees (one per state) forming the big committee of states that created our federal government, is merely a group or groups of people. The committees can take actions, and their individual members can take other actions. The odd part about our national situation is the big committee is stealing from the members of its fifty constituent committees.

[2]The classic example of a tragedy of the commons is when several families use a field not owned by any of them for grazing. If each family only uses their fair share of the field's grazing resources, everything is fine. The tragedy happens because, as explained by Hardin, building on Lloyd [p. 17 of 199], each family has an economic incentive to graze more than their fair share. Each family knows the other families know this, so they all end up competing to graze as much as possible before the field gets ruined, and sure enough, the field gets ruined.

from the collective spending a lot of money identifying and solving problems. As of the mid-2020s, this commons exists in the form of an approximately \$7 trillion yearly national budget.[3]

The same as for other commons, it is in the best interest of individuals, families, companies, and so on to get as much as they can from the collective's giant pot of money while contributing as little as they can. The mechanics of the tragedy in this case are a result of the fact that, all else being equal, the representative who votes to spend more of that giant pot of money on the people she represents than does her competition, and tax them less, has the better chance of being reelected [ch. 19 of 192]. Also, all else being equal, representatives who vote to spend more money on guns, tanks, bombs, and aircraft carriers to protect us have better chances of being reelected [201], especially if those weapons contracts are awarded to their constituents.

The result has been a tendency for our elected representatives to find more ways to spend our national treasure than replenish it,[4] making it difficult for our treasury to fund the national budget. Our Treasurers have closed the gap with borrowing,[5] which unfortunately has become a more or less permanent feature of our national budgets. Christopher Whalen makes this point in his book *Inflated*, noting, "The great un-

---

[3]According to our federal government's Office of Management and Budget report, national yearly outlays are expected to be \$7 trillion in 2027 [p. 123 of 200].

[4]A representative example of the collective's spending problem is its \$1.25 trillion as of 2019 [202], and steadily growing, up to \$1.5 trillion as of 2023 [203], yearly military budget. According to some estimates, more than half of everyone's federal government taxes are spent on our military institutions [204].

[5]Sadly, the new nation, thirteen states initially, has never *not* been entangled in a debt trap. The entanglement began when speculators, including James Madison, Alexander Hamilton, and others, purchased so-called Continentals from the heroes of the revolution against King George. They only paid pennies on the dollar because too many of the notes were in circulation. When issued by the Continental Congress and the Continental Army between 1775 and 1779, recipients were promised the notes were redeemable at face value in specie, meaning gold or silver. But they were issued in great excess of the available specie, causing their market value to crash. From 1775 to 1779 the supply of Continentals increased by 5,000 percent, and their market exchange rate crashed from \$1 in 1775 to less than a penny by the end of 1779 [193, 205]. After scoring the notes for cheap, Madison, Hamilton, and others cooperated to create a national government with the power to tax, borrow, and spend. Finally, in the conclusion of their scheme, they had the new government borrow money to pay them face value for their Continentals, for a many thousands of percent profit [ch. 11 of 206, 207].

spoken secret in American life is the refusal to maintain anything like fiscal balance in the national government [p. 255 of 208]."

The problem with borrowing is finding lenders.[6] As the collective's national debt and deficits have grown, lenders have become less interested in helping it. As with any irresponsible borrower, at some point the credit risk becomes too great. The prospective lender knows if the debt gets too big the collective will eventually be unable to pay. This causes a conflict. We keep voting for representatives who promise more money and lower taxes, and the only way they can deliver is to complete the budget shortfalls with borrowing. But we, operating in our capacities as individuals, families, or companies, aren't willing to lend more to the reckless spender.

Our growing individual reluctance to lend to the collective manifests as lowered demand for its debt notes, or bonds, which tends to lower their sale prices. Lower bond prices effectively means the collective must pay higher interest rates[7] to borrow money. For example, if individuals and companies are more willing to lend, bond prices will rise, and a $1 bond may sell for $0.99. If the bond matures in one year, the collective will have paid an interest rate of about 1 percent per annum. But if those individuals and families become less willing to lend, the going price for a $1 bond may drop to, say, $0.90, for an effective annual interest rate of about 11 percent. The more market prices for treasury bonds drop, the more bonds our treasury is forced to sell to make the budget, driving their prices down and effective interest rates up even more.

This dynamic should be sufficient to decrease funding for the collectively irresponsible borrower known as "We, the People," and in a peaceful world would force it to be fiscally responsible. But the rules are different for this collective. It maintains a monopoly on violence within the geographic combined territory of our fifty states[8] and has taken advantage of this monopoly to violate the rules of civil engagement. This collective enforces tax and legal tender statutes, causing an artificial demand for its fraudulent gold receipts (the mechanics of this demand

---

[6]Anyone can lend to the national treasury by purchasing its IOU notes, known as treasury bonds or bills.

[7]The interest rate is the price, in money, of borrowed money [30].

[8]The national-level collective shares the monopoly on violence with the collectives of each of these fifty states through the federation power-sharing structure, but the point remains.

are described in Chapter 9). By effectively forcing us individuals to use its fraudulent receipts, this third-party vault owner has enabled itself to succumb fully to the temptation to print more receipts than there is gold.

4. LAUNDERING FRAUDULENT RECEIPTS FOR GOLD

RATHER than changing its evil ways by becoming fiscally responsible, the collective We, the People, acts like a two-year-old, stamping its feet and insisting on spending as much as it wants. It gets its way by cheating, like the old-school vault owners. In addition, it adds a new twist, by hiding the cheating behind a money-laundering operation. Through the actions of its government agent/employees and some accomplices, the collective creates fraudulent gold receipts (dollar *bills*), runs them through a money-washing machine, and lends them to itself. The money-washing machine in this case is two federal government departments and certain large commercial banks working together, making the new fraudulent gold receipts indistinguishable from receipts already circulating.

The collective, with its metaphorical left hand, replenishes the treasury by selling bonds on the primary market[1]. With its metaphorical right hand, it prints up fraudulent paper receipts for gold[2] on which the words FEDERAL RESERVE NOTE are printed, and buys its own bonds with them [209] on the secondary market.[3] It doesn't do the fast move straight from left hand to right, buying its own debt from itself, right out in the open for all to see. Instead it buys the bonds from those who purchased them directly from our left hand; specifically, from certain large commercial bank accomplices [30, 185, 206, 210–212].[4] The metaphorical left hand of the collective is the federal Department of the Treasury, while its metaphorical right hand is the central bank (Figure 4.1). Here in these fifty states, the central bank is known as the

---

[1]The primary market is where the collective first sells its bonds

[2]Also known as funny money [186].

[3]The secondary market is where investors trade the collective's previously issued bonds

[4]See Appendix A for a simplified example showing how the numbers work when printing new money to borrow and then repay.

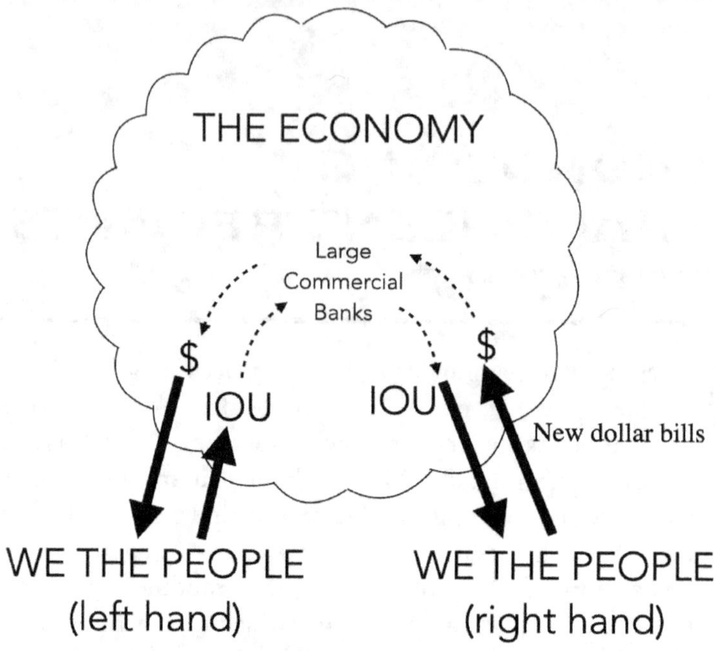

Figure 4.1. *Right hand buys debt sold by left.*

Federal Reserve System, composed of twelve regional branches [213, 214].

In a classic money-laundering scheme, the fraudulent gold receipts flow through the collective's accomplices, mixing with receipts already in circulation before making their way to the treasury. This extra step in the magician's trick of transferring fraudulent receipts from right hand to left gives us, the audience, a distraction. We end up focusing on the money transfer from right hand to middle-man, or middle-man to left hand—the extra step distracts us from paying attention to the whole chain of money movement. This magic trick gives the collective a way to plausibly deny the laundering, which it needs when spending the fraudulent cash on guns, tanks, bombs, aircraft carriers, cannon fodder, charity, bureaucrats, and so on. The metaphorical right hand of the collective, the Federal Reserve System, is depleting the bond supply by removing bonds from the secondary market, putting upward price pressure on bonds in both the secondary and primary markets.

The collective, which must redeem the bonds when they mature, is happy with their higher prices since its cost of borrowing is lower. But it isn't happy when the new fraudulent receipts for gold in circulation cause general price increases, and neither are we individuals. Other countries have their own central banks, for example, the Bank of Japan and the Bank of England, doing the same tricks and experiencing the same consequences.

Making the situation even worse, since the tragedy of the commons-induced spending pressures never go away, the collective is never able to complete its budget without borrowing. Because part of the budget is debt payments, the collective is forced in a sense to pay old credit cards with new, causing a compound-interest runaway in debt (Figure 4.2). Because the collective regularly purchases its own debt, the amount of paper money in circulation also rises in a compound-interest fashion, meaning faster and faster over time.

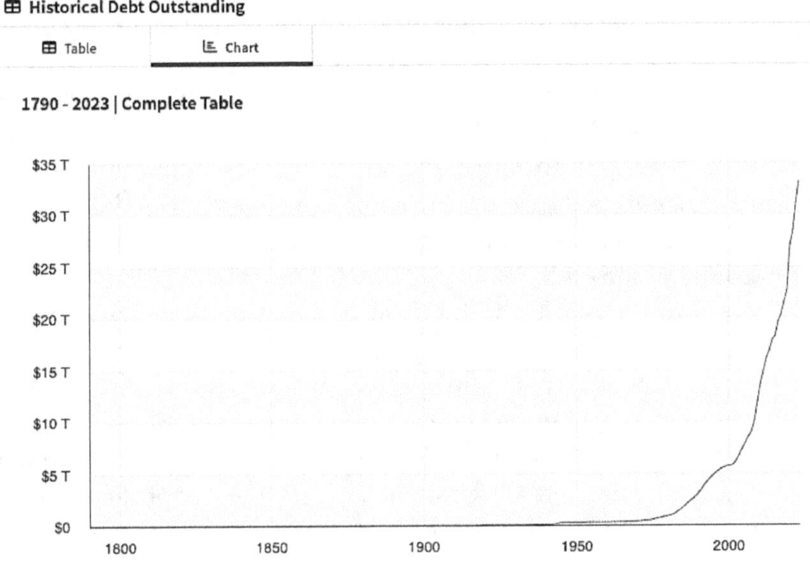

Figure 4.2. *Federal government debt (1790–2023). (Plot courtesy of US Department of the Treasury.)*

Like any money launderer, the collective denies the laundering, claiming it's not the party printing the fraudulent gold receipts with which to purchase its own debt notes. The collective makes this denial through Federal Reserve spokesmen, who claim the money printer, the Federal Reserve System, or the Fed, is independent of our federal government. Those spokesmen claim this to persuade us individuals the collective isn't doing the thing it's in fact doing—creating demand for its own debt notes. As reported by many people in the know, the Fed spokesmans' claims of independence are well-known to be lies.

In one of these reports about the Fed's claim of independence, J. P. Koning pointed out in the comments section of his article [215] the five Federal Reserve Board of Governors members are appointed by the President, with congressional approval. He noted, too, the presidents of each of the twelve districts are appointed by district boards of directors who themselves have been appointed by the Board of Governors—Federal Reserve shareholders have almost no management control over the system. This story is corroborated by the Library of Congress [216]. Stephanie Kelton also calls out the non-independence of the Fed in her 2020 book *The Deficit Myth* [217], informing us the Fed is a creature of Congress and no more independent of the federal government than the Department of Energy, the Department of Transportation, or any other federal government department. Economist T. Windsor Fields, too, refers to the Federal Reserve System as the government in his analysis of government bond sales and purchases [211]. Therefore, importantly for the mechanics of our escape from this never-ending inflation of fraudulent paper gold receipts (explained in Chapter 19), the Federal Reserve System will be treated as part of the federal government for our business purposes here.

Whereas in the old days, the third-party vault owner would surreptitiously print fraudulent receipts and spend them into circulation directly, this modern-times third-party vault owner is craftier. It sells debt notes to accomplices, and with a hidden-in-plain-sight central bank, which loudly and often proclaims it is independent of the vault-owning collective selling the notes, buys them back with newly printed fraudulent receipts for gold. The collective makes sure to cut its laundering accomplices in with a percentage, paid by purchasing its bonds from the secondary market for a higher price than it received for them on the primary market. This devious method helps the collective get away with the money printing without causing a run on the bank because too few are aware of it. As British economist John Maynard Keynes observed in his 1919 book, *The Economic Consequences of the Peace*:

> There is no subtler, no surer means of overturning the existing basis of Society than to debauch the currency. The process engages all the hidden forces of economic law on the side of

destruction, and does it in a manner which not one man in a million is able to diagnose. [218]

That we individuals may not be aware of the hidden-in-plain-sight money printing doesn't prevent it from causing us trouble. By spending new money into circulation in this fashion, the collective is able to siphon away our life energies quietly, draining us like a vampire every time we touch its money.

In summary of our price problems and their cause: Prices are running away because We, the People, as a collective, are effectively compelled by tragedy of the commons dynamics to spend more money than we have. The spending problem is so bad even borrowing can't supply sufficient funds, so the collective has resorted to purchasing its own debt with newly issued, fraudulent receipts for gold. The new fraudulent receipts increase the quantity of money in circulation, causing prices to run away. Because we pay old debt with new, the required spending, and circulating money and therefore prices, increases faster and faster in response to the demands of compound interest. Helping keep us in this debt trap, most don't understand what's going on because the collective launders the new money into circulation.

Next: How is the collective's spending problem causing poverty, and what other trouble is it causing? In Chapter 5, we'll find it is the mechanics of the spending causing prices to rise faster than most peoples' incomes. Chapter 6 will show us how the collective amplifies the rising-prices-induced poverty by varying the speed of entry of the new money into circulation. In Chapter 7 we'll find the collective's spending problem is causing assault, corruption, and dangerous experimentation as a side-effect of the spending mechanics described in Chapter 5. Chapter 8 details some of our (failed) efforts to mitigate the runaway prices problem, and Chapter 9 explains the statutory trap effectively forcing us individuals to use the collective's problematic money. Finally, in Part II we'll commence taking Grandfather Zed's advice, from Terry Goodkind's *Sword of Truth* series, to "think of solutions not problems" [219].

5. CHEATED WITH AN INFLATION TAX

THE collective's combined counterfeiting and laundering operation has serious consequences. By purchasing its own debt on the secondary market with newly printed fraudulent receipts for gold (dollar *bills*), the collective is cheating its customers, those of us who use its money. We get cheated by the collective from the time after each fraudulent gold receipt was printed to the time when we get to spend it, as the new notes bid against the existing mixture of real and fraudulent notes already in circulation [137, 192, 206, 210, 220, 221]. Cheating people out of their money this way, by diluting it with more monetary units, is commonly referred to as an inflation tax.

The inflation tax is known by few and understood by fewer [193], with many blaming greedy business owners for the ever-increasing prices. But greedy business owners aren't the cause—people who own businesses are victims of rising prices the same as everyone else; the money itself is the problem. The effect of the inflation tax is the same as that of the more well-known statutory taxes because it causes you to work more to get more money. The difference is with the inflation tax, you have to work more to get more money to pay bills rather than work more to get more money to pay statutory taxes. When you have both, though, as do we, you get to work more to pay the bills and then work even more to pay the statutory taxes. We know the reason we have to work more to pay statutory taxes is fear of the revenuers' brute squads, but why do we also have to work more to pay bigger and bigger bills? We know the general reason is spending money into circulation results in more money chasing the same amount of goods and services, causing price increases, but why do we have such a hard time keeping up? If there's more money in circulation, we can expect prices to rise, but there's more money in circulation, so we all should have more money, making it a wash, right? While it is true we tend to end up with more money when the amount in circulation increases, some get the new money before others, enabling them to outbid those others for real products and services. The later receivers get the new money after the earlier receivers have bid prices up, and the longer it takes the new money to come their way, the higher prices are relative to their available cash. The mechanics of this process can be illustrated with an analogy of water flowing from a spigot into a tub (Figure 5.1).

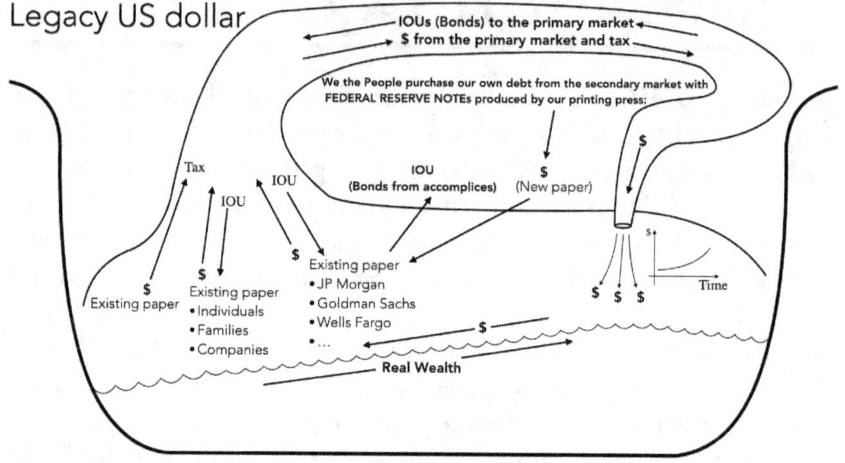

Figure 5.1. *Legacy monetary flows.*

In the figure, market participants are arranged from left to right as a function of how close they are, economically, to the spigot. The spigot is analogous to the spending of the collective, and the amount of money in a participant's account is analogous to the water level at their location. For example, a defense contractor or social security recipient receiving money from the central government is immediately under the spigot, while the person selling trinkets on the side of the road is further from the spigot because the new money changed hands one or more times before he or she received it.

When water/money flows from the spigot into the tub, the level is higher near the spigot when the water/money is flowing. This happens with water because it takes time for the new water molecules entering the tub to move to the lower-level parts of the tub. Similarly, it takes time for new money entering circulation to move from the first hands receiving it to later hands. Known as the Cantillon effect [222], named after eighteenth-century banker and philosopher Richard Cantillon, the faster the new money enters circulation, the bigger the differential in money held, on average, between those closer to the spigot and those less close. The result is the rich getting richer [223]—as Janet Yellen put it (paraphrased): "The bigger and powerful get money first, and the small and weak get money last" [222]. In 2011 Christopher Whalen reported the average wage of public sector employees, who are immediately under the metaphorical federal spending spigot, was twice that of those in the private sector [p. 329 of 208].

Our metaphorical left hand (Figure 4.1) is causing the bond and dollar *bill* flows in the pipe between the primary bond market and the spigot. The right hand is the sneaky part below that, where the collective operates a printing press outside the regular money flows in the system, hidden in plain sight. The further individuals are economically from the spigot, the more they are cheated as market prices adjust for the increased money supply and decreased available economic output.[1] Being able to print money rather than earn it, the paper money printer has an advantage when bidding, causing real property to move toward the money printer. In contrast, money moves in the opposite direction (Figure 5.1), out into circulation.[2] Those less close to the spigot eventually get the new money, but late, after the real wealth has been consumed and prices have run up [220, 224, ch. 18 of 192]. The water/money level in the whole tub is rising so even the individuals further from the spigot eventually end up with more money in their pockets. However, at any given time, the differential in the average pocket holdings between those closer and those not as close to the spigot remains.

---

[1]When you purchase anything, like a house or a car or a tube of toothpaste, you've removed it from the marketplace, and thus decreased its economic supply, and thus put upward price pressure on the remaining supply.

[2]Imagine you are the one printing the new paper money and spending it into circulation. The money flows away from you, the money printer, while the real property you purchased with it, such as real estate or food or clothing, flows to you. If it costs you less effort to print the money than it costs others to earn it, you can always outbid the others. The new money you're adding to circulation causes upward price pressure on the economic supply, and the economic supply you're removing from the market causes upward price pressure on the remaining supply. Viewing this process through the lens of a market price fraction, say dollars/apple, when you purchase an apple with new money, you've increased the numerator and decreased the denominator for everyone else because there are now more dollars bidding for fewer apples. Both of these changes operate to increase the purchase price of apples for those trying to buy them after you did your dirty deed. If you do this continuously, like the collective We, the People, is doing, you will continuously cause real property, apples, to flow to you, while the money you printed flows away from you, out into circulation.

Even once a person acquires the new money, he or she continues to get cheated as the value of each new unit decreases during the time it is held. For those who adopt a strategy of spending the money soon after earning it, the spending power lost in this way is minimized. But those who wish to spend it on value-retaining assets to save for a rainy day are cheated by the extra work needed and risk taken on to accomplish that [220]. The problem for many of us is other investors are smarter, and we're dumber. Yours truly, for example, excels at buying high and selling low.

Businesses also suffer when prices continually rise as contracts must regularly be adjusted to compensate, retail prices adjusted, and countless other administrative tasks must be paid for with both money and time. Consistent with those mechanics, we know empirically countries with high price inflation rates tend not to be very economically productive [ch. 16 of 192].

Variations in the inflation tax are also known to amplify the damage caused by so-called boom-bust business cycles.

6. CHEATED BY BOOM-BUST BUSINESS CYCLES

THE collective spends new money into circulation from a central economic location faster and faster, causing a transfer of value from the small and weak to the big and strong. This effect of the collective's spending problems causes continuous poverty on a mass scale, but unfortunately, there's more.

The collective's metaphorical right hand doesn't print and then spend new money into circulation predictably, such as if it reliably purchased the same amount of its own debt every week. Predictable bond purchases would result in more predictable interest rates, causing less unfavorable business conditions due to less impairment of the ability of businesses to make and execute plans. Instead, bond purchase rates often vary week over week, and month over month, due to politically influenced committee decisions.[1] This has the effect of making interest rates unpredictable and, therefore, business planning even more difficult than it is with regular price increases, reducing the number of people gainfully employed and the products and services they supply to consumers. In short, it makes us poorer. This interest rate manipulation is also a source of monetary policy-induced so-called boom-bust business cycles [220, 225].

By way of explanation, and to help the reader appreciate one of the huge problems we'll solve by fixing our US dollars, a boom-bust business cycle can start when business "booms," meaning economic activity increases. Business booms can result from various causes, such as increased supply and demand, but the cause relevant to our problematic US dollars is high-priced debt, implying low interest rates. Low interest rates can occur in an economy that isn't being interfered with, and can be caused artificially by the central bank. Considering the case of an economy free from central bank interference, if consumers

---

[1]An example of a politically influenced committee making bond purchase decisions is the "Federal" Open Market Committee (FOMC) [209].

are done consuming and have surplus funds, they may seek to use their money to make money by lending it out.

This additional supply of money to the debt market increases the price of debt as those surplus funds compete for it. The increased price to purchase debt, in effect, is a lower interest rate, encouraging businesses to borrow money to expand and use that money to consume the economic output not consumed by individuals who are now loaning out their surplus money. In other words, the consumption of economic output is being transferred from consumers to producers. Since the surplus economic output now being consumed by the expanding businesses existed in the first place, causing the lowered interest rates, all is well in the economy. Only economic output that existed is being consumed, and the economy is booming since people are producing more than they're consuming.

In such a situation, a run on debt can ensue due to fear of missing out (FOMO) among lenders, and the resulting high prices can cause companies who shouldn't go into debt to do so regardless. At some point, debt prices may have drawn in most or all of the available lenders, and some of the early lenders might sell their debt for a profit, driving prices down. Drops in prices could then draw in more sellers, driving prices down more in a runaway selloff. If too many companies got in on the boom debt binge, consuming too much economic output and causing prices of that output to rise, even more debt consumers might exit the market to raise money, driving debt prices down even more. If debt prices decrease too much in this part of the cycle, and companies that shouldn't have borrowed are forced to borrow again to stay afloat, the price on offer for their debt may no longer be able to sustain them, and they may fold. If too many companies get in trouble in this way, it can be called a bust.

These kinds of business boom-bust cycles are normal, short-lived, and typically cause minimal economic damage. However, if an external entity like a central bank purchases companies' debt, keeping debt prices high and, therefore, interest rates low for an extended period of time, the boom-bust cycles can be longer, causing much more damage. When a central bank prints new money to purchase bonds and thereby artificially lowers interest rates,[2] businesses are incentivized to borrow the low-cost money to expand production for the same reason as before:

---

[2]Federal government bond price increases drive bond buyers into other debt markets, causing price increases there, or, in other words, lower interest rates.

the money is low cost. Businesses are more or less forced to borrow when interest rates drop because if they don't borrow and expand, their competitors will, possibly stealing customers from them.

Furthermore, when the central bank lends new money into circulation, the new money drives prices up for everyone, enhancing the price-increasing effect of the excess economic output consumption caused by the excess of expanding companies. An undesirable chain of events can then result in which the savings, or capital, of the economy is depleting simultaneously with an increasing money supply, causing prices to rise and decreasing consumer demand for both debt and non-monetary goods. Decreased consumer demand reduces sales for the expanding businesses and thus increases loan defaults. Loan defaults begin accelerating when the price-increasing effects of monetary inflation and economic output depletion impact the economy.

When companies default on payments, it reduces demand for debt because debt consumers value risky debt less. If prices are rising, the amount of consumer capital available to purchase debt will decrease proportionately. Decreased demand for debt, along with decreased available capital, causes lower prices for debt. This implies increased interest rates and, therefore, reduces the number of companies borrowing money to expand. However, if the central bank keeps buying debt, regardless of actual market demand, the high prices companies can get for their debt maintains the pressure on them to keep borrowing to expand. This ongoing borrowing happens even though there isn't sufficient surplus production available for the companies to consume and even though there is less demand for products and services from consumers because their capital is being consumed by higher prices. Companies continue to default even on the central bank-enabled low-interest-rate loans and continue going out of business, in the so-called bust phase of this central bank-caused cycle. Shareholders then frequently get painful financial haircuts as share prices plummet. These share price collapses are in addition to the money problems caused to consumers by the price inflation, which in turn was caused by the monetary inflation combined with the excess business consumption.

For the cherry on this cake, it isn't unusual for the central bank to stop purchasing bonds with their newly printed paper money at this point in the cycle [192, 193]. When the central bank stops purchasing at this worst of times, it magnifies the effect of the bust as the companies that were staying alive with low-interest-rate loans go out of business.

Stock market crashes such as those in 1929, 1987, 2001, and 2008 are examples of the problems caused by the bust phase of these cycles.

7. CHEATED: DEATH BY A THOUSAND CUTS

As if we don't already have enough bad news, these metaphorical left and right hands of the collective, selling us down the river with hidden-in-plain-sight fraudulent gold receipt printing, do more than "just" launder new paper money into circulation faster and faster from a central spending point. The collective also assaults individuals to keep them using its ever more diluted money, takes actions unfairly benefiting some asset holders over others, causes corruption, and exposes us all to the consequences of large-scale planning errors.

Assault.   From the collective's metaphorical left hand, which is the US Department of the Treasury, we're assaulted. This department of the federal government uses credible threats of violence[1] to force individuals, families, and companies to obey federal government tax and legal tender statutes. This is essential for the collective's spending, giving it both funds and consumers who will accept the funds in exchange for doing the collective's work. The mechanics of turning the collective's statutory threats into individuals' actions are described in Chapter 9.

Unfairly benefit some asset holders over others.   The metaphorical right hand of the collective, which is the central bank, known here in the fifty states as the Federal Reserve System, or Fed, also does more. By way of the Fed, the collective prints up additional fraudulent gold receipts and purchases other financial assets with them. For example, this metaphorical right hand has been known to use these fraudulent receipts to purchase items such as mortgage-backed securities to bail out companies deemed by certain interested parties to be "too big to fail" [226–228]. Such purchases have the effect of thwarting markets'

---

[1]In the Anglo-Saxon customary law tradition, which is the basis of law in this country, the word "assault" means a credible threat of an imminent battering. As we all know, some of us have had this threat, to pay the revenuers or else, carried out by battering of our persons, sometimes to death.

"efforts" to shed money-losing operations. The metaphorical right hand in other countries has also printed up new *bills* with which to purchase shares of companies, to support their prices [229, 230]. Investors owning shares in unsupported companies are thus robbed as their shares lose value relative to those of the supported ones.

Corruption.   We're cheated again by competition to get closer to the metaphorical money spigot, which exposes us to the corruption of some of the competitors. Our monetary system creates a large pot of government budget money in full public view, attracting unsavory people who use that hoard to acquire power over us [231–240].

This side effect of government money, of enabling some to acquire power over others, is not a fact to be taken lightly. As the late Professor R. J. Rummel observed, the iron law of human nature is power kills [241]. As long as we're allowing concentrated financial value via our large central government budget, each of us is exposed to the possibility of murder by his own government agents.[2] Historically, government-money-fueled government power tends to concentrate; that power has already resulted in hundreds of millions of murders by the victims' own government employees [241–245].

Things have become so bad that, if you didn't know better, you might conclude some of these people are trying to kill us all [116, 117, 246, 247]. To add insult to injury, much of this murder has happened due to the same political arrangements ostensibly [207] put in place to guarantee life, liberty, and property for all [248, 249].[3] Rummel informed us concentrated power is the most dangerous thing on earth, having killed far more than floods, storms, earthquakes, fires, tsunamis, diseases, and even wars. He reported governments murdered around 262,000,000 (plus or minus 50 percent)[4] innocent people in the twentieth century alone, compared to "only" 36,000,000 killed in combat. Laid head to toe, these twentieth-century government murder victims would circle the earth four times [241].

---

[2]So far, knock on wood, our governments here in the states haven't murdered nearly as many of us as some other governments have their people.

[3]Part 1, Article 4 of the 1977 version of the constitution of the USSR states the government will "safeguard the interests of society and the rights and freedoms of citizens."

[4]It's an inexact science to count all those corpses. Note that 262 million minus 50 percent remains a hideously large number of murder victims.

Large Scale Planning Errors.   Another side effect of the large flow of money from a single source is exposure to large-scale planning errors, which can occur due to spending decisions of governments or wealthy individuals or families. For example, if our representatives in the federal government, along with at least some popular support and at least some amount of indifference or learned helplessness among the rest of us, decide we need another aircraft carrier, we get another aircraft carrier, regardless of actual market demand. This happens because those of us struggling to pay bills while prices are rising will gladly accept some of that government contract money in exchange for building the aircraft carrier.

Other large-scale planning error exposures come from some of those who manage to accumulate vast sums due to spigot proximity, or due to barrier-to-entry-type statutes[5] enforced with direct-from-the-spigot federal government money. Those fortunes are often spent philanthropically—here in the states, the top 1 percent of income earners make about a third of all charitable contributions [250]. This is a good thing, and of course we're all grateful for their generosity. But it gives them power over the inflation tax victims who aren't as close to the central government monetary spigot, who are therefore more willing than they otherwise might be to do what the top 1 percent wants in order to get paid. For instance, if a wealthy philanthropist decides a new vaccine should be developed and distributed, those falling behind while chasing prices may accept some of her or his charitable contribution in exchange for producing and distributing the vaccine, regardless of actual market demand.

In effect, this large flow of money from a single source puts us all at risk by causing us to put more eggs in fewer baskets, going against

---

[5]An example of barrier-to-entry-type statutes are those providing for licensing or intellectual property (IP) such as patents, copyrights, and trademarks. Companies must be able to raise enough cash to pay for the state-provided license, or the IP license fee, to enter the market. Therefore, in effect, companies already in the market enjoy tax-subsidized protection from competition since newcomers must surmount a financial barrier before they can compete with the incumbents. In another barrier to entry example, compliance and licensure costs disproportionately damage smaller firms in the financial services industry. A large-cap financial services provider does not have to allocate as large a percentage of its resources as a small company to ensure it doesn't run into trouble with the Securities and Exchange Commission (SEC), Truth in Lending Act (TILA), Fair Debt Collection Practices Act (FDCPA), Consumer Financial Protection Bureau (CFPB), Federal Deposit Insurance Corporation (FDIC), or a host of other agencies and statutes.

the maxim warning us not to put all our eggs in one basket. It creates large spenders who can conduct large spending experiments, such as massive capital expenditure projects like aircraft carriers or vaccine production runs, rather than the fewer-eggs-in-more-baskets approach resulting from individuals conducting their own experiments. The smaller number of bigger experiments method is dangerous because, when a large experiment causes trouble, it can cause a lot of trouble, whereas smaller experiments are less able to cause too much trouble.

Overall, the collective's counterfeiting and laundering operation enables it to steal financial value on a large scale, by diluting the money supply. Worse, it sometimes dilutes faster and sometimes slower, causing sporadic bursts of economic destruction. The operation also effectively forces the collective to assault people to keep the spending scheme going, unfairly benefits some asset holders over others, and causes corruption and large scale planning errors. These effects are well known, and various mitigation efforts have attempted, but failed, to reverse them.

8. FAILED MITIGATION EFFORTS

SOME have tried to mitigate the damages caused by the collective's incessant paper money printing and spending with talk. For example, some have explained the excess money entering circulation is not harmful, while others have explained our federal government taxation system protects people from its harms. Others have taken actions designed to mitigate the paper printing-induced damages. For example, central banks have been loaning out new money, ironically to mitigate harm they've caused by loaning out new money, and organizations like the Council on Foreign Relations have been brainstorming mitigation ideas like printing new money and giving it directly to consumers. However, when these thoughts are examined carefully, we find the explanations false and the ideas flawed. The excess money entering circulation is in fact causing great harm, our federal government taxation system can't protect people from the harm caused by compound-interest-induced new money spent into circulation from a central source, and the central bank and others' mitigation efforts actually make things worse.

Mitigate with talk: Excess money printing isn't causing harm

The case has been made that money printing has not made people poor as prices rise [251]. The argument is productivity-induced wage increases[1] have matched money supply increases, so the purchasing power of workers' wages has remained approximately constant [138, 141, 252] (Figure 8.1). Furthermore, the argument goes, if you were

---

[1]Productivity-induced wage increases take the form of more production per time if the worker is paid according to the amount of product produced. They take the form of higher wages per time if the worker is paid according to time worked, which works for the company if the more productive worker is taking less time to manufacture the same amount of product.

smarter than the other investors you would have protected your increased wages from price increases. This argument not only blames the victims of the runaway prices for not being smart enough investors, but ignores the fact price increases due to money printing have cheated workers out of real wage increases due to productivity they would have received in the absence of the money printing [253, ch. 16 of 192]. We've probably all experienced the dismay of getting pay raises but at the same time watching real estate and grocery prices increase as much or more [254].

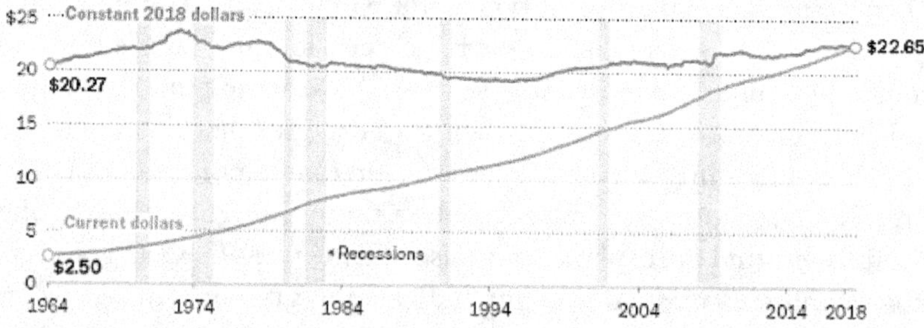

Figure 8.1. *Since 1971, workers' real wages have remained flat. (Plot courtesy of Pew Research Center.)*

To finance its spending addiction, the collective is spending new fraudulent gold receipts into circulation from a single economic location, imposing an unjust inflation tax on late receivers. Because it's repaying old loans with new, the collective is experiencing a compound interest-induced [223] runaway in debt (Figure 4.2 [255]), and in the quantity of money in circulation and, therefore, in prices.

Dilution-caused value loss turns the money into a kind of hot potato, incentivizing its users to do more work to get rid of it after they first had to do work to get it. These fraudulent gold receipts implicitly teach us savings and thrift don't reward as well as spending and consuming [220], incentivizing people to harm their living world by turning it into products and waste. After all, what is the point of saving if one can't enjoy the fruits of one's labor [p. 20 of 186]? Those economically further from the new money are additionally incentivized to turn our living world into products and waste, as explained in Chapter 1, because they're chasing prices while the new money travels to them. The collective vault owner is committing the crime of using force and tricks to create demand for its ever-increasing output of fraudulent receipts for gold, thereby causing poverty, crime,[2] and environmental degradation.[3]

Mitigate with talk: our federal government progressive income tax fixes inequities

Another story we're told is we individuals aren't being cheated, and the value transferred from us to our federal government is spent on our behalf, transferring the value back to us individuals. Exactly how it gets spent is decided by majority-rules polls of our federal government senators and representatives. These senators and representatives are themselves chosen, also by majority-rules polls,[4] to represent the rest of us in a system political scientist Jane Mansbridge refers to as adversary

---

[2]These crimes have even caused airplanes to crash as cutthroat competition between operators resulted in irresponsible cost-cutting by manufacturers [256]. They've also resulted in deadly pharmaceutical pills as cutthroat competition among drug producers led to fraud and deception at their manufacturing facilities to evade the FDA [257], and they've sickened people with "filthy" food [257].

[3]The grinding stress resulting from continual price chasing even causes suicides. A tragic example, sadly but one of many, is the story of Matsuri Takahashi in Japan, who died from *karoshi*, or "overwork death," after being worked into an unrecoverable depression [258].

[4]The Seventeenth Amendment to the US Constitution changed the group who chooses senators. Per the original Constitution, they were chosen by the state legislators; the framers' intent was for the senators, thus chosen, to ensure the states' control over the federal government they were creating. The House of Representatives was intended to give the people a more direct voice in the federal government. The Seventeenth Amendment changed the group of senator-choosers to the people of the states, destroying the federalist concept of a decentralized group of peer-to-peer states giving a "federal" government strictly limited powers [259].

democracy [260].

Furthermore, the progressive income tax levels out unfair value accumulation (Figure 5.1) by taking more from the rich than the poor. In effect, the progressive income tax attempts to even out the water/money level in the tub/circulation by filling the wave troughs with the wave peaks. If we vote for the right representatives, who vote to spend the money in the right ways, the peaks of the money/water waves in the tub will be lowered and the troughs raised, benefiting society by reducing inequities in financial wealth.

Regardless of how close this story is to truth, it only has a partial bearing on the inequity caused by the compound interest-induced supply of new money from a single spender. Individuals economically closer to the new money get taxed at the same rate as those less close and thus retain their spending advantage at any tax rate. Existing progressive taxation systems treat all equally, regardless of proximity to the new money. In other words, the tax bracket as a function of income is the same for the person selling trinkets by the side of the road, who is one or more spending steps away from the federal spending spigot, as it is for the defense contractor receiving the new money first, directly from the spigot.

It is true the closer someone is to the central government spending spigot, the more money he or she's likely to earn. The higher earnings put the him or her into the higher tax brackets, so the progressive tax codes do at least partially achieve their goal of reducing income inequality. Furthermore, we can imagine it may be possible to concoct a taxation system progressively taxing individuals and companies more the closer they are economically to the new money.

However, given federal government budget constraints, progressive taxes based on economic distance from newly printed money can't happen because such taxes would have the effect of increasing its costs. This is because such progressive tax rates would force the federal government to pay more to workers, to make up for their taxation-reduced wages, so it could remain competitive in the labor marketplace. In other words, progressive taxation based on economic proximity to the new money would reduce the inflation tax, which is what allows governmental departments to spend more—the whole point of the inflating money scheme. Progressive taxation based on economic proximity to the new money would also reduce support for the federal government in general as those benefiting handsomely from large, money printer-enabled, federal government budgets would find their percentage reduced and therefore wouldn't support it [232]. Even if such a progressive taxation statute were to be signed into law, politicians who voted for it would likely find themselves replaced in the next election, with the statute's lifetime sharply curtailed soon after.

Therefore, the progressive income tax only partially counteracts the inflation tax, and does not and can not negate the dynamic of compound interest caused by a mob of spendthrifts. Because of the compound interest caused by the loans our federal government is repaying with new loans, the new money must enter circulation faster and faster. It enters circulation faster and faster from the single federal government spending spigot, causing inflation-tax-induced poverty, and thus we can't stop killing our living world as we chase prices.

Mitigate with action: central banks have our backs

Central banks have also been attempting to reduce inflation tax-caused poverty, by introducing money into circulation. The central bank methods are essentially to lend or give money to people on the periphery, so the federal government isn't the only new money entry point. The intent is to get the water/money level on the left-hand side of the tub (Figure 5.1) closer to the level on the right-hand side. Simply put, the central banks have been attempting to even out the water/money level in the tub/circulation by filling in the wave troughs with new money, as opposed to the peak-chopping/trough-filling method of the progressive income taxes.

In an example of central banks reducing poverty by lending, many have been reducing interest rates. In some cases, banks have gone so far as to use a warehouse business model, charging customers to hold their money and paying them to borrow—the equivalent of paying negative interest rates.[5] (When lending to governments, negative interest rates

---

[5]A positive interest rate is when the bank depositor is paid for the use of their money, and a negative interest rate is when the depositor is charged a fee to store their money. The flip from negative to positive interest rate first happened with early goldsmiths, who owned vaults [193]. Initially, vault owners would charge customers to store gold in their vault in what was a situation of *depositum*, with an effectively negative interest rate. This is a warehouse model because the vault owner provides the warehouse service of storing customer gold. Later, they would

can be mechanized by bidding the price of bonds up to greater than face value.) In two recent examples of this business model, interest rates paid by the European Central Bank became negative starting in June of 2014 [261], and Swiss central bank interest rates have been near zero or negative since 2009 [262], neither becoming positive again until the early 2020s. In addition to supporting government bond prices, one of the purposes of negative rates is to encourage depositor banks to lend their money out to businesses rather than keep it on deposit with the central bank. The hope is for these loans to reduce poverty by getting money into circulation, supporting more businesses, consuming more inputs, selling more products, and creating income for owners and employees.

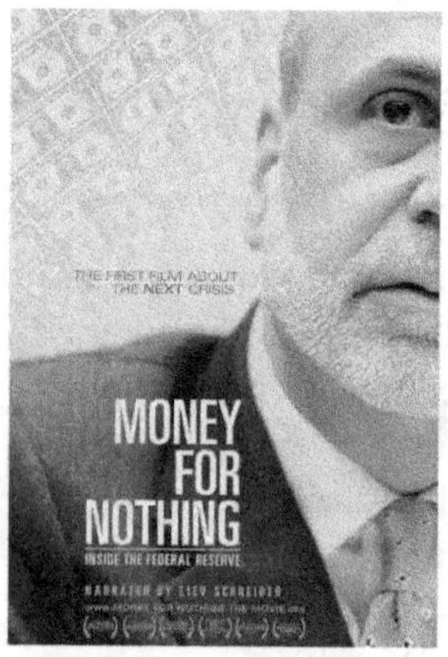

Fig. 8.2. *The Ben Bernank. (Image courtesy of Jim Bruce.)*

In an example of central banks reducing poverty by giving money away, in August of 2014 the Council on Foreign Relations published a recommendation for central banks to deposit money into retail bank customers' accounts. This was to be without any action by the owners of those accounts [263], *à la* the famous Ben Bernanke (Figure 8.2) helicopter drop [264].

Federal Reserve System Chairman Ben Bernanke became known as "Helicopter Ben" after his 2002 deflation speech proposing the US Congress deficit spend, with a combination of public works spending and tax cuts, to get cash into people's accounts [265]. Dr. Bernanke proposed the central bank cover the deficit with a credit, or gift, to our treasury. Bernanke's proposal would have new money enter people's bank accounts surreptitiously, by way of some of them receiving income through employment in the public works projects and all of them by having less tax money removed from their accounts. It would be the same as the standard money-laundering method in use since 1913, except it would switch the middlemen from large commercial banks to

pay customers for their deposits since they could earn income on those deposits by lending out, at positive interest rates, surreptitiously printed fraudulent receipts for gold while assuring depositors all of their gold was in the vault as promised. The gold deposits, in this case, were in a *mutuum* [184].

public works and tax cuts. Milton Friedman understood Dr. Bernanke's proposal amounted to the same old money-laundering scheme even before he proposed it, and knew it might not be sneaky enough and might arouse widespread public suspicion. Friedman had already illustrated his concerns about handing out money by using a helicopter example in his 1969 book *The Optimum Quantity of Money* [266]. In the book, he presciently pointed out Dr. Bernanke's method would be similar to flying over a community in a helicopter, dropping $1,000 in *bills* from the sky, and hoping everyone believed it was a one-time event.

Both of these poverty reduction methods have negative consequences. One of the main problems with the "loaning new money into circulation" method is the new money leaves circulation when the loan is repaid [193, 211].[6] Loaning new money into circulation and removing it from circulation when the loans are repaid is known to amplify the economic destruction resulting from boom-bust business cycles (described in Chapter 6), causing poverty rather than alleviating it [193, 206, 210, 220, 225, 267, 268].

One problem with the Council on Foreign Relations' idea to distribute money for nothing is it would turn people into dependents, stealing their dignity. Another problem is it would make our world less pleasant socially by depriving recipients of some of their incentive to help others. Although humans are naturally born with the instinct to help others, this instinct is stronger with family and friends than with strangers. In areas with dense populations and the resulting high likelihood of interactions between strangers, a beneficial feature of a high division of labor is helping others is also a way to help yourself, increasing the chance you'll help others even when they're not family or friends. For example, if someone pays you to manufacture a car for them, both you and the customer know each of you is helping the other. You're providing a useful car to the customer, and the customer is providing useful cash to you. Mutual exchanges such as this trigger a gratefulness response in each of your brains, thereby making everyone a little happier than they were. Getting something without giving something in exchange deprives us of that little bit of extra gratefulness and feeling of satisfaction.

---

[6]Griffin explains the mechanics of the "loaning new money into circulation" poverty reduction method in Chapter 10, "The Mandrake Mechanism," of *The Creature from Jekyll Island* [193]. Those mechanics are also illustrated in a simplified example in Appendix A.

Our mitigation efforts have failed

Our gold US dollars are causing a compound interest-induced runaway in paper money printing and, therefore, inevitably, a runaway in prices (Figure 2.1). If we keep using them, we'll continue to be incentivized to work supply chains harder so we can pay our bills as prices run away, resulting in more environmental degradation (as explained in Chapter 1).

Governmental attempts to fix the environmental degradation symptoms of our gold US dollars have focused on the symptoms, the damage caused by people responding to runaway prices, and not the root cause, the inflating money supply. As we know, none have succeeded. The schemes to get our federal government to save us nearly always involve printing more money, to borrow more money, to spend more money, to control individuals more, to prevent them from working supply chains harder. But people are incentivized to work supply chains harder by the poor-quality money the collective is spending into circulation to stop them from working harder to pay their bills as prices run away. It's like we're caught in a Chinese finger trap—the harder we try to escape with more taxes and controls, the tighter the trap gets as the resulting price runaways incentivize individuals to tear up the world faster.

Attempts by private organizations to make our world healthy, while achieving impressive results, have not helped nearly enough. The problem is private organizations rely on donations from the same people being robbed by the inflation tax caused by that flood of new money, limiting their ability to donate, and, again, incentivizing them to work supply chains harder and damage our living world more. The poverty caused by the inflation tax simultaneously limits damage-fixing donations and increases the damage needing fixed with those donations.

In addition to causing an inflation tax and the resulting poverty and environmental degradation, our gold US dollars also cause crime. They cause crime both as a result of poverty and by corrupting people, because the national spending spigot has the undesirable trait of being a giant pot of money in plain view. It causes a financial shark feeding frenzy, leading to disasters such as the military-industrial complex President Eisenhower warned us about in his farewell address [269].

Finally, the collective is bankrupt. Like olden-days vault owners, it's been printing fraudulent receipts for the gold in its vault. Because so many of these fraudulent receipts, or dollar *bills*, have been spent into circulation in response to the demands of compound interest, prices have been running away. The runaway prices have caused tragedy-of-the-commons-induced spending pressures on the collective to increase over time, in turn increasing the number of dollar *bills* spent into circulation, causing prices to run away more, and round and round it's been going. Because of these dynamics, there's no realistic hope the collective can ever make its creditors whole [270, 271]. At least there's no hope without some sort of big change, which is why we're here. As with all bankruptcies, this one too will be settled, either painfully, or unspeakably painfully. If settled voluntarily, it will be painful for its creditors, the holders of US dollar *bills* worldwide, who will receive only a small fraction of a penny on the dollar when they redeem their dollar *bills* for dollars. If it is settled involuntarily, it will be in the form of an unspeakably painful, catastrophic price runaway, the inevitable result of this monetary system [185]. As a reminder of what unspeakably painful means here, remember the tragic story of the starvation of Maximilian Bern in Chapter 1, and again remember to multiply the victims by millions. Then add in the horrific crimes that happen routinely during hyperinflationary runaways as destitute, starving people become desperate [4, 5, 19] and even insane, as their property losses obliterate the basis of their human personalities [272].

So it has gone, and the world has been flooded with paper money and US federal government bonds, and subjected to repeated boom-bust business cycles [273], theft, and murder. The collective gold vault owner is cheating with money by printing new fraudulent gold receipts to lend to itself because individuals and companies declined to lend to it. We are being harmed by the chaos unleashed during the bust phases of boom-bust cycles, the inflation tax, and all the other negative consequences of our gold US dollars. To top it all off, as of the mid-2020s there is a serious risk of our US dollars losing their de facto world reserve status.[7] If this happens, the US dollars' negative consequences we've endured so far will seem like a cakewalk—a loss of world reserve status would mean those trillions of newly printed dollar *bills* we've been spending around the world for all these decades will "come home to roost" as the saying goes, all at once. Those trillions will return

---

[7]Our US dollars effectively acquired world reserve money status with the 1945 so-called Bretton Woods Agreement, in which the 44 allied countries who had just won World War II agreed to use US dollars as the money of the other national moneys [274, 275].

home as foreign investors diversify out of US notes [276], causing price inflation the likes of which has never been seen in this country.

Again, both for financially struggling people and our ailing world, time isn't our friend. In the absence of a voluntary bankruptcy settlement, our world continues getting sicker, and inexorably closer to the inevitable hyperinflationary runaway. Almost unbelievably, our situation is even worse than all that because we seemingly can't escape with a voluntary bankruptcy settlement—we're trapped by tax and legal tender statutes, unable to escape this destructive national money.

9. TRAPPED BY TAX AND LEGAL TENDER STATUTES

P RINTING the fraudulent receipts for gold in a sneaky way helps the collective of We, the People, get away with adding to the circulating money supply, keeping us in this ruinous monetary and biological trap by keeping the populace ignorant. Few understand the collective holds a 7,413 tonne[1] hoard of gold in our Fort Knox vaults, and theoretically, both individuals and the collective are conducting business using that gold in the form of paper claims on it. Most don't understand each dollar *bill* is a paper receipt for one of the dollars in the vault, where each dollar consists of $1/42\frac{2}{9}$ ounces of gold [180–184]. We're mostly unaware the collective has succumbed to the same temptation every third-party vault owner ever has, by surreptitiously issuing more paper receipts for dollars than there are dollars in the vault.[2]

The excess dollar *bills* have been driving prices up the same as in previous surrenders to temptation, so why hasn't there been a run on the bank? Even if few of us are aware of the fraudulent receipts surreptitiously added to the money supply, we've all noticed the price increases. There hasn't been a run on the bank partly because our worldwide monetary systems now completely depend on paper money (due to its improved divisibility and portability over gold [ch. 8 of 192]), and partly because we're effectively forced[3] to use the dollar *bills* by tax and legal tender statutes [210, 224, 277]. The portability and divisibility improvements of paper and electronic claims to paper over gold are a legitimate, technical reason for their widespread use, but the same can't be said for the statutes; tax and legal tender statutes lock us in by creating an unfair market demand for US dollars, each in its own way.

---

[1]As noted earlier, the exact amount is in question. All that matters, though, is for us to discover the exact number when the time comes to settle our bankruptcy.

[2]A more detailed history of our US dollars can be found in Appendix B.

[3]Actual force is rarely used because assault, as described in Chapter 7, usually suffices to get us to do what the brute squads say.

Tax statutes create a market demand for whatever kind of money is demanded by the statutes. Here in these fifty states, they demand US dollars, and therefore, there is a market demand for US dollars. The statutes accomplish this by using credible threats of violence to compel market participants to surrender a percentage of their profits as if they had used US dollars, even if the transaction were completed directly using barter or indirectly using non-US dollar intermediaries such as barrels of whiskey, cigarettes, Greek drachma, bitcoin, or whatever. If an exchange is completed without the use of US dollars, the participants are compelled to use extant market prices to compute profits as if the transaction had used US dollars, then do more work and incur additional expense to buy US dollars to surrender to the revenuers. It's almost always easier to skip the extra hassle and complete transactions with US dollars in the first place; therefore, virtually all of us transact with US dollars. It works the same way in other nation-states, locking people into their respective national currencies.

Legal tender statutes also create market demand for US dollars, but in a different way. Instead of forcing people to use US dollars, they discourage the use of alternatives by causing tax-subsidized courts to limit civil remedies to US dollars. To explain the mechanics of this limitation with an example, imagine two parties enter into a contract in which the first party promises to deliver gold to the second. Imagine further, that instead of delivering gold, the first party offered the equivalent amount of US dollar *bills*. If the second party sues for breach of contract damages in a tax-subsidized court, the court may refuse remedy on the basis of legal tender statutes, and on the court's presumption that a dollar *bill* is as good as a dollar. Legal tender statutes back up the verbiage on the *bills*, which assert "THIS NOTE IS LEGAL TENDER FOR ALL DEBTS, PUBLIC AND PRIVATE." Again, legal tender statutes in other nation-states work the same way. Gold clauses in contracts were specifically, and in violation of the foundational bedrock of our Anglo-Saxon contract law traditions, rescinded by our federal government agents in 1933 [183, 186].

The two types of statutes, along with paper and electronic ledgers' natural market demand, work synergistically to trap people into the network of US dollar users, effectively forcing market participants to use US dollars to complete transactions. Since the dollar *bills* say on them they are legal tender, and since a US dollar is statutorily defined as a fixed weight of gold [182, 183], these statutes lock us into a monetary system that directly causes environmental degradation by paying land parcel owners to excavate their land. Adding insult to injury, they also lock us all into a funding system in which revenuers force us to pay them to force us to pay them to force us to pay them. . . This customer capture happens in most or all nation-states and is responsible for unspeakable misery and suffering when national currencies burn up in catastrophic hyper-inflationary runaways [4, 5, 25].

Tax and legal tender statutes, along with the divisibility and portability improvements of paper and electronic ledger entries, create a large pool of users for our fraudulent receipts for gold, which enables the spending problem, leading to the price runaways, the thefts, the murders, the boom-bust business cycles, and so on. The tax and legal tender statutes enable the spending problem because they guarantee buyers for US dollar *bills*. Buyers of US dollar *bills* are needed when our employees in the federal government, per the budgets approved by our senators and representatives, purchase various items, and labor, and pay for them with US dollar *bills*. The statutes have the effect of creating a pool of workers throughout the supply chains who will accept payment with US dollar *bills*, enabling the federal government to purchase things and pay workers. In addition to creating a pool of workers who will accept US dollar *bills*, the tax statutes, along with the borrowing, give the collective We, the People, funds with which to pay those workers. The general price increases are a direct result of the newly printed fraudulent receipts for gold surreptitiously added to the circulating money supply by paying workers with them.

Thanks to our gold US dollars, we residents of Spaceship Earth [2] appear to be spending our way into an economic collapse as we murder our living world. We need new US dollars.

In a great stroke of luck, getting the US dollars we need is easier than one might think, and doesn't even require anything particularly new. It turns out we can acquire new and lifesaving US dollars simply by choosing the requirements those dollars must meet, then request proposals for a monetary product meeting those requirements.

Part II.

Paradise Planet: Cheating with Money

10. BRIBING PARCEL OWNERS

I N Part I, we followed the money to determine our situation, and discovered our gold US dollars are at the root of many or most of our problems. In Part II, we'll determine our future by engineering new US dollars to reverse those problems, by design.

The news about the problems our gold US dollars are causing, especially the part where they expose us to mass murder as described in Chapter 7, is really bad news, but it's also really good news, for the same reason it's bad. The trouble our US dollars are causing is due not so much to their substance but to statutes making us use them despite their ill effects. The really good news is our US dollars can be changed, and statutes can be voted out of existence the same as they were voted into existence. We know doing so will enable their improvement because already our US dollars have improved in spite of being somewhat frozen in form by the statutes. Tax and legal tender statutes effectively force us to use them, but US dollars have nevertheless become more useful to their users by transmuting into the form of the more divisible and portable paper and electronic ledgers used to track them. As will be seen in the following, We, the People, are presented with the opportunity to continue the evolution of our US dollars. We are going to find we can keep, and even improve, the divisibility and portability of our current paper and electronic ledger entries while sacrificing neither scarcity nor our living world.

If we accede to Supreme Court Justice Douglas's dissenting opinion in Colten v. Kentucky, in which he affirmed We, the People, are the true sovereign, nothing, or at least no law of our material reality, prevents us from tasking our federal government agents with engineering new US dollars and adopting them.[1] Similarly, nothing, or at least no law of our material reality, prevents We, the People, from repealing our

---

[1] A way to cause our federal government employees truly to act as our agents, as per the constitutional theory noted by Justice Douglas, is described in Part III.

federal government tax and legal tender statutes, freeing our US dollars to improve and serve their users better.

> Since when have we Americans been expected to bow submissively to authority and speak with awe and reverence to those who represent us? The Constitutional theory is that we the people are the sovereign, and the state and federal officials are our agents. We who have the final word can speak softly or angrily. We can seek to challenge and annoy, as we need not stay docile and quiet. (Justice William O. Douglas, dissenting, Colten v. Kentucky, 407 U.S. 104 (1972))

Nothing prevents us from using an orthodox design process to engineer new US dollars that eliminate poverty, *and* crime, *and* environmental degradation rather than cause them. As will be seen, we can engineer money that will accomplish these ends in a safe, decentralized way. We can create a machine that provides market actors with valuable price information, leading them naturally to behave in such a way these curses of poverty, crime, and environmental degradation disappear, seemingly by magic. Simultaneously, we can design our new US dollars in such a way we get to exit our co-owned money production business.[2] How can we do this?

Anchoring our new US dollar requirements in our living world

The orthodox design process to engineer new products for use as money is the same as for any product—first, write a formal set of requirements, and second, use those requirements to build product. Here, we'll take the first step by conducting an analysis leading to a formal set of requirements (a proposed set is presented in Appendix C). We'll take the second step by acting like the owners of the production of US dollars we are, as detailed in Chapter 17.

In the analysis step of engineering our new US dollars, the obvious way to begin is by triaging the big problems caused by our gold US

---

[2]As mentioned in the introduction, our co-owned money production business means the production, by the federal government Treasury Department, of gold US dollars and paper claims to them. According to the principle of *E pluribus unum*, we're all getting together and acting as one to produce those.

dollars—the unholy trinity of poverty, crime, and environmental degradation. The solution to this triage is found by observing that, while poverty and crime are the primary and most observable symptoms of our gold US dollars, environmental degradation is the deeper and more threatening problem.

Environmental degradation can be considered the most important of our problems because our very lives depend entirely on our nonhuman fellows who share this small spaceship with us; those no longer with us need not be concerned with poverty or crime. Without our plant brethren, we don't get to breathe breathable air, drink drinkable water, or eat edible food, and without our animal brethren, our plant friends don't get to live to provide us those services. Starting with the imperative to correct our environmental degradation problems is analogous to the instruction to passengers on commercial airplane flights to put the oxygen mask over their own faces first.

This isn't to dismiss or sidestep the vital truth that a healthy living world only helps so much if you're a dirt-poor crime victim. Importantly, these problems won't be set on the back burner with the proposed solution. As we'll find instead, the obvious design for our new and improved US dollars eliminates poverty and crime as a side effect of eliminating environmental degradation.

We'll find starting from the goal of reducing environmental degradation leads to a method requiring no more than a minor modification of an environmental health-improvement technique already in use. We'll also find we can accomplish that minor modification with just one small change to our legacy gold US dollars. Finally, we'll discover a wise detailed design choice can also gift us the elimination of poverty and crime.

Cheating with money by bribing parcel owners

Once we've decided to focus on environmental degradation as the starting point for redesigning our US dollars, the question of how arises. How do we redesign our US dollars to achieve the end of reducing environmental degradation? We can approach this question by considering the basic concepts of property and ownership.

One way of thinking about environmental degradation, which is used in this analysis, is to think of it as a collection of land parcels, each owned by someone, that may not be as healthy as we'd like. When we approach the problem from this angle, we find there are two possible ways to make those parcels healthier: the right way and the wrong way.

If you were the owner of a parcel of land, you could imagine some do-gooders trying to reduce environmental degradation by getting you to do this or that to your parcel to make it healthier. Perhaps they wanted you to spare your trees or not fill in a swamp. But imagine you wanted to harvest your trees and fill in the swamp. You wanted to cut the trees near your house because they dumped debris on it, you wanted to harvest some others to sell, and you wanted to put a shopping mall in the swamp.

From your point of view, what approach would you prefer the do-gooders use to get you to make your parcel healthier? One possibility is they could make you an offer you couldn't refuse. They could use tax-subsidized brute squads to enforce various statutes, rules, and regulations regarding your parcel. However, forcing someone to do something isn't nice, and for good reasons is proscribed by our Anglo-Saxon customary law traditions. Forcible methods are clearly the wrong way to reduce environmental degradation.

Another way to persuade you to make your parcel healthier is to make you an offer you'd be dumb to refuse. For example, if the do-gooders asked extra nice, with a cash bribe thrown in, you might be persuaded to do it their way. It might not be enough for them to offer you a one-time bribe either because they would be competing with the cash flow you could be getting from the shopping mall. They might need to offer you a competitive payment every month to keep you interested. This would work well for everyone. The parcel owner, you, would get a positive cash flow, the do-gooders would get a healthy ecosystem, and the brute squad would be out of work. Bribery is clearly the right way to reduce environmental degradation.

In a lucky precedent, the bribery approach is already in use. The collective We, the People, through the actions of our federal government agents, pay some parcel owners for certain ecosystem services provided by their lands:

Large-scale government Payments for Ecosystem Services (PES) were initiated in the 1985 Farm Bill with the creation of the Conservation Reserve Program followed by the Wetlands Reserve Program, Forest Legacy Program, the Forest Stewardship Program, and the Stewardship Incentives Program in the 1990 Farm Bill. Nearly 20 Federal programs currently pay private forest landowners to enhance ecosystem services through improved forest management, retention of lands in forest or undeveloped uses, protection of soil and water quality, preservation of forested wetlands, and wildlife habitat improvement. [143]

Private organizations have been helping too, some by contributing payments for various ecosystem services [110], and others by providing financial assistance to private landowners who adopt ecosystem beneficial conservation practices [127]. Additionally, private landowners have been selling the ecosystem service of huntable game:

Many privately funded PES programs are operated in the United States. Conservation organizations have been paying forest landowners for decades (through conservation easements) to provide or protect ecosystem services. In addition, a thriving market has long existed comprising hunters purchasing the rights to access wildlife habitat and species through hunting leases with private landowners, especially in the South. [143]

Most recently, in an action put forward for approval by the collective on September 27, 2023, the New York Stock Exchange (NYSE) published a proposed rule change with the Securities and Exchange Commission (SEC). The rule change proposes to establish a new listing standard for a company category called Natural Asset Company (NAC) [120, 278]. NACs are "corporation[s] whose primary purpose is to actively manage, maintain, restore (as applicable), and grow the value of natural assets and their production of ecosystem services" [Proposed listing rules: 1. Charter: 1. of 120].

As demonstrated by these examples, it is well understood bribing parcel owners to provide ecosystem services is a logical way to reduce environmental degradation. The idea is ecosystem services can be used as a proxy for parcel health and, thus, for environmental degradation, or lack thereof. A first-order approximation can be made that the more ecosystem services a parcel provides, the healthier it is. Therefore, paying parcel owners for those services tends to make their lands healthier since we expect them to take the opportunity to keep their parcels healthy in order to be paid. The beautiful part of making parcel owners offers they'd be dumb to refuse is they can still refuse—for example, if they choose to build a shopping mall on their parcel. This part of the idea behind bribing parcel owners is described further in Chapter 12.

Using this method to reduce environmental degradation can be thought of as cheating with money in the same way bringing a store-bought pie to the party, rather than baking it yourself, can be thought of as cheating with money—you cheated[3] by hiring the job out instead of doing it yourself. In the case of fixing our environmental degradation problems, cheating with money means hiring the job out to parcel owners rather than attempting to do it ourselves as a collective. By "cheating," and hiring the job out to the many individual parcel owners, the collective can bypass the flawed and dangerous method of central planning.[4]

Bribing parcel owners to provide ecosystem services is the right thing to do for the utilitarian reason of helping us reduce environmental

---

[3]It's a catchy way to use the word "cheat" since in our high division of labor economy you have to cheat with money to obtain almost everything. You likely didn't make the clothes you're wearing right now, the soap you washed with, the shelter you're living in, the food you'll eat today, or the paper book or electronic gadget you're using to read these words. You cheated with money for each of those by paying others to make them for you.

[4]Central planning is a fundamentally flawed decision-making method because it can't, even in principle, accomplish its stated ends; central planners can't have the knowledge needed to make good plans [279–281, ch. 16 of 192]. Specifically, in this case of reducing environmental degradation on the various land parcels, the planner's conceit would have him determine what trees should grow in what areas and how old or big they should be, what other plants and animals should be on that parcel and where and how old, what cultural knowledge both the animal [84] and human people should have and pass along, and a myriad of other details. As with other central planning fantasies, it isn't possible for the planners to acquire enough information to achieve their goals. Hiring the job out to parcel owners shrinks the central planning problem down to individual parcels, where competition and cooperation among the parcel owners can be expected to produce the best decisions.

Central planning, when accompanied by concentrated power, is also known to be incredibly dangerous, as described in Chapter 7. Witness the millions murdered by the centrally planned regimes of nationalist and communist China, the USSR, and National Socialist Germany, to list what Rummel referred to as the deca-mega murderers, having killed tens of millions of their own people. As Rummel informed us, power kills [241].

degradation without the problems associated with central planning. It is also the right thing to do for the ethical reason of ensuring every supplier in our high division of labor economic system gets paid.

Landowner bribery rights a wrong

The function of money in a high division of labor economy is to enable that high division of labor by helping people make deals with one another. By using certain products, like gold coins or receipts for gold coins, as money, people can make equitable trades with each other. People's hands or pockets or strongboxes can be thought of as ledger entries, and the amount of money recorded in an entry can be thought of as the amount of gold held in someone's hand, pocket, or strongbox. The monetary amounts recorded in those ledger entries can be moved from one entry to another by the easy expedient of handing gold over to another person.

Products used as money allow their owners to get paid by people different from those they supplied by moving those products from one ledger entry to another. For example, a doctor might accept X dollars to treat John's injury and then use those X dollars to purchase fuel for his car. The doctor supplied services to one party, John, and was paid with what he needed, fuel, by another party, the owner of the fuel. The same thing could have happened, but without the patient John, if the fuel owner had an injury the doctor treated, with no money changing hands. Such a situation would be known as a coincidence of wants since the fuel owner, who could provide fuel, wanted injury treatment, and the doctor, who could provide injury treatment, wanted fuel.

Coincidences of wants practically never happen, so an accounting device is needed to track who supplied how much and who received how much.[5] Such a device is needed because few people are willing to do work for others without materially benefiting themselves. In addition, most of us don't want to take advantage of others, so we want to make sure our suppliers get paid a fair price. Therefore, our high

---

[5]The classic example of why a high division of labor economy can't exist without products that can be used as money is to imagine you wanted to pay your doctor with eggs. What if the doctor doesn't want eggs or already has too many because his other patients are also paying with eggs? And is the doctor supposed to pay his suppliers with eggs, in which case he would be using the eggs themselves as money?

division of labor economy is a tit-for-tat-style one, where I'll scratch your back if you scratch mine, and at the same time it's a type of gift economy, where most of us voluntarily take care of our suppliers.

In both tit-for-tat and gift economy-type deals, the parties usually will participate only if the books are right. In other words, everyone must get paid or the deal won't happen. In a high division of labor economy, which, as explained above, of necessity means money is half of practically every deal, the suppliers of the non-monetary parts of deals must be paid with money by the suppliers of the monetary parts. For example, if Ralph buys a sheep from Frank, then Frank has to supply Ralph the sheep, and Ralph has to supply Frank the money. If either participant suspects the other will breach the contract, the deal isn't made. Focusing on the monetary side of deals, all the suppliers of non-monetary goods and services in deals must be paid with money so they can pay their own suppliers. If suppliers don't get paid, they can't pay their suppliers, and so on, and production stops, and people die. One must pay the grocer for eggs, so the grocer can pay the farmer for eggs, so the farmer can pay the feed company for chicken feed, so the feed company can pay wheat farmers and others for their feed ingredients, and so on. Suppliers of medicine, tools, parts, and a mind-bogglingly long list of the economic outputs of this global high division of labor must be paid so we can stay alive.

Importantly for the redesign of our US dollars, the people whose living lands supply us with essential services, like breathable air and drinkable water, are currently exceptions to this rule. This is a significant omission from humanity's financial books.

Urban woodlands in the fifty states produce over $18 billion annually in benefits to society [282]. Trees and other green plants provide us animals with our most important supply, breathable air. Trees provide aerosol pollution reduction, slope stabilisation and water flow regulation within urban catchments [283]; they shade houses, reduce air temperatures, and block winds, resulting in reduced power plant emissions while slashing home energy bills by $5.4 billion a year in the United States alone [282]. Trees reduce stormwater runoff, decreasing flooding and the pollution carried into waterways [284], and they absorb excess nutrients from the soil, preventing algae blooms in waterways [285]. Forests in the United States currently sequester almost 15 percent of the carbon dioxide emitted into the atmosphere from fossil fuel combustion [286], with our national forests, parks, and monuments sequestering 17.2 billion tonnes of carbon [287]. Our lands provide an untapped opportunity—proven ways of storing carbon and reducing carbon emissions in the world's forests, grasslands, and wetlands [288]. The entirety of our living world may be providing us all with more than $100 trillion worth of ecosystem services every year [120, 130, 289]. In a real sense, these ecosystem services are priceless since we don't get to be alive without them.

If we choose to redesign our US dollars so this omission from our books is corrected, by paying *all* our parcel owners for their valuable ecosystem services, those parcel owners would be given a financial incentive not to cut down their trees or pave over their parcels. All other things being equal in such a scenario, we would expect them to leave more of their trees standing and their parcels healthier, and all of us would benefit from the ecosystem services provided by those healthier lands. Without correcting this omission, much of our living world is worth more money dead than alive, so what did we think would happen?

Means, motive, and opportunity to pay our parcel owners

There are good reasons for the previous lack of payment for ecosystem services to parcel owners. In the long long ago, certain ecosystem services like breathable air and drinkable water were plentiful and not easily measured, so the providers of those services, the parcel owners, were not paid. No one had the means or opportunity to do such a thing or the motive to even think about it—it would have seemed silly and absurd at the time.

That said, these times aren't those times. Breathable air and drinkable water can no longer be taken for granted [289], and ecosystem service data, which can be used to calculate landowner payments, is already available from sources such as the USA Forest Inventory and Analysis program and LiDAR-based re- mote sensing [290], Planet.com, Landsat, Moderate Resolution Imaging Spectroradiometer (MODIS), eddy covariance flux tow- ers [291], wildlife maps [292], and DNA samples from rivers and lakes [293].

The state of the art of this ecosystem service data collection has been improving for more than half a century and continues to improve. In one example, progress in remotely sensing solar-induced chlorophyll fluorescence (useful for the production of plant respiration estimates) is accelerating, using innovative sensors and advances in modeling [294]. Furthering these capabilities, in 2026 the European Space Agency is scheduled to launch the FLuorescence EXplorer (FLEX), a satellite custom-engineered to measure chlorophyll fluorescence [295]. We either have or can get the data needed to compute landowner payments [296–310].

Our ecosystem service data collection productivity may be on a path to further increases, thanks to personal data collection devices [311]. People will be able to wear gadgets to collect ecosystem service data like plant respiration rates. Evolutionary descendants of Metaverse™ glasses could fill such a role, as could video and photographic surveillance from automobiles, such as dashcam video recorders and the Google Street View surveyors. Data from the newly developed internet of living things (IOLT) [312] also could be incorporated into ecosystem services measurements. The entire planet will benefit from high-quality ecosystem service data through innovations such as these.

The information needed to pay lawful landowners exists too—much or most of the land on the earth is delineated into parcels owned by individuals, families, companies, and collectives,[6] with that ownership information theoretically recorded somewhere.

Thanks to the ecosystem service and land ownership data, we have at least part of the means to pay our land parcel owners for their breathable air, drinkable water, and other ecosystem services. Thanks to our knowledge of our poverty and environmental degradation problems, we have a utilitarian motive, and thanks to our innate selfishness and sense of being fair to others, we have ethical motives. We're going to have the opportunity when We, the People, of these fifty states agree to the present proposal. We will have the final piece of the puzzle needed to bribe parcel owners when we obtain the rest of the means, which is paying them their due. We will be able to bribe our parcel owners to keep their parcels healthy with our new, redesigned US dollars.

---

[6]Examples of land owned by collectives include the national forests, parks, and monuments co-owned by We, the People, of these fifty states, the lands of the Lakota Sioux people, the parks of the Republic of Dagestan, the parks of the city of Rio de Janeiro, the parks of the state of Hawaii, and so on.

We need a way to obtain the bribe money

Bribing parcel owners to provide ecosystem services is the obvious thing to do, so obvious it is already being done, on a limited scale. It is also the right thing to do, to make sure all our suppliers are paid in this worldwide high division of labor economy. It's even more so the right thing to do because our living world is in big trouble, and paying parcel owners to make it healthier will help. Furthermore, we have almost everything we need to do it—most importantly, ecosystem service data and land ownership data. There are then only two pieces missing from this parcel owner bribery puzzle—where to get the bribe money, and how big to make the bribes. We'll discover the answer to the first question in Chapter 11, and the second in Chapter 12.

Regarding where to get the bribe money, it would not make sense for it to come from our existing federal government payments for ecosystem services, which are obtained by taxing and borrowing. It would be terrific if the bribe money could be provided by privately funded charity organizations [110], who have been contributing what they can, or from hunters who have been paying private landowners for the ecosystem service of wild game to hunt, but we shouldn't hold our breath for these methods either. Private or public payment streams have obvious limitations—the efficacy of both federal government and private payments is limited by the availability of cash, and hunting rights sales only make sense on a minority of parcels. The problem with federal government payments is they increase poverty and environmental degradation as explained in Part I. The problem with private payments is there isn't enough cash available from the private sector; again as explained in Part I, most of us are already struggling to keep up with prices, let alone take on the additional expense of paying parcel owners for their ecosystem services.

Another idea, closer to where we're going with all this, is if we can't get the funds to pay landowners for their ecosystem services from money already in circulation but really want to pay them, nothing prevents the collective from doing more of what it already does—it could print new money to pay the parcel owners. How would that work? Easy—the collective could print up a certain number of US dollars for each ecosystem service provided by a land parcel and pay them to the owner. But wait, a US dollar is 1/42.22 ounces of gold [180–184], and alchemists haven't succeeded in "printing" any of it, aside from the hard way—by mining ore and manufacturing coins or bars.

How about printing up fraudulent paper receipts for gold and paying them to the landowner? Or better yet since it would be expensive to print all that paper and drive around delivering it to all the landowners, how about printing up new electronic receipts for fraudulent paper receipts for gold and crediting each landowner's bank account with a certain number of them? This seems like a step in the right direction, but it isn't—it would be vulnerable to political changes, and would leave gold as the definition of a US dollar—and thus continue to pay parcel owners to harm their land by excavating it. In addition, it likely would have no effect on the exponentially increasing supply of newly printed fraudulent paper receipts for gold being spent into circulation from a central point by the cheating vault owner, with all those resulting problems.

To deliver ecosystem service payments with new claims on US dollars within the existing monetary system, the central (Federal Reserve) bank(s) would have to give each parcel owner an account and credit it in direct proportion to the ecosystem services their parcel renders. Under existing fractional reserve rules, the Fed would also have to purchase federal government debt in direct proportion to the parcel owner payments, thus continually exacerbating We the People's debt problem. This one organization would have to measure ecosystem services accurately and credit parcel owners the correct amounts, and we would all have to trust it not to cheat or make mistakes. On the face of it, it sounds complicated and possibly dangerous. With this idea, we're almost there, but not quite. We need new US dollars, not more of the same.

Another option is to abandon this idea of fixing our US dollars and instead attempt to pass all the right statutes that will allow us to keep our existing compound interest inflationary monetary system, but without the poverty, crime, and environmental degradation. To be complete, some arguments do support the idea of governmental protection, rather than outright buying and selling of ecosystem services, because these types of protection have worked in certain circumstances, in certain ways, for certain things [313]; but again, a known risk of forcible government methods is mass murder [241–243], making this method not an option. The governmental option has been chosen for centuries, yet here we are. Our purpose here is actually to fix things, so let's keep trying.

How can payment be made to land parcel owners while simultaneously eliminating the dynamics of centrally produced fraudulent gold receipts? Do we expect every parcel owner on this small spaceship to send an invoice to each of us every month, and each of us voluntarily to write them a check every month? In addition to logistical objections to such actions, most of us simply don't have the cash as mentioned earlier. So what can we do?

By not paying parcel owners for their ecosystem services, we reduce their incentive not to harm their parcels, while our inflationary US dollar *bills* increase their incentive to harm them, so we can't do nothing. However, as noted, it's not practical or even possible for each of us to write checks to the world's land parcel owners, and we can't blindly abandon our inflationary money trap because many people depend on checks from our federal government. We can't throw all those families out on the street, but we also can't keep our money monopoly and let it continue to wreck our world. A way or ways must be found to escape the dilemma.

An examination of the money flows in our existing supply chains reveals a logical, easy means to that end. It will be similar to the idea of printing up fraudulent paper receipts for gold and yet different, in a lifesaving way. We have an opportunity to use a power we already exercise to reduce the unholy trinity of poverty, crime, and environmental degradation—the power of the monetary printing press. We have the opportunity to cheat with money and pay for ecosystem services with a new kind of US dollar that inverts the energy flow of conventional money. Surprisingly, this one simple change to our US dollars is going to transform our small world into a paradise for us all, and in the same way number two wood pencils are built; that is, without any one of us knowing how to do it [29].

11. BRIBING PARCEL OWNERS WITH ENTROPY MONEY

"You see things; you say 'Why?'
But I dream things that never were; and I say 'Why not?'"
~ The serpent [314]

I F we're serious about fixing our US dollars, an easy way becomes obvious upon consideration of how any products are made, both those intended for use as money and those not. Human-manufactured artifacts are produced by people making trades with each other in what are known as supply chains.

In our worldwide high division of labor economy, we cooperate to use raw materials from our world, processed through supply chains, to manufacture retail products and services. The general flow of materials and energy in supply chains is progressively processed raw materials flow from people in the agriculture, timber, and mining sectors to people in the retail sector. In an example of one small part of a supply chain, a parcel owner may mine iron ore from his parcel and sell it to a steel manufacturer. The steel manufacturer could sell steel to a screw manufacturer, who could sell screws to a car manufacturer, who could sell cars to retail or end users. This supply chain unavoidably removes energy, in the form of raw materials, from our living world since that's the only known way to manufacture things like houses, iPhones, and cars. Energy flows from land parcels supplying raw materials to completed retail products (Figure 11.1).

An argument can be made that people use energy removed from land parcels to live. The energy exists in the form of the raw materials used to manufacture houses, iPhones, cars, and so on. This argument can be made due to the physical relationship between mass and energy embodied in the special relativity formula, $E = mc^2$, where E is energy, m is the mass of the timber or iron ore or whatever, and c^2 is the speed of light squared. The energy removed, in the form of matter from the

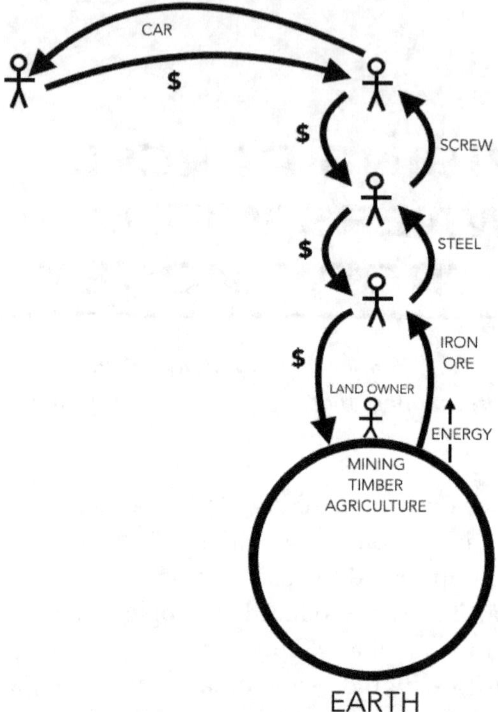

Figure 11.1. *Supply chain.*

parcel providing the material, is given by the formula. In effect, we're paying supply chain participants to remove energy from land parcels in the form of raw materials. This abstract argument will become concrete when we apply it to the human-manufactured products we use as money.

We have to use energy from our world to manufacture houses, iPhones, and cars, but what about the money used in the supply chain transactions? Must we do the same for it? In addition to bulk steel and screws, things that can be used as money, such as gold coins, are needed to manufacture artifacts like cars. As noted in Chapter 10, this is because coincidences of wants among trading parties are vanishingly rare. Things that can be used as money are also manufactured with the use of supply chains and have historically suffered from the defect that they, too, in effect consist of energy removed from land parcels.

Products used as money are no different from any other products of supply chains in that their raw materials must be removed from land

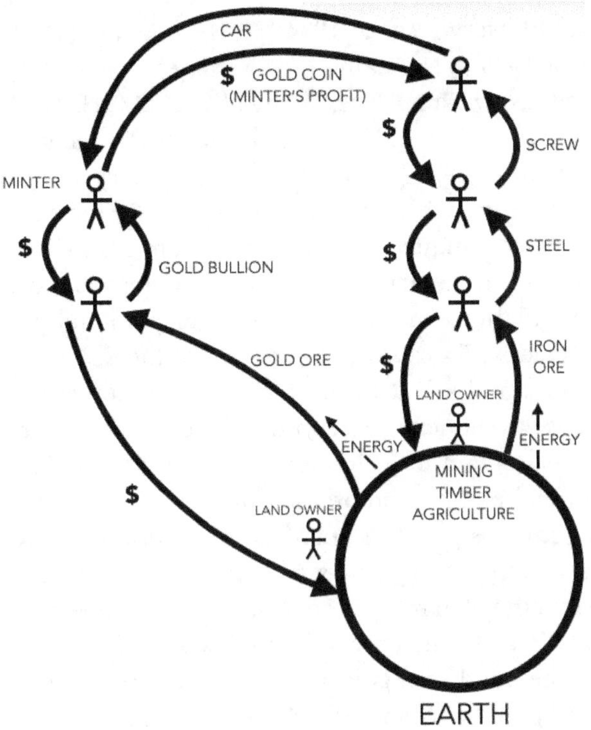

Figure 11.2. *Gold money.*

parcels. In various times and places, a diverse collection of commodities
that come from the land in one way or the other have been used as
money. Some examples include cows or *pecca*, hence the word *pecu-
niary* [193, 206], sheep, gems, and salt; for example, salt mined in Italy
and carried over the *via salaria*, or "salt road" [206], was commonly
used to pay first-century AD Roman soldiers—they received a *salarium*,
or "salt money" [p. 40 of 191], the Latin origin of the word *salary*.
Other examples include skins, shells [315, ch. 2 of 192] (i.e., to "shell
out" [p. 39 of 191, 316]), rice, nails, tobacco, cocoa, enormous stones,
feathers, beads, grain [ch. 2 of 192], whiskey, cigarettes [317], cotton,
canned mackerel [318, 319], copper, and so-called precious metals like
silver and gold [185, 206].

In modern times, gold has won the monetary arms race [p. 216 of
185]. Gold's win in this race has come in the form of the Coinage Act of
1792 [**CHAP. XVI**, Sec. 9 of 187], the US Coin Act of 1834 [**CHAP. XCV**,
Sec. 1 of 188], the Gold Standard Act of 1900 [**CHAP. 41**, Sec. 1 of

320], the Gold Reserve Act of 1934 [3], the so-called Bretton Woods Agreement of 1945 [321], named for a monetary conference held in Bretton Woods, New Hampshire, in July of 1944 [322, 323], the Par Value Modification Act of 1972 [SEC. 2 of 179], and the Par Value Modification Act reenactment of 1973 [180], along with the fact our gold treasure is officially recorded with a book value of $42.22 for each Fine Troy Ounce of our gold [August 31, 2025 report from 181].

Similar to non-monetary supply chains, to get the modern money, gold, into circulation, landowners mine gold ore and sell it to gold bullion producers (Figure 11.2). Bullion producers process the gold ore into bullion and sell it to minters, who manufacture gold coins suitable for use as money. These minters are, in effect, "printing" new money and spending it into circulation. Some of the coins are used to pay the minters' bullion and other suppliers, and the remainder, the coin manufacturer's profit, is spent on retail products. As with non-monetary products, energy flows from the land parcels supplying the raw material to the final retail products. For simplicity, and to aid in the discovery of a replacement for our gold US dollars, we're ignoring for the moment the fraudulent gold receipts used to complete transactions since, according to the Official Story, each of those is as good as 1/42.22 ounces of gold. We'll return to those when discovering how to put this all together in an escape plan (Part III).

Not all our suppliers are being paid

This system of producing retail products from raw materials appears to pay all suppliers needed to manufacture those retail products, but as noted in Chapter 10, for good historical reasons does not. The land parcel owners, whose living lands supply products like the breathable air and drinkable water necessary to keep retail supply chain partici-pants alive, have not been paid, nor have economists yet factored those contributions into their models [324]. For example, as things stand today a parcel owner can get paid for his tree by harvesting it, but typically can't get paid to let it stand and provide its valuable ecosystem services to us all [120]. His tree was worth more money dead than alive, giving the tree a smaller chance of staying alive than if the parcel owner had been paid for the services his tree was producing. Because of this dynamic, much of the land on the earth is worth more money dead than alive, and therefore, much of our living world is dying. However, the fat lady has not yet sung—we can still save our beautiful world. Acknowledging the properties any product must have to be suitable for use as money reveals a way to make our living world worth money both dead and alive, without robbing Peter to pay Paul.

A small change from gold can get everyone paid

In our existing supply chain structures, gold, by way of paper receipts and electronic receipts for paper receipts, is used as the monetary middleman, enabling suppliers to get paid. Gold is used for this purpose because it has better monetary properties than the competition. Gold won the monetary arms race over competing monetary products like silver, copper, rice, etc., partly due to its superior qualities of scarcity, durability, fungibility, divisibility, portability, and ease of use. Among gold's monetary competitors, silver is nearly as good as gold in those qualities; however, it's less durable, and less scarce, and therefore less portable.[1] In addition to its superiority in these three qualities, gold won the monetary arms race over silver because it's less useful for non-monetary purposes. Although its uselessness is decreasing as more industrial applications are found for it, such as electronics and medicine [326], as of the early twenty-first century the most popular use for gold, by a substantial margin, is monetary in nature.[2] In contrast, silver has a large and rapidly growing portfolio of non-monetary uses [328].

Counterintuitively, the lack of non-monetary uses for gold makes it more useful monetarily because that lack has helped produce a large and effectively invariant aboveground supply. Because it is (mostly) industrially useless, the amount of gold in circulation has grown steadily as people hoard rather than consume it, and is now large and relatively constant year over year. Backing up this claim, at current usage rates

---

[1]There are about 2.5 billion ounces of investment gold in the world and about 4 billion ounces of investment silver [325]. Due to silver's greater above ground supply, and its inferior durability, prices in silver historically have been greater than in gold. Users therefore have had to carry more silver than gold for purchases, making it less portable.

[2]These monetary uses include jewelry, art, and decoration, which are typically simply aesthetically pleasing ways to store gold [327].

it would take around 70 years to consume the world's aboveground gold supply if production stopped today, as contrasted with about 20 years for silver and a year or less for commodities such as crude oil, copper, corn, wheat, and frozen concentrated orange juice (FCOJ) [192, 328, 329].

This relatively constant supply, with a small amount added every year from mining operations and a small amount consumed every year in the electronics, medical, and other industries, gives gold utility to users by removing money supply from the price discovery process. If money supply, product supply, and consumer demand are the three things determining price, when money supply is constant the only price determinants are product supply and consumer demand. This allows consumers and producers to communicate economic preferences to each other without the information-corrupting influence of money supply variability [329].

Eliminating money supply influence on prices enables producers to make production decisions more accurately, based on perceived demand [ch. 16 of 192]. It also enables consumers to make consumption decisions more accurately, based on perceived supply. For example, if the money supply is constant, and the price of apples increases, both consumers and producers correctly perceive the supply of apples has decreased and/or the demand for apples has increased. This signals consumers to consume fewer apples, which makes sense because there are now, apparently, not as many apples available as they would like. It also signals producers to produce more apples, for the same reason.

Although neither consumer nor producer is necessarily aware of variations in supply or demand, the price signals incentivize them to behave as if they are. However, if supply and demand pressures have not changed but an increased money supply causes the price of apples to increase, suppliers can be tricked into producing more apples, and customers into consuming fewer. In such a case, the market might paradoxically produce more apples and consume fewer, possibly leading to a glut of apples and a waste of valuable resources that could have been better used elsewhere. Here, we propose to design a new US dollar that retains this valuable property of gold, in that it will remove money supply variations from the price discovery process. This new money will provide accurate price signals that enable people to cooperate to save the world, without any of us necessarily knowing how we're doing it.

To summarize, our supply chains use gold, formed into products such as coins and bars, as money because it is scarce, durable, fungible, divisible, portable, easy to use, and, so far, mostly useless for non-monetary purposes. These properties are all necessary for high-quality money.

The property of gold not required for high-quality money is that it is, in effect, a measurement of how much harm has been done to the earth (Figure 11.3).[3] This is because the size of the gold mine is directly proportional to the amount of gold mined. In other words, if you know how much gold you obtained from the mine, you know roughly how big the mine is. Similar to non-monetary products, a reasonable argument can be made that we use energy removed from parcels as money, and gold is a way to measure that energy and track it in a form suitable for use as money. A thermodynamically equivalent way of thinking about

Figure 11.3. *The amount of gold recovered (coin on right) is a measurement of the harm done to the parcel (open pit mine on left). (Gold mine photograph courtesy of Mhy, Gold Eagle photograph courtesy of WikiImages, both from Pixabay.)*

this idea, useful for bribing parcel owners, is that entropy[4] added to parcels is being used as both non-monetary and monetary products.

If the unrequired feature of the world's premier money incentivizes

---

[3]Brazilian wildcat gold miners [330] provide a dismaying example.

[4]Joules per kelvin. Entropy is a measurable physical property most commonly associated with a state of disorder or randomness. In the Classical thermodynamics sense, entropy is energy that is no longer available to do work. In the statistical thermodynamics sense, entropy is the probability of a given arrangement of matter and energy. Further discussion of the concept of entropy as related to our living world is included in Appendix D.

us to harm the land, is it possible to engineer a replacement reversing that incentive while retaining the premier money's monetarily needed properties? Can we metaphorically keep the baby and throw out the bath water?

What if a way can be found to manufacture a scarce, durable, fungible, divisible, portable, non-monetarily useless product that effectively consists of entropy removed, or mined, from the earth rather than added to it? Could such a product facilitate our escape from the unholy trinity of poverty, crime, and environmental degradation?

Entropy money

Whereas legacy monetary products like gold are, in effect, a way of using energy mined from a land parcel as money, this new kind of monetary product would reverse the energy flow. This energy flow reversal can be illustrated using a part of the supply chain required to manufacture a wood pencil rather than a car as in the previous two examples (Figure 11.4), and is inspired by Leonard Read's essay *I, Pencil* [29]. The

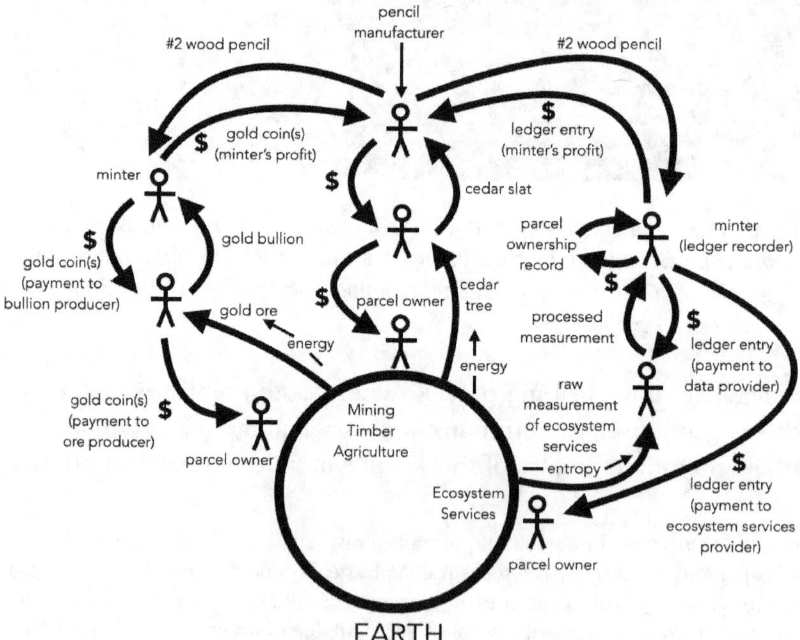

Figure 11.4. *Entropy money pays landowners not to cut down their trees.*

differences between the two monetary supply chains are summarized in Table 11.1. When entropy added to a parcel, or equivalently, energy mined from it, is used as money, the amount added or mined is estimated by measuring the health diminishment of the land (left-hand-side of Figure 11.4). This measurement is accomplished by using the amount of material excavated as a proxy for that diminishment, and estimating the amount of excavated material by measuring the amount of gold recovered.

If entropy mined from a parcel were to be used as money, the amount removed could be estimated by measuring the health enhancement of the land (right-hand-side of Figure 11.4). The land's health enhancement could be measured in the same way your doctor gauges your health: by measuring its respiration rate. While respiration rates are only a rough approximation of yours or a parcel's health, they are a good starting point, and can be improved with further measurements (see Chapter 14). In the case of a parcel's respiration rate, that rate could be estimated by measuring its oxygen production rate.[5] In addition to being used as a gauge of land health, the parcel's oxygen production rate can be treated as a measurement of its breathable air production rate, which in turn can be thought of as the rate it supplies ecosystem services[6] to us all. In our new monetary system we'll use the health of the parcel, as measured[7] by its respiration rate, approximated in turn by breathable air production rates, as the money "printed" by parcel owner(s).

If gold can be thought of as a type of energy money, considering it consists of a material used as a proxy for the energy removed, or mined, from a parcel, a material used as a proxy for entropy mined from the parcel can be considered a type of entropy money. Consider that any land parcel owners with gold on their land effectively own a type of

---

[5]Carbon absorption rates or carbon dioxide absorption rates could be used if desired. Counted on a molecule-by-molecule basis, the oxygen production rate is numerically identical to either of those. The oxygen production rate will be used here because it is the magic ingredient making our air breathable.

[6]Note that using provided ecosystem services (as measured by produced breathable air) as a proxy for health enhancement is just one way of skinning this cat. It will be used in this portion of the monetary analysis as a straightforward way to obtain a first cut at our new, world-saving money, but it is not the final word in the use of removed entropy as money. Speculation on future entropy money developments is presented in Chapter 14.

[7]Details about how and when such measurements can be made, and by whom, can be found in Part III.

Table 11.1. *Entropy money makes parcels healthier*

	Energy mined	Entropy mined
Measured by:	diminished parcel health	enhanced parcel health
Inferred by proxy:	material excavated	respiration rate (ecosystem services provided)
Proxy measured by:	gold	oxygen (breathable air)

monetary printing press because they can fashion it into coins and spend those coins into circulation. With this new kind of money, entropy-type money or entropy money, parcel owners with living creatures on their land will also effectively own a monetary printing press.

When energy removed from a parcel is used as money, the minter records the monetary amounts onto a type of physical ledger entry, in the form of fungible gold coins (left-hand side of Figure 11.4). The minter pays some of the coins to his ore supplier and keeps the rest as profit. The parcel owner and the minter have turned energy from the earth into products that can be used as money. In other words, they've "printed" money.

When entropy removed from a parcel is used as money, the minter converts processed ecosystem service data into a monetary number (right-hand side of Figure 11.4). He then records that monetary number onto several ledger entries, each spendable by the appropriate parties. He records the bulk of the monetary number in the lawful parcel owner's ledger entry and records certain portions of the monetary number in the ledger entries of the ecosystem service data and land ownership data providers. Finally, the minter records a portion in the ledger operator's entry and keeps the rest as profit. The parcel owner, data providers, and minter have turned entropy, instead of energy, from the earth into products that can be used as money. In other words, they've "printed" money.

When energy removed from a parcel is used as money, the amount removed is estimated by measuring the parcel's health diminishment, using the amount of material excavated from the mine as a proxy for that diminishment, and estimating the amount of excavated material by measuring the amount of gold recovered. The gold is spent by forming it into fungible coins or bars, keeping them in a vault, and trading paper notes denoting ownership of them. The gold coins or bars can be thought of as ledger entries in physical form, and the paper notes can be thought of as a more divisible and portable set of physical ledger entries pointing to the first set. Here in these fifty states, the first set of physical ledger entries are known as dollars, where each dollar consists of 1/42.22 ounces of gold, and the second set of ledger entries are known as dollar *bills*, where each dollar *bill* is an IOU for a dollar. This brief description ignores the vault owner cheating enabled by ownership claims (such as paper dollar *bills*) to the gold in the vault.

In contrast, when entropy removed from a parcel is used as money, the amount removed can be estimated by measuring the parcel's health enhancement, using the amount of ecosystem services provided by the critters as a proxy for that enhancement, and estimating the amount of ecosystem services provided by measuring the amount of breathable air produced. If produced oxygen, for example, is used as the entropy measurement, it can be treated nearly the same as gold, but by recording the measured amount directly on a ledger rather than doing something with the oxygen first. The difference from gold is the oxygen wouldn't be stored in a vault, but instead would be left in the atmosphere for us animals to enjoy. This will make the initial measurement more important since it won't be possible to go into the vault to check the previous measurement. Therefore, provenance and other metadata must be recorded and packaged with oxygen production rate data to ensure user confidence in the money.

Our legacy US dollars were each defined, or could be thought of as, a fixed quantity of energy removed from a parcel, where a fixed quantity of excavated material, as measured by recovered gold, is used as a proxy for that energy. These legacy US dollars can be considered a type of energy money, or energy-type US dollars. By way of comparison, new and improved US dollars could each be defined as a fixed quantity of entropy removed from a parcel, where a fixed amount of provided ecosystem services, as measured by produced oxygen, is used as a proxy for that entropy. Rather than energy-type money, such new and improved US dollars could be considered a type of entropy money, or entropy-type US dollars. If our US dollars were redefined as a type of entropy money, using ecosystem services as a proxy for removed entropy, we would, in effect, be using provided ecosystem services themselves *as* money. Table 11.1 compares the two types of money and their measurements.

Since modern commerce substantially depends on the ability to complete transactions remotely, it makes sense to track and trade the measured oxygen production numbers on an electronic ledger. Because a ledger that is both reliable and accessible to everyone is needed, a decentralized autonomous ledger (DAL) similar to the bitcoin ledger will be ideal because it will not require us to trust any individuals or institutions. The network maintaining the ledger will be nothing more than an inanimate machine. This will give us a trustless way to complete our books by paying everyone in our supply chains, including the suppliers of ecosystem services like breathable air and drinkable water.

Using an appropriate DAL will also give us a way to add monetary qualities to our produced oxygen—durability, fungibility, divisibility, portability, and lack of non-monetary uses—to make it a good store of value and means of exchange. If the ledger records land parcel-produced oxygen faithfully, the ledger entries are automatically scarce, meaning finite, since the parcel produces oxygen at a finite rate. Other monetarily needed quantities can be added by the DAL: the ledger units on DALs are durable, as long as the Internet routers are functioning. The ledger units are fungible or can be made fungible by making transactions private. The ledger units are divisible, within the limits of floating point arithmetic, and portable, for anyone with Internet access. For the needs of doing business remotely, ledger units on a DAL are effectively infinitely portable compared to gold since it is easy to transfer ledger units to anyone in the world with Internet access. DAL portability can be compared to the difficulty of getting gold, or paper claims to gold, to someone on the other side of the world. Finally, the ledger units can have no other value than to be transferred reliably by their owners to other ledger entries.

Completing our books in this way will allow us to eliminate the ill effects of gold while keeping the good—we will have solved both of gold's problems. Using entropy removed from a parcel as money will do the opposite of what using energy removed from it does, because it pays parcel owners to make their land healthier rather than sicker. Tracking it on a DAL, rather than a physical ledger in the form of gold coins or paper notes, will eliminate the possibility of excess claims on the entropy, and the resulting price inflation, by turning the tracking over to a machine that cannot be corrupted. Taking the two steps of using entropy removed from land parcels as money rather than using energy removed, and using an incorruptible machine to track it will automatically reduce poverty, crime, and environmental degradation.

12. ENTROPY MONEY REDUCES UNHOLY TRINITY

I F something from the land is used as money, people can be expected to remove it from their land voluntarily. Conversely, if there is a need for people to remove something from their land voluntarily, a way to make it happen is to use that something as money. Using entropy removed from our world as money will give parcel owners a financial incentive to remove entropy from their land, and therefore, we will expect landowners voluntarily to keep their lands healthy so they remove entropy.[1]

We all depend for our lives on land parcel owners who allow the living creatures on their parcels to live and therefore remove entropy from their lands. If all the plants and animals on the earth were to die today, its surface would soon look more like the surface of our moon or Mars because the rest of the universe is always adding entropy to the earth. In other words, our universe is trying to kill us. Every day, the non-earth part of the universe adds entropy to our world, making it look more like our moon or Mars. Also every day, we animals and plants are removing about the same amount of entropy from our world by living and growing, powered by supplies of low entropy [p. 10 of 324] from the sun and the earth's hot, molten core.[2]

Our living biological world exists as a relatively stable system in which the net amount of living beings, breathable air, and drinkable

---

[1]This dynamic will apply even to very wealthy individuals and families, owning very large tracts of land. They will be incentivized to remove entropy for the same reasons as smaller owners—partly due to wanting a healthy living world, partly to keep up with the price inflation to be caused by the linearly inflating money supply, and partly because it generally isn't smart to turn away money as there's always a possible use for it (for example for charity). More details regarding who will get what are presented later in this chapter.

[2]The earth's hot, molten core nourishes the creatures surrounding deep-sea hydrothermal vents.

water in our gravity well remains about the same, day to day. If put in the form of an equation, we could say the rate of change of the entropy of the surface of the earth is the rate of change due to entropy added by the rest of the universe plus the rate of change due to entropy subtracted by us living beings:[3] [4]

$$\frac{d}{dt} Entropy_{\text{Earth}} = \frac{d}{dt} Entropy_{\text{Universe}} + \frac{d}{dt} Entropy_{\text{LifeOnEarth}}. \quad (12.1)$$

Therefore, increasing the rate of entropy removal by us living beings decreases the rate of entropy increase on the surface of the earth, resulting in reduced entropy there at any given time, all other factors remaining unchanged.

However, with the explosion of industrial civilization in the past few thousand years, especially the past century or so, it appears the rate of entropy removal by living creatures, the last term on the right-hand side of equation 12.1, has been reduced. This is because it generally pays more to decrease the ability of our living world to remove entropy, such as by harvesting trees, than it does to increase that ability, such as by planting trees [120]. Consistent with this supposition of a reduced rate of entropy removal by living creatures is the news of pollution and animal die-offs. This is where our new and improved US dollars come in—if parcel owners are paid for the amount their living land contributes to the last term in equation 12.1, we can expect the entropy of the surface of our world to decrease, all other things being equal. This will mean a healthier biosphere, including every one of us human occupants of this world.

We're considering using removed entropy as money, but an important practical consideration is that to do so, it must be measured. If we consider the rate at which the ecosystem service of breathable air is produced, as measured by the rate of produced oxygen, to be a first-order approximation of the second term on the right-hand side of

---

[3]The notation $\frac{d}{dt}$ means the derivative, or rate of change, with respect to time.

[4]The equation is a summation because the value of the rate of entropy increase due to the universe is positive, while the value of the rate of increase due to us living beings is negative. Quantitative details of the terms in the equation, using both the Classical and statistical thermodynamics paradigms, are included in Appendix D.

equation 12.1, a numerical approximation of the integral of the oxygen production rate can be used as a proxy for the amount of removed entropy. Therefore, we can use removed entropy as money by measuring the produced oxygen rate for the various parcels. As noted in Chapter 10, this needed rate data used to compute landowner payments either exists or can be made to exist relatively easily for nearly the entire surface of the planet.

Setting aside for a moment the question of how to measure removed entropy, let us instead ask what if, to see if there is any point in asking how. What if every parcel owner received regular bribes with an automated printing press that, in effect, printed new and improved US dollar *bills* at a rate directly proportional to the health of the parcel? The consequences of these new and improved entropy-type US dollars are far-reaching and profound.

Entropy money reduces environmental degradation

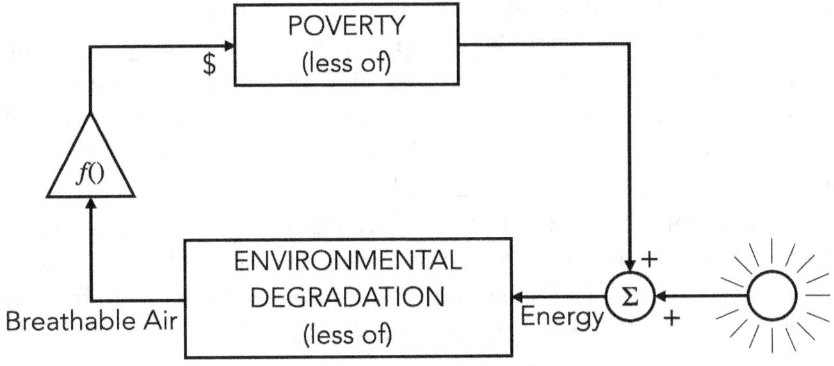

Figure 12.1. *Entropy money puts our living world in harmony with our financial world.*

US dollars improved in this way will introduce a positive feedback loop between our financial and biological worlds (Figure 12.1). This loop is effectively an automatic control system,[5] with money used to close the feedback loop.

---

[5]This control system is unstable by design, in contrast to most industrial control systems, which must be stable.

This feedback loop operates in the following way: The parcel owners in the **POVERTY (less of)** box in Figure 12.1 either work their parcel, making it either less or more healthy, or they don't work it. The parcel owners' energy, provided in the form of work, plus energy from the sun, are inputs to the land in the **ENVIRONMENTAL DEGRADATION (less of)** box. If the land gets some sun energy and the owners let at least some of the creatures on it live, it may produce some breathable air as a byproduct of plant photosynthesis. If the land has living plants producing breathable air, it may also produce drinkable water and other services as a byproduct of other functionalities of the living creatures on the parcel.

Considering only the breathable air portion of the provided ecosystem services, the rate of its production is treated as an approximation of the rate of provided ecosystem services, and the numerical values of that measurement are converted through the function $f()$ into a number representing the amount of entropy money the parcel owners have "printed." This number is added to the owners' ledger entry, giving them a financial incentive to keep the parcel healthy.

Even if a parcel owner were being paid for entropy removal, he or she would still have the option to make the land less healthy. For example, the owner may want to build a shopping mall and parking lot on his or her parcel to earn money. In that case, however, he or she would no longer receive payments for ecosystem services, and the potential income loss would be factored into the decision to build or not build the mall. Whereas entropy money would have been added to the owner's ledger entry in proportion to the breathable air and drinkable water produced by the parcel, if it were razed the entropy removal income would cease, at least until trees and critters resided there once again. In another land-health preserving incentive, if a parcel owner or natural event causes the ecosystem service production rates to decrease (such as from a clear-cut or fire) and the owner decides to sell the parcel, the reduced ecosystem service production rate would of course factor into the sales price. This dynamic gives the parcel owner a financial incentive not to clear-cut his parcel and to protect it from fire, while not forcing such behaviors.

Considering this dynamic for all land parcels, we can expect environmental degradation to decrease with the use of entropy money, other factors remaining equal. Due to the respiration of those spared trees, entropy money will also supplement existing efforts [331] to reduce the atmospheric concentration of the greenhouse gas carbon dioxide [288, 332, 333].

Entropy money eliminates federal government taxation and borrowing

In addition to reducing environmental degradation, the positive feedback loop added to our world by entropy money (Figure 12.1) will reduce poverty. The positive feedback loop between our financial and biological worlds will reduce poverty by paying land parcel owners for the health of their land. The more health, the more payment.

The first, and extremely beneficial, poverty reduction consequence is revealed when we consider who owns the parcels. There are many among us lucky enough to own a parcel or parcels, but one owner in particular gives us a very interesting possibility. This owner is the collective We, the People, of these fifty states. Composed of approximately 270 million politically competent peers, this collective owns 202,133,000 acres of trees [Appendix 1 of 334, which excludes interior Alaska], plus many acres of grasslands, scrublands, wetlands, and other ecosystem types on its national forests, parks, and monuments. If parcel owners are bribed to mine entropy, and We, the People, as a collective are a parcel owner, We will be among those receiving bribes to mine entropy. Here's where the concept of entropy money becomes even more interesting due to the two obvious questions: one, how big will our bribes be, and two, can we use them toward our federal government budget?

Since We, the People, as a group are the sovereign, we can define our new US dollars so our national land bribes work out to whatever size we like, and yes, of course we can use them toward our federal government budget. If we were to fund our federal government with them, the newly printed money received from those national lands would reduce that government's need for taxation and borrowing. How much entropy money would our national lands produce and thus reduce taxes and borrowing? In other words, how many ecosystem services would be counted as a dollar? We haven't yet said, and since we're redesigning our US dollars, this is a degree of design freedom available to us. A wise choice will calibrate our new entropy money to eliminate the need

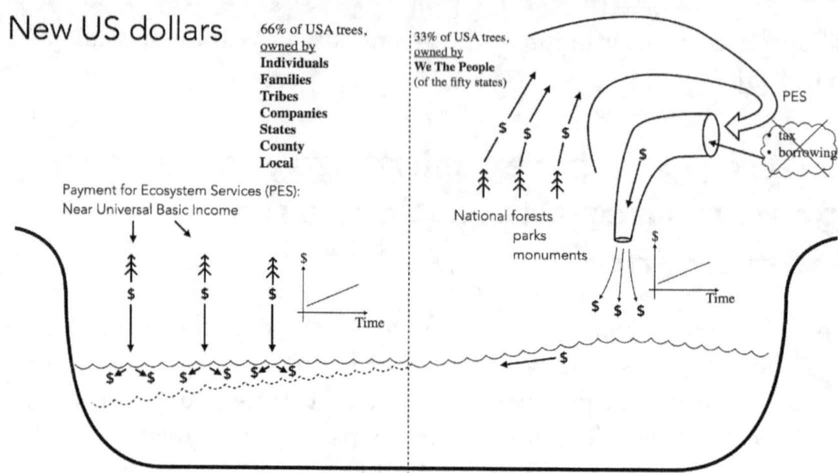

Figure 12.2. *Entropy money enters circulation equitably.*

for both federal government taxation and borrowing (Figure 12.2).

We currently use energy from land parcels as money, measured by the amount of gold recovered, and call every 1/42.22 ounces of gold a dollar. If someone produces an ounce of gold from his parcel, then mints it into a coin and spends that coin into circulation, he has effectively "printed" 42 and 2/9 (~42.22) new US dollars and spent them into circulation.[6]

Similarly, if we were to redesign our US dollars so they consist of a given amount of entropy mined from a parcel, as measured by the amount of ecosystem services produced, the owner could "mint" that entropy by recording those provided ecosystem services on a spendable ledger entry and subsequently spend it into circulation. In other words, he could "print" a new US dollar and spend it into circulation.

If our national lands produce $X_{national}$ ecosystem services per year, and our national budget is, say, $7 trillion per year, we have design freedom to choose the K dollars per ecosystem service that causes our collectively owned trees to fund our entire national budget (equation 12.2).

---

[6]Ignoring, for the purposes of description, the fact that, under the current rules and regulations, We, the People, will send a brute squad after anyone who does such a thing.

$$X_{national}\left(\frac{\text{ecosystem services}}{\text{yr}}\right) K\left(\frac{\$}{\text{ecsosystem service}}\right) = 7\text{T}\left(\frac{\$}{\text{yr}}\right) \quad (12.2)$$

As mentioned earlier, we could use produced oxygen as a measurement of the ecosystem services provided by any given parcel of land. If we do that, a value for K allowing our nationally owned trees to cover the entire federal government budget can be computed by assuming We, the People, own approximately 202,133,000 acres of trees [334], and each of those acres produces, on average, 1,060,000 grams of oxygen[7] per year. If our federal government budget needs $7 trillion per year, and we choose to size our new and improved US dollars so our national lands produce enough new US dollars every year to cover it, all we have to do to find the number of grams of oxygen that would be defined as a US dollar is solve equation 12.3 for K. Solving, we find K = 1/30.6, and thus to cover our national budget our new definition of a US dollar will have changed from 1/42.22 ounces of gold to 30.6 grams of oxygen produced by living plants on living lands.[8]

$$202,133,000 \,(\text{acres})\, 1,060,000 \left(\frac{\text{g/acre}}{\text{yr}}\right) K\left(\frac{\$}{\text{g}}\right) = 7\text{T}\left(\frac{\$}{\text{yr}}\right) \quad (12.3)$$

K could be scaled up to provide help for those among us not lucky enough to privately own any land. For example, if the definition of our new oxygen US dollars is rounded down from 30.6 to 30 grams of oxygen, those of us who don't individually own any land will each receive $42/month. As another example, if we change our definition of a US dollar to 20.67 grams of oxygen, those who don't own any land would receive $1,000 per month, and each of the millions of owners of 1/8th acre parcels (if they're half covered by trees) would receive $1,267 per month. Such a change to our money would help many survive, and the number can be adjusted to whatever number the collective chooses.

---

[7]This number was found by a brief Internet search for how many grams of oxygen an acre of trees produces in a year and must be updated by the appropriate biologists.

[8]Up-to-date, correct numbers must be used to recompute immediately prior to making the change.

Extra payments such as these could be considered a type of universal basic income (UBI, briefly discussed in Appendix E).

Even without explicitly scaling up K, a computation that only accounts for our forested national lands would allow for a UBI on its own. We would obtain this benefit because equation 12.3 only considers forested lands. If our forested lands by themselves are funding our entire national budget, the extra from our non-forested lands can be distributed out to us individuals as a UBI. Either of these methods, gaining up K or using only our forested lands to compute it, could be used to produce a UBI. We could also choose to do both, or neither and not have a UBI, to minimize the number of new US dollars entering circulation. It would be the choice of We, the People, and We could change Our minds at any time because We, as a group, or collective, are the sovereign.

Continuing for now to defer the question of how exactly one would go about using plant-produced oxygen molecules as US dollars, if these new US dollars are initialized with the correct value of K, with its value thereafter held constant, and if the number of our new oxygen US dollars produced by our national and private lands is established by reliable ecosystem service measurements, several consequences will ensue, starting with the obvious: our national lands will get healthier, our national debt will be eliminated after a period of time, and our national taxes will be eliminated immediately.

Our national lands will get healthier because a positive feedback loop (Figure 12.1) will be established between them and our national budget, giving us all financial incentive to conserve and preserve them. It will reduce the number of trees sold to timber companies due to the income stream from those trees that would be lost if they were harvested and sold.[9]

New oxygen US dollars, with the correct scaling of K, will allow us to repeal our federal government tax statutes since the national lands will be supplying the entire yearly budget. Federal government budget needs will be reduced by the amount no longer needed to pay revenuers, and the excess can be distributed back to us individuals as a UBI.

If our national lands provide for our entire national budget, our national debt will also begin shrinking, on its way to zero. The debt will shrink because debt service is part of the budget, and we will no longer

---

[9]The high division of labor price discovery machine will adjust timber prices to match supply with demand, such as for houses or paper.

be borrowing, again since additional debt will no longer be needed to complete the budget. Our federal government budget will shrink even more and continue to shrink, thanks to steadily decreasing interest payments as the debt is paid down. Again, any resulting budget surplus can become a UBI.[10]

Eliminating the federal government revenuers will also cause almost everyone's health to begin improving immediately, thanks to reduced financial- and revenuer-induced stress. It will save us the $409 billion currently wasted every year on tax compliance and "tax planning" [335, 336], give us back the time and energy previously wasted filling out revenuer forms, and increase our monetary wealth as we suddenly get to keep the money previously lost to federal government revenuers.

Entropy money reduces poverty

Entropy money "printing presses" improve cash flows by introducing money into circulation, but without the negative side effects caused by the central bank and Council on Foreign Relations methods described in Chapter 8. Rather than being loaned into circulation, and subsequently leaving circulation when the loans are repaid, entropy money will be spent into circulation by land parcel owners and remain in circulation thereafter, with no one put on the dole. The parcel owners will rightfully be paid for the entropy their living land removed from our world, or equivalently, the ecosystem services provided by their parcels. In addition to entering circulation through our national forests, parks, and monuments, entropy money will benefit us all by entering circulation

---

[10]Some may argue holders of our US debt notes won't accept payment in entropy dollars. Given that the market discovered price of entropy dollars will reflect its superior temporal and spatial monetary policy, entering circulation linearly and equitably, as compared to the federal reserve notes currently paid to US debt holders (Figures 12.2 and 12.5), entering circulation exponentially from a central spending point, it is likely debt holders and others will be happy to be paid with entropy dollars. Also, if We, the People, choose to change our definition of a US dollar as We have many times before, and continue to pay Our debts with Our redesigned US dollars, it isn't like bond holders will have much choice. Bond buyers won't be able to boycott Our bond sales because there won't be any more of those—our national lands will be covering our entire budget without further borrowing. Finally, see Chapter 13 for the solution in case consumers of money aren't happy with Our new, improved US dollars.

through our state, county, and local government parks and through our private landowners' parcels.

We'll all benefit thanks to the improved budget funding for our states, counties, and cities due to the new entropy money income streams from their parks. We, the People, will be presented with the option to partake of some sweet government rebate checks and/or reduced taxation, thanks to the money newly supplied by our parks. Everyone in the states will receive a piece of the $189 billion/month going to the states, counties, and cities (assuming we set the definition of our new oxygen US dollars at 30 grams and those collectives own a total of 64,095,000 acres of trees [334]).

With the help of central banks and revenuer brute squads, the current federal government budget is funded with explicit taxes, inflation taxes, and borrowing, but a properly calibrated entropy money will fund the government with an inflation tax only (Figure 12.3). This inflation tax

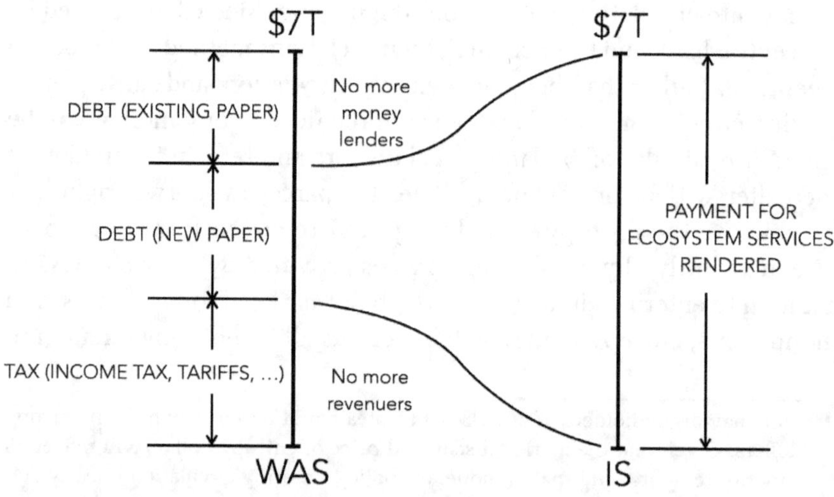

Figure 12.3. *Entropy money gets federal government money lenders and revenuers out of our lives.*

will be similar to our legacy inflation tax in that it will be paid with increased prices due to the new money entering circulation. However, the inflation tax used to fund our federal government with new entropy-type US dollars will be smaller than it was with legacy energy-type US dollars because federal government spending won't be the only circulation entry point for new money. The new money will enter circulation from many locations, including our federal government, our city, county, and state parks, and our companies, Indian tribes, and families, decreasing everyone's inflation tax by getting us all closer to a monetary spigot. Entropy-type US dollars will improve cash flows, by getting money into circulation and by doing it more equitably than in the before time, reducing the Cantillon effect [222]. It will do this by entering circulation from the many economic locations of the various land parcel owners, similar to how gold enters circulation.

One of the reasons for gold's win in the monetary arms race is its relatively even distribution in the earth's crust, causing it to enter circulation somewhat equitably. This can be contrasted with central bank fraudulent receipts for gold, which enter circulation by way of a relatively few people, who are therefore first to the bidding wars with this newly printed money. As noted previously, price increases resulting from the fraudulent receipts tend to precede the money itself as it flows out into circulation, and thus increase poverty through a transfer of real wealth from the many late recipients of the new money to the few earlier recipients [211, 220, 222, 224].

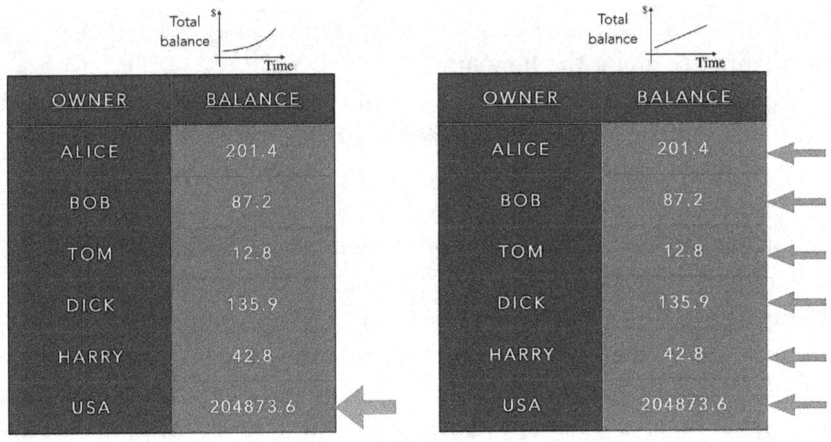

Figure 12.4. *Entropy money enters circulation equitably and linearly.*

Paying parcel owners for their ecosystem services, by giving them metaphorical printing presses with metaphorical cranks mechanically turning at rates directly proportional to their land's provided ecosystem services, has a poverty-reducing effect similar to that of gold. These payments won't directly affect our federal government spending, which will remain numerically unchanged from the legacy monetary system. However, the new entropy money cash flows will affect the other land parcel owners, who will benefit from the more equitable entry of new money into circulation (left-hand side of Figure 12.2[11]). As noted in the figure, payment for ecosystem services rendered will be a form of universal basic income for parcel owners who keep their lands healthy.

The old and new money systems also can be juxtaposed in their ledger forms (Figure 12.4). The legacy US dollar *bills* enter circulation faster and faster over time into the one ledger entry of the collective, operated by its agents in the federal government. In contrast, new and improved US dollars enter circulation at a steady rate through the collective's ledger entry and all of the many private parcel owners' ledger entries, as well as the ledger entries of states, counties, cities, and so on.

The new entropy money entering circulation from our private landowners will benefit both them and those of us not lucky enough to own any land privately. In addition to the benefits we'll obtain by virtue of being co-owners of public lands, those of us who don't own any land privately will benefit by getting closer to the new money entering circulation. Our private landowners will benefit by virtue of being directly under the new monetary spigots.

Using a US dollar definition of 30g of oxygen, considering forested lands only and excluding the interior of Alaska, corporations, conservation organizations, Native American tribes, and others, owning about 24 percent of the trees in the country [334], will receive a total of $488 billion per month, while family forest owners, comprised of nine and a half million people who collectively own 272 million acres of trees [334], will receive about $801 billion per month. By far the largest group of family forest owners, those owning from 1 to 9 acres of forest, consisting of 5.9 million people who own a total of almost 19 million forested acres, will receive a total of nearly $55 billion per month [334]. This monetary benefit to our private landowners will prove important for reducing both poverty and environmental degradation—as reported by the US Forest Service, "America's 10 million family forest owners are diverse, dynamic, and numerous. They are pivotal for the protection

---

[11]The area between the lower and upper ("water" level) lines in the non-central government portion on the left-hand side of Figure 12.2 is the amount we will have effectively shrunk our central government spending by using this type of money.

and sustainable management of our forests across the landscape, yet they face ever-increasing pressures and challenges. . . . only 1 in 5 acres of family forest land is owned by someone who has a written forest management plan, and only 2 in 5 acres are owned by people who have received forest management advice" [337].

Entropy money will benefit us all by helping our forest-owning families care for their lands. Choosing to track our new money on a programmable ledger will give us design freedom to help those families improve the care they can provide their life-giving forests. In one of many possibilities, entropy money algorithms could be encoded to pay family forest owners bonuses for forest management plans, as mentioned by the US Forest Service. The huge benefit of tracking our new entropy-type US dollars on programmable ledgers is that paying a bonus for land health assistance, such as forest management plans, is merely one possibility out of many. As will be discussed in Chapter 14, bonuses could be paid for anything entrepreneurs might dream up—for example, biodiversity. Paying land owners bonuses for improved land health will result in bonuses for everyone. It will result in monetary bonuses to people employed by parcel owners to make their lands healthier and to the people subsequently getting business from those employees, to provide them things like shelter and food. It will also provide health bonuses to the rest of us, who will get to enjoy the benefits of a healthier living world.

In addition to the benefits provided by entropy money to forest-owning families and their employees, benefits will accrue to farm-owning families and their employees. Farmers will be paid for the ecosystem services provided by their crops during the time when the crops are living and growing, and various companies could benefit by selling farmers the service of helping them increase crop yields in healthy ways [338–341, ch. 2 of 342]. Modifications to the entropy-to-US-dollars conversion algorithm could also be made to encourage healthy farming practices.

Practically every home-owning family in the country will also benefit from the new entropy money as it pays them for their ecosystem services—nicely manicured grass lawns produce oxygen, as do the shrubs and trees on those lots. Best of all will be the environmental degradation reduction benefits of entropy money as each of those homeowners will have monetary incentives to make their yards healthier. Entropy money will provide incentives to plant native vegetation and make other changes to help the critters on homeowners' parcels, such as pollinators and other valuable ecosystem contributors. Furthermore, similar to the case for forested parcel owners, the entropy money computation algorithm could be modified to pay a bonus to homeowners for certifications such as the wildlife habitat certifications awarded by the National Wildlife Federation [343]. With programmable entropy money, our options to incentivize landowners to make their parcels healthy are limited only by our imaginations.

Entropy money reduces poverty

Ecosystem service printing presses will reduce poverty by creating new jobs. Jobs will be created for biologists, remote-sensing specialists, and computer programmers to measure ecosystem services and credit lawful parcel owners.

More jobs will be created for people like arborists and foresters to help landowners keep their parcels healthy. Jobs will be created for lawyers, to help parcel owners sue for damages those who trespass against them by harming the living creatures on their lands, such as by hunting without authorization or polluting the parcel. Even more jobs will be created for speculators to trade and hedge the new money.

Entropy money will improve cash flows by giving businesses back the cash they'd previously wasted on tax compliance and planning. Business conditions will also improve because the elimination of federal government taxes will result in reduced prices throughout the various supply chains.

Entropy money will benefit us all with a good temporal monetary policy. The expected number of monetary units in circulation and their rate of entry into circulation as a function of time can be compared for three different temporal monetary policies (Figure 12.5). The left-hand-side column of the figure shows the amount of money in circulation as a function of time, and the right-hand-side column shows its entry rate as a function of time. The number of fraudulent receipts for gold in circulation and their rate of entry is shown in the first row. Due to compound interest effects, the more of this type of money in circulation the faster even more enters circulation, in a runaway. This type of money is known as easy money because it's easy to get more—in the case of paper US dollar *bills*, by printing them. As some say, the easy

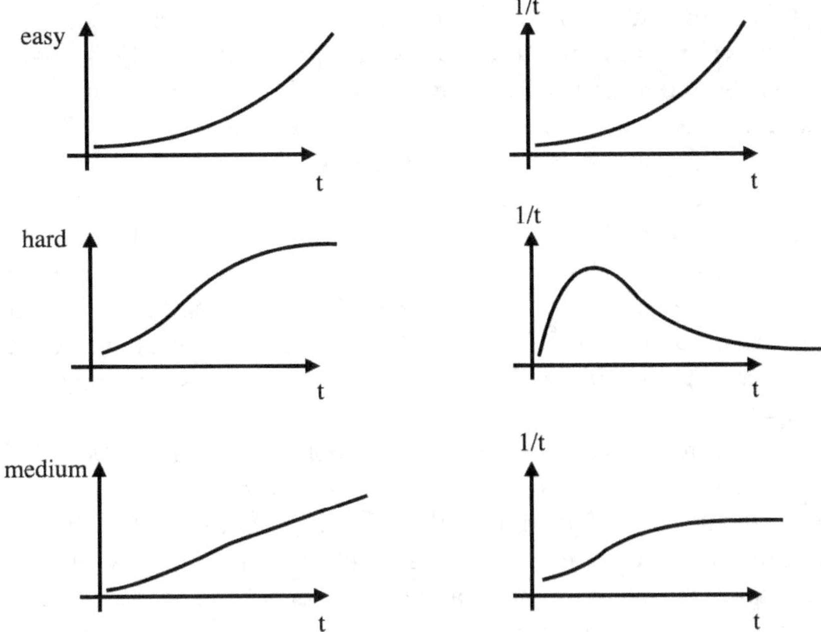

Figure 12.5. *Entropy money enters circulation linearly and predictably.*

money printing machine goes "Brrrr."

The middle row shows an example of a monetary product with a hard monetary policy. Gold coins and bitcoin are examples of hard money. Hard money means it's hard to introduce new units into circulation. Gold monetary policy is hard because of the mechanical and chemical work needed to produce new coins or bars. The monetary policy of bitcoin is hard because that particular temporal monetary policy is hard-coded into the software. As seen in the middle right plot, the rate of entry into circulation for hard monetary policies rises at first and then decays, eventually to zero or near zero.

The number of units in circulation and their entry rates for entropy money, with its linear inflationary monetary policy, is shown in the bottom row. Since our sun-powered land parcels continuously produce ecosystem services, the quantity of entropy money in circulation increases linearly and predictably, entering at an approximately constant rate—day-to-day, or month-to-month, the overall health of our living world is approximately constant.

Thanks to that linear and predictable entry into circulation, entropy money will result in reduced commodity price volatility [344][12] and predictable interest rates. Reduced price volatility will improve business planning success due to improved knowledge of future price conditions. Similarly, in contrast to our existing situation, in which notoriously unpredictable interest rates ruin business plans and can exacerbate boom-bust business cycles, predictable interest rates will also improve the ability of businesses to make and execute plans. These improvements will help us all become wealthier thanks to the newly available and improved products, services, and employment opportunities resulting from improved planning capabilities, lowered costs, and increased competition between more successful businesses.

Entropy money's linearly increasing supply will also spur additional human activity to increase land health, to get more value from people's lands as the value of the money those lands produce steadily shrinks. As a result, more plants and animals will get to live happily, and we can expect thorough pollution and unexploded ordnance cleanups to be completed. It is even possible entire buildings will be moved underground to free up land space for plants and animals. We can also expect many buildings to acquire trees and other plants on their exteriors as this process continues, as illustrated by the Liuzhou Forest City depicted in *Architect* magazine [345]. Dreaming more, landowners' needs to increase their parcels' entropy removal rates could result in mathematical work completed leading to genetic diversity restoration for species that have been nearly wiped out [346, 347], and even the resurrection of recently extinct species [347–350]. It isn't impossible that, eventually, enough buildings and roads get moved underground for mastodons and other mega-fauna from the Pleistocene epoch to be resurrected and resume their role of fire-ladder suppressors [351]. The possibilities of entropy-type money are seemingly endless. Entropy money is the middle road between easy and hard money that turns our world into a paradise planet.

---

[12]The 2018 Macleod article refers to gold, but entropy money will provide the same benefits to users as it enters circulation linearly, predictably, and equitably.

Entropy money improves gold

Entropy money will reduce gold mining due to the cash flow loss incurred to excavate gold ore.[13] Reduced gold mining will increase stability in the aboveground gold supply, further removing (gold) money supply from non-monetary supply and demand relationships.[14] Entropy money will therefore reduce environmental degradation while simultaneously preserving and improving a well-known and well-used monetary commodity.

Entropy money launches our science-fiction future

Changing our US dollars into a type of entropy money initialized as described, enabling our national forests, parks, and monuments to cover our entire national budget, will have the effect of putting our federal government on a monetary leash. As previously noted, this is because it will allow us to repeal our national tax statutes and national borrowing as they will no longer be needed to supply our federal government spending needs. It would be a big deal to reinstate those activities and likely wouldn't happen—once the monkey of the government tax man is off our backs, we're not likely to let it climb back on, and it would be the same with borrowing. Once we all see the national debt decreasing, we probably won't be keen to see it increase again. These two likely outcomes will prevent increased federal government spending and may have an additional, beneficial side effect: many individuals may get ideas about freedom and reduced government spending.

---

[13]Similar to the question of timber for houses due to the cash flow lost for landowners to harvest their trees, gold prices in an entropy money world will continue to be discovered by the high division of labor price discovery machine. It is conceivable reduced monetary demand for gold, combined with increased industrial demand, will cause the world's above-ground gold hoard to supply more and more of the industrial demand as time goes on, with less and less supplied by gold mining. In such a case, if industrial demand for gold continues after that above-ground hoard has been consumed for industry, asteroids could supply the industrial gold demand rather than gold mines here on the earth.

[14]As an aside, keeping some gold around as a backup after the transition to entropy-type US dollars could be a smart idea in case of a global electrical infrastructure wipeout like the Carrington Event (a strong geomagnetic storm in 1859) [352].

These individuals may, for some reason, get into their heads the possibility of repealing our national intellectual property (IP) statutes and thereby turning innovation rates up to eleven [353]. The repeal of IP statutes would cause this because it turns out that, in addition to falling outside the bounds of moral thought and behavior, IP has been hampering innovation rather than aiding it.

At the heart of the problem with IP statutes is the fact ideas are not naturally scarce, and can only be made scarce by using tax-subsidized brute squads to force everyone to behave as if they are—therefore, the entire IP edifice is built on the quicksand of trespass. As in other areas of life, we shall know the tree by its fruits, and in the case of IP the fruits come from a poisoned tree. The poisoned fruits produced by this tree, IP "rights," have the effect of giving producers of intangible works, such as sequences of written words in the form of books, or sequences of audible tones in the form of musical works, control over the tangible property of others [354]. This creates sources of conflict in society where there should be none as people try to catch others doing things with their own property, and use brute squads to take control of that property forcibly. As Kinsella observes, "To ask whether a law should be enacted or exist is to ask: is it proper to use force against certain people in certain circumstances" [p. 15 of 354]? He concludes instead, "We should re-assert the primacy of individual rights over our bodies and homesteaded scarce resources" [p. 45 of 354].

To add insult to injury, and as should be expected from the fruit of a poisoned tree, forced IP obedience fails not only on moral grounds, but on utilitarian grounds as well. This is because the principal effect of IP statutes has been to harm us all,[15] by causing inventors to waste time preventing competitors from improving on their inventions instead

---

[15]Based on empirical data from the last century or so, Barnett makes the utilitarian case that "insecure IP rights appear to shelter entrenched incumbents from the entry threats posed by smaller but more innovative firms" [p. 7 of 355]. His (utilitarian) argument for the benefit of IP is in effect that we can forcefully put the public's fingers on the scales of competition, in this case in favor of smaller and presumably more innovative firms, over larger, more entrenched, and presumably less innovative firms, to bring benefits to us all from the presumably increased innovation. Boldrin & Levine, on the other hand, claim in *Against Intellectual Monopoly* "there is no evidence that intellectual monopoly achieves the desired purpose of increasing innovation and creation," and therefore has no benefits [356]—perhaps Barnett is reporting one of the exceptions that prove the rule. Furthermore, regardless of any benefits to some, moral considerations inform us such benefits do "not justify the use of force against the otherwise legitimate property of others" [p. 15 of 354].

of inventing more themselves. Many others, such as lawyers, waste time helping inventors with such unproductive pursuits, and modern times have seen the rise of the patent trolls, firms that do nothing but purchase patent rights for cheap then use dirty tricks to pursue others they claim are "stealing" their "property" [357]. IP statutes even cause legal wrangling over molecules and compounds gifted to us by our living world [p. 223 of 132]. We all lose the benefits helpful people would have provided had they not been wasting their time quarreling over "ownership" of ideas. In well-known examples of such time-wasting behaviors, James Watt, the Wright brothers, Guglielmo Marconi, and others made marginal improvements to existing technologies, then used IP statutes in attempts to monopolize their industries. The time wasted on these unproductive monopolization efforts retarded technical progress by years and even decades [p. 234 of 356].

The Official Story informs us inventors won't have an incentive to invent if they can't get paid, and they can't get paid without the protection of tax-subsidized patents. As we now know, however, patent protection statutes historically only appear after innovation has occurred and major players in the industry are seeking to protect themselves from competition [356].

David Levine and Michele Boldrin summarize the problem and the solution forcefully in their 2008 book, *Against Intellectual Monopoly*, concluding intellectual property is a cancer, and our long-term goal should be the repeal of all IP statutes [pp. 299–300, 302 of 356].

The lives of us all could be so much better now if the evil of these ideas had never corrupted our political ancestors, and will improve incredibly rapidly once we excise the rot. If we get lucky and enough of us get it into our heads to repeal or nullify our IP statutes, we're going to launch ourselves on the rocket ship bringing our science-fiction future to the here and now practically overnight.

Entropy money is better

In general, entropy money is superior to its predecessors by improving on the two most important qualities of anything used as money—monetary policy and the side effects of producing and using it. As long as those are right, everything else takes care of itself. We can summarize the superiority of entropy money over the competition by comparing the monetary policies and side effects of various kinds of moneys, using the following format:

1) Monetary policy:

    a. Spatial (Where does it enter circulation?)
    b. Temporal (When does it enter circulation?)

2) Side effects: (What are the costs of producing it?)

As an example of hard money, the important qualities of bitcoin, a type of energy money, are:

1) Monetary policy:

    a. Enters circulation through many hands, reducing inflation tax.
    b. Enters circulation slower and slower over time, eventually shrinking slowly as private keys are lost. (Private keys enable ledger entry owners to spend their ledger entries, and can be compared to the key to your house or mailbox.) This is a slightly deflationary monetary policy, leaving supply and demand as the main determinants of prices.

2) Side effects: Costs electrical power to produce and use, typically causing some sort of environmental degradation.

As an example of easy money, the important qualities of legacy US dollars, also a type of energy money, are:

1) Monetary policy:

    a. Enters circulation through a single organization, for US dollar *bills*, causing an inflation tax, and therefore poverty, and therefore crime.
    b. Enters circulation faster and faster over time due to compound interest, for US dollar *bills*. This adds money supply to supply and demand as determinants of prices, and exacerbates the inflation tax resulting from single-point entry

into circulation, causing more poverty and therefore more crime.

2) Side effects: Causes environmental degradation in the form of gold mining, for US dollars (although President Nixon "temporarily" suspended redemptions in 1971 [358], a US dollar remains implicitly defined as a fixed weight of gold [August 31, 2025 report from 181]).

Finally, the important qualities of new, improved US dollars, now a type of entropy money, scaled to cover the entire federal government budget and featuring no federal government tax statutes, are:

1) Monetary policy:

    a. Enters circulation through many hands, similar to gold or bitcoin, reducing inflation tax.
    b. Enters circulation at an approximately constant rate over time. This is an inflationary monetary policy; however, it is predictable, leaving only supply and demand to determine prices.

2) Side effects:

    a. Reduces environmental degradation by paying parcel owners to remove entropy from their lands.
    b. Reduces poverty by paying parcel owners to remove entropy from their lands.
    c. Reduces poverty by creating jobs.
    d. Reduces poverty by creating improved business conditions.
    e. Reduces poverty by eliminating federal taxes in supply chains.
    f. Reduces poverty by eliminating federal tax compliance labor.
    g. Reduces crime by reducing poverty.
    h. Reduces concentrated power, the most dangerous thing on the earth [241], by allowing for the repeal of federal government tax statutes.

i. Costs electrical power to produce and use, assuming it is tracked on an electronic ledger or ledgers, typically causing some sort of environmental degradation.

Due to its side effects of reducing poverty, crime, and environmental degradation, entropy money is a strong improvement over the competition. Its linearly inflationary temporal monetary policy is equivalent to the slightly deflationary policy of bitcoin in terms of predictability, and its equitable spatial monetary policy reduces poverty by reducing everyone's inflation tax, similar to gold. The design analysis completed so far supports the immediate adoption of entropy money as a replacement for our legacy gold US dollars. Furthermore, the obvious solution to a potential fly in this beneficial ointment will lead us even faster and further into our science-fiction future.

13. FREE ENTROPY MONEY MITIGATES RISK

IN Chapter 10, the idea was introduced that We, the People, of these fifty states can choose, if we become so inclined, to repeal our federal government tax and legal tender statutes. In Chapter 12, we found once we've decided to use entropy removed from a parcel by the living creatures on it as money, it's easy to calibrate some measurement of the removed entropy so our national forests, parks, and monuments provide for our entire federal government budget. We found if our national budget is covered by our living lands, we no longer need to raise money by other means, like taxes and borrowing, and can therefore stop those activities. We can stop the borrowing by no longer selling debt notes, also known as Treasury bills or Treasury bonds, and we can stop the taxes by repealing our federal government tax statutes.

If we were to repeal federal government tax statutes, legal tender statutes would remain as the sole, and unfair, market support for our US dollars. As explained in Chapter 9, legal tender statutes act in concert with tax statutes to create economic demand for US dollars by biasing tax-funded courts against contracts with non-US dollar monetary settlement language. If we're going to make this big change of reversing the energy flow caused by the production of our legacy gold US dollars, we need to repeal our federal government legal tender statutes too. We need to do this because every approach to solving our big problems carries risks, and this proposed adoption of entropy money is not excepted. Factors such as unfavorable consumer response to entropy money monetary policy or degradation of the money due to criminal activity could result in widespread consumer flight from the new money.

The monetary policy of our proposed oxygen US dollars could cause problems because our forested national lands, from which $7 trillion will be spent into circulation every year when the present proposal is accepted, comprise only about a third of the forests in the country [334]. If we define our new US dollars as 30g of oxygen, almost $25 trillion will enter circulation every year with the inclusion of private, tribal, state, county, and city lands, plus non-forested living lands, and even that wouldn't be the total amount in the world.

Since this money is intended to improve the health of all us planet earthlings, not only the ones within the political boundaries of the fifty states, quite a few more trillion US dollars would enter circulation in the course of paying the parcel owners of the rest of the world for their ecosystem services.[1] This new money could total up to something like the $125 trillion per year estimated by the World Wildlife Federation [289]. This much money entering circulation every year could cause a catastrophic hyperinflationary runaway, the same as similar monetary disasters that have happened over and over in our world. This is an unspeakably horrific possibility, and exposing ourselves to it is not an option. In fact, that's why we're here in the first place, seeings how we're being pummeled by price inflation that will only get worse if we don't do something about our compound interest fraudulent receipts for gold—it would be like jumping from the frying pan into the fire.

Other problems could result as well. For example, through human error a measurement of ecosystem services vulnerable to exploitation by bad actors could be chosen and result in the reduction or even elimination of some of our hoped-for benefits. It is also possible for problems to arise that aren't foreseeable from this point in time.

Once we realize these risks, we're faced with the same stark choice as before. One option is to abandon this innovative attempt to reduce poverty, crime, and environmental degradation, return to the old methods, and watch our once beautiful world swirl down the drain of an environmental nightmare on top of a hyperinflationary runaway. Another option is to move forward with this entropy money approach and cross our fingers and hope and pray our fancy new money doesn't burn up in a hyperinflationary runaway. There is a third option, however, that benefits us without exposing us to danger—we can go forward with our world-saving monetary gamble and hedge our bets.

---

[1]For the reader asking by whom will those parcel owners be paid, remember, in this work we're asking "what if?" we use entropy removed from the earth as money. The answer of who pays is the same as when we use energy mined from the parcel, as measured by the amount of gold recovered, as money—we all pay them by using their gold as money, so they can spend it into circulation. Similarly, with entropy money we'll pay them by using their produced oxygen as money so they can spend it into circulation. See again the discussion in Chapter 11.

The obvious way to hedge our bets is to make our money free, and the obvious way to make it free is to repeal our national legal tender statutes. We made the wise design choice to scale the new and improved entropy-type US dollars so the ecosystem services provided by our national lands cover the entire federal government budget, which allowed us to repeal our national tax statutes. But if we did only that, our legal tender statutes would remain on the books and give these new and improved entropy-type US dollars an unfair competitive advantage. In this case, a faulty monetary experiment could cause damage before it's inevitably corrected. In such a case, even though market forces eventually would cause the faulty money to be replaced, a bull-in-the-china-shop scenario is a risk while the markets work their magic. This risk can be mitigated by repealing our national legal tender statutes and thereby making our money free, as in free to compete.

If we choose to adopt these new and improved entropy-type US dollars, and hedge our bets by making them free, we'll be protected from failure of the new money by allowing consumers to substitute with monetary alternatives. If we do that, we'll do more too—not only will we eliminate our risk exposure in case our new entropy money fails, but we'll be able to do the opposite and buy our way all the way out.

14. FREE ENTROPY MONEY OPENS THE DOOR TO FOREVER

W E have a design for our new and improved US dollars that will make our world a better place, but adopting it exposes us to the risk of a catastrophic failure of this new money. The obvious way to have our cake and eat it too, meaning to have our fancy new money but without risk, is to hedge our bets. The obvious way to hedge our bets, in turn, is to finish the job of making our new money free, by not only repealing national tax statutes but also repealing our national legal tender statutes. With legal tender statutes out of the way, anyone will be free to compete in money production markets, protecting us from a failure of our new money—and much more.

This freeing of our money hedges our bets because, if an unforeseen problem, such as a hyperinflationary runaway, causes our new and improved US dollars to become unusable, consumers will be free to use substitutes. It does more, too—in addition to the excellent attribute of preventing a negative thing, hedging our bets this way accomplishes something extremely positive for us all.

Making our money free will turn the "volume" of the previously described optimizer up to eleven. By freeing the monetary production market to all, we will have removed limitations on improvements to the control system linking our living biological world with our human financial world. The control system using land entropy measurements will improve, along with the measurements themselves.

Freeing our money to improve will create jobs in the new field of entropy measurement optimization, to research and produce improved estimates of land parcel entropy removal rates. It will also create jobs to improve the algorithms converting entropy estimates into parcel owner monetary ledger entries. These two types of jobs will implement a machine that automatically searches for the optimal version of the automatic control system that increases everyone's health and wealth, resulting in the most possible benefit to us all.

The mechanics of this optimizer of our monetary health and wealth automatic control system are found in the basic fact that entrepreneurs attempt to steal customers from each other with better mousetraps. Entrepreneurs will attempt to steal customers with improved products intended for use as money, whether or not there are any serious problems with our new entropy-type US dollars. And this is where we truly escape. All the way—not just reducing poverty, crime, and environmental degradation, but quickly and permanently eliminating them on our way to a paradise planet full of healthy, happy people.

This transition to a paradise planet won't be due to luck either—it will be due to our deliberate actions. We have the power to cause this to happen because money is at the center of our economic universe, being half of practically every transaction, and our landowners will be able to earn it by keeping their parcels healthy. We will make this power a superpower when we free our money to improve.

We previously contemplated printing up new fraudulent gold receipts to pay parcel owners for their ecosystem services, but without making any other changes. Using entropy removed from the parcel itself as the new version of our world reserve money, and freeing this money to evolve and improve, converts the entropy-money idea into a world-saving one. Our new world reserve money will be free to improve, and therefore will improve, because entrepreneurs want your business. In attempting to get that business, they discover prices. These prices guide them to the most profitable product development and production strategy, which is to obey what can be called the laws of manufactured products. These laws will cause our new entropy-type money to improve over time.

Laws of product creation and evolution

Things used as money, such as gold coins, cigarettes, barrels of whiskey, and so on, are manufactured products and therefore obey the laws of manufactured products. These laws cause products to enter the world and improve over time.

The first law is economic demand causes economic supply, presenting itself in a demand for products that improve your life. It is known as Keynes's Law, articulated by the economist John Keynes, who observed that any economic supply with no economic demand can't sell and will inevitably be a loss—only supply met with demand can profit. For example, we know there is an economic demand for transportation since some people are willing to hire others to move them or their belongings from here to there. Therefore, eventually, an economic supply in the form of horses, cars, airplanes, boats, and so on entered the world. Similarly, we know there is an economic demand for remote communication methods since some people are willing to hire others to help them communicate remotely with each other. Therefore, eventually, an economic supply in the form of pens, pencils, papyrus, paper, printing presses, telephones, and the Internet entered the world. One could say there were economic niches that could be, and were, filled by transportation or communications products.

Relevant to our efforts here, we know there is an economic demand for intermediaries to facilitate transactions because some people are willing to use things as money by accepting them in exchange for their valuable goods and services even though they don't want them. Therefore, eventually, an economic supply of products that could be used as money, such as blocks of salt, bags of rice, and gold coins entered the world.

The law of supply and demand can be likened to money lying in the corner, waiting to get picked up by someone. People who are willing to pay for something are like the money in the corner. When an entrepreneur finds a way to provide a paying customer what he or she wants, it's like he picked up the money lying in the corner. The prospective customer's money was sitting in his or her pocket, and the entrepreneur found a way to get the money from that pocket into his own by providing the customer with a product or service he or she valued enough to trade money for. Providing the customer with the product or service is like when the entrepreneur bends over to pick up the money in the corner, and when the customer pays the entrepreneur, it's like when the entrepreneur's hand grasps the money. Economic niches can be thought of as human needs that can be satisfied by products or services, and when they are filled, it is like the money in the corner was picked up.

The second law is competition improves the breed. In addition to acquiring customers in new economic niches by offering new products, entrepreneurs try to steal customers in existing niches by offering improved versions of existing products. For example, entrepreneurs trying to steal customers caused the Wright brothers' first flight airplane, carrying one passenger 120 feet, to evolve into jumbo jets carrying hundreds of passengers thousands of miles. Other entrepreneurs, competing in the communications segment, caused hieroglyphs in stone to evolve into iPhones. Still others caused seashell money to evolve into gold money, where up to the present, its development has been frozen by tax and legal tender statutes.

We can expect these rules to apply evolutionary improvement pressures to monetary products when manufacturers are free to compete for customers. We users of money like improved products, and we'll buy better monetary products just like we buy better transportation and communication products.

Automatically searching for the best money

"You can never be too rich or too thin."
~ Wallis, Duchess of Windsor (1896–1986)

If we redesign our US dollars so they consist of entropy removed from our world by living land parcels, and free them to improve like any other product, what might the improvement look like?

Because of the second rule, that competition improves the breed, we can surmise new versions of US dollars might be produced with upgraded measurements of provided ecosystem services to obtain more accurate estimates of removed entropy. For one possible example, a bonus could be paid for biodiversity [130], so the more biodiverse parcel on the right-hand side of Figure 14.1 pays better than the less biodiverse parcel on the left-hand side of the figure. Bonuses could also be paid for other supplemental measurements of ecosystem service [359, 360].

If biodiversity is used to pay bonuses, paying better for it can be mechanized by scaling ecosystem service payments as a function of the biodiversity of the parcel. Whereas the first version of our new and improved US dollars, call it version 1.0, might blindly pay K times

Figure 14.1. *Biodiversity pays. Left-hand side—less biodiversity. Right-hand side—more biodiversity. (Photographs courtesy of Leopictures and HarryJBurgess from Pixabay.)*

produced breathable air (top input-output pair of Figure 14.2), the number of version 2.0 US dollars credited to the parcel owner's account might be scaled by a number directly proportional to the measured biodiversity of the parcel. Using this method of paying for biodiversity, the number of new and improved US dollars to be credited to a parcel owner's account at any particular sample instant could be, for example, the number of produced ecosystem services, times K dollars per ecosystem service, times 1.75 (bottom input-output pair of Figure 14.2).

Paying parcel owners a bonus for biodiversity will give them a financial incentive to maintain and improve the biodiversity of their lands, and thus we can expect increases in biodiversity. Keep in mind the jobs of improving entropy removal payouts will be hired out to professionals like biologists and remote-sensing experts, who may choose to improve them with some quantification of biodiversity, but could also choose alternate means. For example, entropy removal payouts could be improved by paying parcel owners to remove the fire ladders caused by forest undergrowth [351].

If these new and improved entropy-type US dollars are programmable, arbitrary payment algorithms can be executed. Arbitrary payment algorithms mean we can expect competition between money manufacturers to give us both steadily improving customer experiences and steadily

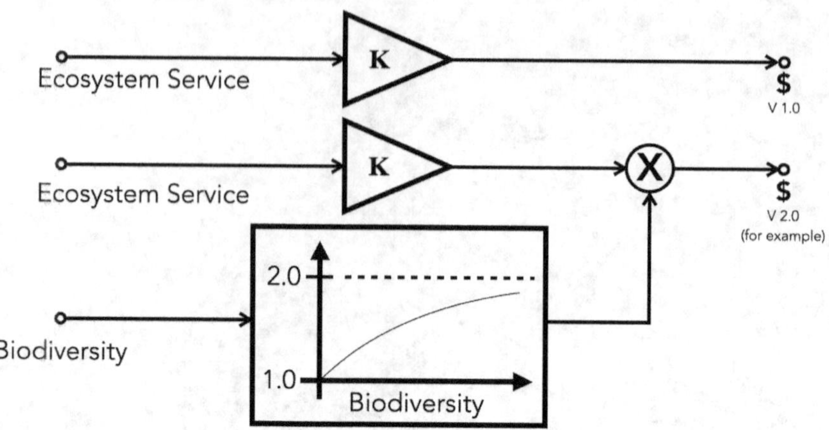

Figure 14.2. *Example: bonus paid for biodiversity.*

improving planetary health. These gifts will be the direct effects of manufacturers exploring ways to earn customers' business by giving them ever-improving usage experiences and healthier environments. We can follow this trend to its logical conclusion by thinking about what money[1] is used for and then about what it will be like for money that does the job better and better. What is money used for?

As all of us who use money know, we get money to get things that make our lives better, the two most important of those being shelter and food. In fact, those two are so important, you could say we use money to buy time. Every night with a roof over your head, and every day with food in your belly buys you a little more time, so when you buy those things, you are effectively buying yourself time. Where this leads monetary evolution can be deduced by noting monetary products are no different than others in that users can be expected to gravitate toward products providing them more of what they value. For example, customers use transportation products to get from here to there, and value safety, efficiency and comfort when doing so—therefore products like cars and airplanes have become more safe, efficient and comfortable over the years. Similarly, customers use monetary products to buy time, and value more time and better time (in whatever sense "better" is defined by the customer)—therefore they can be expected to gravitate to products helping them buy more and better time. For one

---

[1]By money, we technically mean products used as money, but here we'll use the colloquial style for brevity.

of many examples, general poverty reductions resulting from improved monetary products could give customers more time and funds to learn about and purchase organic foods or supplements, or more funds to hire nutritionists, thus increasing the quality of their time thanks to improvements in their health. We can expect monetary products to evolve to help customers buy more time and better time.

How much more time might we be able to buy, and how much better might it get? To start with, thanks to our wise choice of adopting a kind of money that pays parcel owners to keep their parcels healthy, we can expect it to evolve in such a way as to help those owners make their lands healthier. As noted, one obvious evolutionary step is to improve land health, or entropy removal, measurements.

Improving entropy removal measurements means making them more accurate, in whatever sense accuracy is determined by the measurer, so the parcel owner who truly removes more entropy is paid more. This process will continually improve the financial feedback provided to parcel owners, helping them do a better and better job of improving the health of their land, and thereby making our world a nicer place to live.

Looking forward in the evolution of entropy money, early versions of the money might use, as described previously, measured plant respiration rates. While such measurements alone would be wildly successful in helping reduce poverty and environmental degradation, they still would be relatively crude measurements of parcel health. As entrepreneurs continue their efforts to earn customers' business, more granular entropy measurement techniques may be developed. To begin with, parcel ecosystem service measurements could be scaled with estimates of biodiversity (Figure 14.2).

Looking ahead in the development of scaling of plant respiration estimates, we expect such scaling may end up including the individual health of each living plant on a parcel, at least those of a certain size.

Virtuous loop

Looking ahead even more, estimates of the individual health of each plant and animal on the parcel could be made using advanced remote sensing and animal tracking and census techniques. Eventually, money that includes the health of the human occupants may appear. With such money, people would be paid to improve their health by being

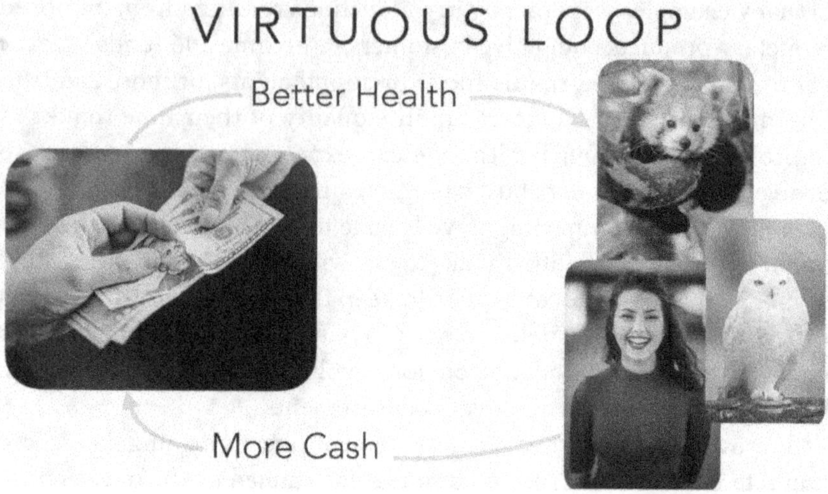

Figure 14.3. *Better health → more cash → better health → ... (Photographs courtesy of Karolina Grabowska, Flickr on Canva, Tim Zänkert, Michael Dam on Unsplash.)*

around more, and healthier, plants and animals, and, in addition, be paid directly for improvements in their own health.

In a possible example of this dynamic, imagine the family patriarch has high blood pressure. If entropy money payouts included the health of the humans on the parcel, the payout for this family would increase if he is able to get his blood pressure down. This virtuous loop would cause a runaway effect, in which getting healthier would improve cash flow, and the extra cash could be used to get even healthier, which would improve cash flow even more (Figure 14.3).

Thinking about the basic definitions of entropy, if we pay people to remove entropy from their parcels, and include the entropy of their own bodies in the payment, might we expect more Beethovens, Gödels and Gausses thinking amazing thoughts in this new world? If the entropy of the matter and energy in a body thinking impossible thoughts is lower than in a body thinking ho-hum nothing thoughts, could clever entrepreneurs trying to earn business find ways to award cash for the entropy no longer existing in a body when it is thinking brilliant thoughts? The possibilities are seemingly limitless.

Implications of improving money

The direct result of freed-to-improve entropy money is expected human lifespans will begin steadily increasing when the new money is introduced, as everyone's health begins improving. As mentioned previously, an expected indirect result of our proposed changeover to new and improved entropy-type US dollars is the likely repeal of IP statutes. If this happens, we can expect an amplification of the direct health benefit effects of the entropy money. We can expect the quality of products and services to accelerate thanks to such repeals, in addition to improvements directly caused by entropy money-induced reductions in poverty. Specifically, we can expect the state of the art in medical and health sciences to continue its relentless advance, now amplified by the repeal of IP statutes.

Due to the synergy of these two effects, from the adoption of free entropy money and the probable elimination of IP statutes, most of us can expect that, by the time our years on this polluted, dying planet were likely going to end, our expected lifespan will almost certainly have increased, possibly by decades. This isn't pure speculation either—due to existing medical and health science improvements, the expected lifespan of a newborn is already 120 years or more [361], and expected to increase, with treatments for atherosclerosis and stem cell therapy for Parkinson's disease already in late-stage research and development [362]. There is much more improvement on the way as well—as Robert A. Freitas Jr. explains, life-extending medical nanorobotic technologies, expected to be widely available by the 2020s or 2030s, can result in average expected lifespans of 1,200 years [362], and JP Errico, Founder of ElectroCore, reports start-ups like Alto Labs and Calico are developing small molecule cocktails to replicate partial cell reprogramming, which can reset epigenetic drift and telomere attrition in human cells to a much younger state [363].

The possibilities for each of us personally become very interesting when considering the dynamic of using our newly gained time to gain even more time [364–366]. For example, if you gain, say, two more decades of expected lifespan [367] during your remaining years, and innovation rates continue at their newly higher levels thanks to the repeal of IP statutes, could you also gain one or two more decades during those extra two decades? Might the speed of approach to your date with the grim reaper slow, pass through zero, and become negative?

If such a thing happened, it would mean free entropy-type money would have bought us expected expiration dates moving into the future faster than our chronological aging. Each of us may experience the miracle of watching our expected date with the grim reaper steadily recede into the future.

We know, too, this miracle almost certainly isn't impossible, as there don't appear to be any theoretical obstacles to the indefinite self-repair of your body [368]. To be accurate, that's how each of us is alive in the first place. You could say self-repairing and eating low entropy to self-repair more is the definition of being alive [p. 10 of 324]. Since in our future economically free world an ever-increasing percentage of us are healthy and happy and probably not ready to check out quite yet, imagine the advancements in the state of the art of medical and health sciences over your steadily increasing expected lifespan, enabling even more expected lifespan increases, buying even more time for medical and health science advancements. Letting our imaginations run wild, could our expected lifespans increase to centuries during the extra decades we bought ourselves early on?

We can't be sure right now, but if it isn't impossible to continue self-repairing indefinitely, maybe seriously extended lifespans are in the cards for us, making the option of not trying unthinkable. All we have to lose is better lives on a healthier planet, and we could gain so much more. Might you be able to enjoy life with your friends and family up until the death of the last stars? If you could, think about the ramifications—we, humanity, would gain hundreds of billions of years, with a network of trillions of human brains, the most powerful computing devices in the known universe, to discover things thought of as crazy or absurd here in the before time. Could we discover a way to escape to a new universe before losing this one? Maybe it's not impossible, so why not try?

Best of all, because everyone will be getting paid to make their land healthier, we won't have to spend the time we've gained on polluted or dying planets, but will instead get to spend it on healthy paradise planets. There's even more entropy money good news. First, thanks to expected health improvements, we expect everyone to get better looking—looking like the healthier people they're becoming. Second, we expect everyone's wealth to improve continuously upon adopting new and improved entropy-type US dollars. We expect this due to the general poverty-reducing effects of entropy money, along with price decreases resulting from continuing advances in the state of the art of automation technology, rocketing forward in a market free from the cancer of IP.

In addition, we expect wealth increases due to the expected new and easy capability of people to save for a rainy day by purchasing monetary products in which prices are increasing less, or even decreasing. For example, while we expect prices to increase linearly in terms of entropy money, we expect these price increases to be mitigated by the new era of free-to-improve money. It will be easy for people to purchase monetary units in which prices are decreasing, such as elemental gold or cryptocurrencies with hard monetary policies.[2] We'll all get to live longer, healthier, and wealthier.

Finally, we'll get to live free. When we get the monkey of the federal government tax man off our backs, we will have set up our system for a painless phaseout of our existing coercive forms of government. Everyone who depends on checks from our federal government will continue to get paid because we wisely priced the new money that way, but what we also will have done is put that beast on a leash.

If our federal government budget continues to expand, our treasury employees may continue to borrow, but we won't care because We took the wise precaution of repealing Our federal government tax and legal tender statutes. Once we eliminate the unfair protections for US dollars, we can foresee that any changes our federal government employees make that decrease the utility of the dollars would cause their price to fall.[3] In other words, such harmful changes would cause price inflation in these fancy new entropy-type US dollars. Price inflation would directly counteract any attempted spending increases and cause users to flee our new US dollars for alternatives. The users would be free to do so because there wouldn't be any tax or legal tender statutes blocking their way. These price inflation and substitution effects would defeat any attempts to increase federal government spending.

What if some of our federal government representatives once again attempted to levy taxes? Hopefully, they would understand they could get shot for even thinking of such a thing. Again, realistically, the chance federal government taxes could ever be reintroduced seems small because we'll all be so happy to be rid of them.

---

[2] A way to make this type of hedging extremely convenient is described in Chapter 18.

[3] For example, if dollars/apple increases, the price of apples in dollars increased, and the price of dollars in apples (apples/dollar) decreased.

On top of all that, two things almost certainly will happen, causing our federal government, in its present form, effectively to evaporate. First, it will lose employees who migrate to more rewarding income streams elsewhere, such as in the new entropy money economy. Second, the collective could either sell our federal lands and equipment, or change the form of our federal government. In the first option, the collective We, the People, could sell all of our federal government owned property as everyone quickly realizes we don't need our federal government, at least not in its present form, and this is our big chance to escape.

Alternatively, the collective could choose to keep it, but change its form. For example, the collective could instantiate a fourth branch of the federal government using social media technology to innovate and install "a system specifically designed to harness the collective empathy and intellectual might of the American people," as advocated by Kevin Bruch in *The Last Old Growth Sawyer* [p. 12 of 351]. For another example, the collective could convert the federal government back into something more like the weak central government formed by the thirteen states with the Articles of Confederation [207].

Using our imaginations more, our federal government could be converted into something like the non-compulsory governmental organization of the Iroquois Confederacy, which was one of the inspirations for our national government. Such an Iroquois Confederacy-style union could grow in the same way our country of fifty states did, by adding states. Alberta in Canada could join up, and then British Columbia, and Chihuahua in Mexico, etc., eventually ending up with a United States of Planet Earth (USPE). This could be the path to the happy state of true anarchy[4] on the entire planet as states are forced to do things like strictly obey bills of rights and reduce taxation to retain populations

---

[4] "Anarchy" was originally the word αναρχια in ancient Greece and later became the Latin word *anarchia*. In the Greek, it was used to denote groups that were αν ("without") a αρχια (military "leader," and later "ruler"), so groups without a ruler. Historically, the word has been used both in the negative sense of disorder and chaos and in the positive sense of free people who don't need and won't tolerate a ruler, big man, or boss [ch. 1 of 369], causing many a "Tastes great! Less filling!" style argument. In the present work "anarchy" will be used in the original Greek sense of no ruler(s).

newly able to get out of Dodge[5] whenever they like, for any reason they like.

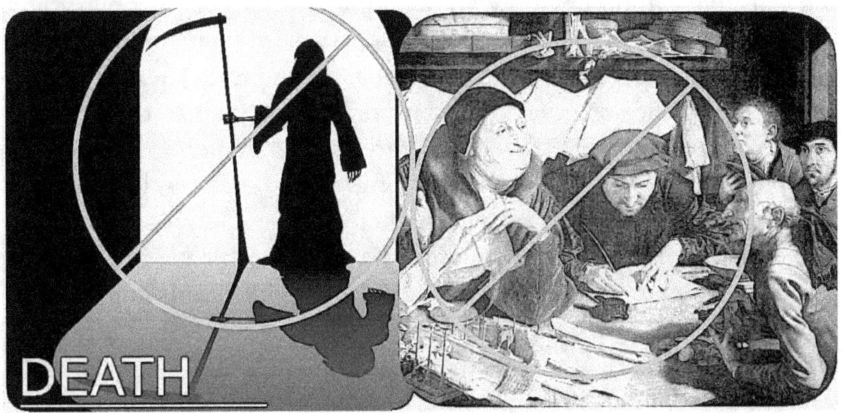

Figure 14.4. *Death to death and taxes. (Grim Reaper courtesy of macrovector on Freepik, The Tax Collector by Marinus van Reymerswaele, 1542, courtesy of Levan Ramishvili on WikiArt Visual Encyclopedia.)*

Such a planetwide result of anarchy could happen because, with a traditional Iroquois-style peer-to-peer grouping, states almost certainly won't be able to collude with other states to control and tax people. Any defector state wanting to attract people in a peer-to-peer system merely has to have lower taxes and/or higher-quality service than the states it's competing with for population. In a truly free world of states befriending states in a worldwide Iroquois Confederacy, individuals, families, and companies will pick up and move at their whim, incentivized to live in more free and less taxed areas.[6] The stable equilibrium in such a space is the condition in which all the state governments have evaporated. The same logic holds for counties and cities, thus the stable equilibrium of a new Iroquois Confederacy is planetwide anarchy, with any attempts to tax probably met with a *posse comitatus*.[7] In general,

---

[5]The phrase "get out of Dodge" means leaving a place you don't like, referring to criminal violence in 1870s Dodge City, Kansas.

[6]Raico, Landes, and others report this dynamic, known as the demonstration effect, has historically resulted in the decentralized system of competing jurisdictions in Europe having the most prosperous populations on the planet [370].

[7]*Posse comitatus*: The entire body of the inhabitants who may be summoned by the sheriff to assist in preserving the public peace (as in a riot) or in executing a legal precept that is forcibly opposed, including under the common law every male inhabitant who is above 15 years of age and not infirm [371].

in a state of planetwide anarchy, trespasses against individuals will be handled peacefully with the help of customary law traditions such as the Catholic Canon law, Jewish Mosaic law, English customary law, the Xeer tradition of Somalia, and so on. Also, in a state of planetwide anarchy, all property would be privately owned and defended, eliminating the chance of invasion of any public space since there would not be any public land. Travel in a world of private property would be an opportunity to profit by making properties healthier, for both the traveler and the landowner (see Chapter 15).

In a world of free entropy money, the stable political equilibrium is planetwide anarchy, and the stable health equilibrium is an expected date with the grim reaper receding away from you into the future. Some say death and taxes are the only sure things in life [372], but it's not true (Figure 14.4). The opportunity to kill them both with a single blow stares us in the face. In summary, free entropy money enables our escape *from* some very bad things, and at the same time, *to* some amazingly good things.

15. ESCAPE

In the category of escaping from bad things, free entropy money, calibrated so as to get the federal government revenuers out of our lives, lets us escape the unholy trinity of poverty, crime, and environmental degradation that has plagued innocents for millennia.

We'll all be gifted the ability to reduce environmental degradation by paying people to remove greenhouse gases from the atmosphere [373, 374]. [1] Free entropy money will do this by giving us all a convenient way to pay parcel owners to keep their lands alive and respiring, filtering the greenhouse gas carbon dioxide from the air. Because the giant parallel computing device consisting of all us smart humans will be making entropy money production decisions, guided by prices, we can expect this system to cause us to optimize, not removing too much or too little carbon dioxide. We can expect the requirements for our new programmable money (Appendix C) to be revised as needed to guarantee this result.

Free entropy money will reverse environmental degradation because landowners will be paid for healthy land. For example, it will help members of the Ethiopian Orthodox Tewahedo Church steward their "biodiverse pockets of forest that improve water quality, house pollinators necessary for the surrounding agriculture, reduce soil erosion, and provide natural medicine" [378]. In another example, it will help the Green Belt Movement, begun by Wangari Maathai in Kenya, plant trees [pp. 402 - 404 of 132]. In general, free entropy money quickly will evolve to become better and better at making our world healthier as entrepreneurs improve land health/owner wealth control systems to steal customers from the competition.

Environmental degradation also will be reversed by giving us all a more garden-like, healing environment. Living in a more garden-like, healing environment is good for one's health, and as Daniel Quinn wrote, the world is a sacred place and we're part of it [136]. As such,

---

[1]To be fair, established forests are carbon neutral. However, when they are maturing, they are net carbon sinks, in addition to their numerous other benefits [375–377].

giving us improved environmental conditions and therefore making us all healthier is part of our reduction in environmental degradation [379–381].

Thanks to park payouts, free entropy money will reduce poverty by reducing taxes the various national, state, county, and city governments collect from their people (Appendix E). Poverty also will be reduced thanks to the new jobs created, improved cash flows, and tax reductions.

Poverty won't only be reduced thanks to free entropy money but will be reversed, thanks to smart and motivated entrepreneurs who will attempt to win your business by producing improved money for you. This improved money will evolve to fill our needs and desires for lower prices and higher quality. We can expect most prices to decrease continually,[2] thanks to both monetary and automation improvements. Practically, this means as time goes on each of us will get to do more of what we think is important because we'll be less and less financially constrained.

Free entropy money will reduce tyranny because our wise pricing of the new money eliminates both federal government revenuers and the national debt. No longer will there be an army of agents prying into your intimate and private financial affairs, forcing you to pay.

Tyranny will be eliminated thanks to free entropy money by allowing We, the People, of Spaceship Earth to sell our various governments. Selling governments means the people of each city, county, state, prefecture, and province will sell off the lands and infrastructures of their governments, likely happening in a domino style starting with the federal government. In the case of our federal government, as noted before, it could be restructured first on the way to an eventual sale.

Once our federal government debts have been paid off, we may choose to have our government employees sell our national forests, parks, monuments, and all other property. We won't worry about those beautiful lands getting covered by malls, apartments, and parking lots because we'll know the new owners of those trees will be paid to let them live. To increase the chance those lands remain healthy, we could encumber them with conservation easements prior to sale.

---

[2]As a point of reference for the concept of decreasing prices, compare the price, both in size and money, of the Electronic Numerical Integrator and Computer (ENIAC) of 1945, the supercomputer of its day, with the supercomputer/cell phone in your pocket.

Additionally, we won't have to stop there—we can sell it all, especially the war departments. Our former government employees will finally get to escape their dreary government bureaucrat jobs [382]. Some of our former federal government employees may find employment in the newly opened security, insurance, and dispute resolution markets resulting from the elimination of the federal government war and police bureaucracies, including the Department of Defense and the Federal Bureau of Investigation.

This sale describes the fate of the federal government, but as stated, it will likely be just the first domino to fall as people come to understand they don't need compulsory governments. All the polities on the planet have parks that will be paying entropy money to the governments of those polities, reducing their needs for taxing and borrowing. It's a good guess that once We, the People, of these fifty states rid ourselves of our federal government, the smart and motivated people of each of those remaining polities will find ways to do the same.

The anticipated escape of our government employees from their dreary government bureaucrat jobs can be considered a reduction in environmental degradation, again on the basis the world is a sacred place and we're all part of it. If those employees are a part of our living world, benefits to them are benefits to our living world and thus reductions in environmental degradation. The rest of us will benefit from this escape because our smart and conscientious former government employees will become available to explore more fully their potential to serve others in our newly nongovernmental world. Think of the benefits in crime prevention and national defense alone. Instead of being cannon fodder in faraway lands, many of our top-notch former army personnel will be able to provide their talents to insurance companies, newly exploiting the national security economic niche recently vacated by governments. Constrained by the imperative to profit and disciplined by customers free to flee, insurance companies in our new world will need defense departments to protect their policyholders from any invading hordes [383, 384].

As governments everywhere evaporate, the talented folks formerly employed by our many local, county, state, and national police departments will be afforded the opportunity to join security services whose mission is to protect customers from criminals, rather than capture individuals who may have violated often victimless "crime" statutes [385, 386]. In the event of disputes, dedicated dispute resolution experts like lawyers and judges will be able to provide their talents to help with problems. Dispute resolution experts such as these will get to change jobs from government institutions oriented toward retribution to free market institutions oriented toward restitution [387]. Our talented road construction and operation experts also will be afforded the opportunity to change employers, from government bureaucracies oriented toward spending their allocated budgets to "the customer is always right" companies oriented toward building and operating safe and affordable roads. Thanks to the efforts of these good people, we'll all be blessed with safe roads, safe flying, and efficient, productive defense.[3]

Free entropy money will reduce environmental degradation in multiple ways by eliminating tyranny. In one example, the elimination of tyranny will allow for improved protection of the law for landowners, affording them peaceful ways to be made whole if others harm their land, so we can expect less harm to the land. These protections exist in the form of the tort, contract, and other customary or common law traditions developed by our Anglo-Saxon ancestors over millennia [144, 388–390].[4] In another example of environmental degradation reduction, the elimination of tyranny will remove obstacles to the best functionality of our price discovery machine, which is the machine we all work together to animate by participating in the high division of labor. By freeing our economic system to allow for the highest quality price discovery and by adding the new feedback of entropy money, our system will be able to make difficult choices, such as, for electric power production, dams versus wind versus solar versus hydrocarbons versus fission versus geothermal [391], and so on. Entropy money will help us make choices like these—not by individuals or committees making them, but instead by setting the search algorithm executed by our newly freed price discovery machine loose on them [279]. Combined with a monetary initial condition that pays landowners for healthy parcels,

---

[3]In a planet-wide anarchy, disputes between road owners and customers, such as if a road-operating company attempted to charge customers a million dollars to use the road in front of their house, will be resolved with low-cost, high-quality assistance from our newly freed dispute resolution agora, or marketplace.

[4]One way our Anglo-Saxon customary law traditions help protect property owners is through the maxim of law stating: "It is prohibited to do on one's own property that which may injure another's." This maxim is also expressed in a slightly different version by the principle of *sic utere tuo ut alienum non laedas*—in English, "So use your own as not to injure another's property." (1 Bl. Com. 306; Broom's max. 160; 4 McCord, 472; 2 Bouv. Inst. n. 2379.)

our new system, with relaxed restrictions on property rights, will solve environmental problems by discovering the price information needed for rational economizing [280]. In the same way number two wood pencils can be manufactured without any one person knowing how [29], an optimal solution for our various environmental problems will be found without any one of us knowing how.

Free entropy money will help us all improve our world by reducing concentrated financial power. Reduced concentrated financial power will increase the ability of people to engage in free and open debate by reducing the present concentration of media ownership.[5] In turn, this will improve humanity's ability to find solutions to big problems.

Our new and improved money will reduce poverty by eliminating tyranny. The elimination of tyranny means economic freedom for us all, increasing everyone's wealth by allowing us to exploit more fully the price discovery capabilities of the high division of labor computing machine [370, 393–398]. The reduction of poverty should, in turn, contribute to easier elimination of tyranny since economic inequality was one of the causes of the emergence of States [ch. 2 of 369].

By reducing poverty, free entropy money will help us reduce crime by helping us eliminate the world child molester network [233, 399]. The heroes catching child molesters will become numerous and powerful thanks to the flood of money headed their way from the newly wealthier people produced by our freed world. Free entropy money will also reduce crime in general by reducing poverty. The legacy of crime that has plagued us children of the agricultural revolution for the last ten thousand years will finally be removed from our lives as poverty disappears, and thus the motive for most crimes disappears. Murder, assault, kidnapping, and probably even most petty theft will become distant memories.

The new money will reduce environmental degradation by reducing cruelty, pain, and suffering. This is the saddest benefit of the new money because it shouldn't even be a benefit. These crimes against us all shouldn't exist in the world, or at least they shouldn't be caused by any humans, so it's sad we stand to benefit from their removal. But at the same time, we're very lucky for this opportunity. Entropy money will aid in the effort to reduce cruelty, pain, and suffering because, by the simple understanding of the word, a human [233] or nonhuman [133,

---

[5]In one example of concentrated media ownership, only five media companies account for 80 percent of the news and information market in the UK [392].

400–404] person experiencing pain is in worse health than one not in pain. Therefore, as our various new monetary products rapidly evolve to be better measurements of the health of the various land parcels, we expect some to emerge that pay less, or even negative, for land with suffering creatures.[6] Even better, it could come to pass that new versions of entropy measurements pay a bounty for information leading to a negative rating for a parcel owner. [7] This means we can expect a quick end to fur farms, dog and cat meat markets [409], factory farms,[8] animal vivisection, prisons with cruel conditions—the list is horrifically long. Our new money will benefit us incalculably.

Free entropy money will deliver another sad but happy benefit in cruelty, pain, and suffering reduction as the various forcible governmental institutions around the world evaporate: the elimination of wars. Leo Tolstoi knew this well, famously observing:

> In all history there is no war which was not hatched by the governments, the governments alone, independent of the interests of the people, to whom war is always pernicious even when successful. [411]

Hermann Göring too understood that without governments you don't get wars, as he reported in an interview conducted by Gustave Gilbert during the post-WWII Nuremberg trials. Göring explained it isn't us poor slobs who decide to raise armies and risk our necks in some war we don't want. It's those who acquire governmental power over us who do that, by telling people they're being attacked and denouncing pacifists as enemies of the people. He said it works the same in any country [412].

The elimination of wars will cleanse from our world the violations of all the innocent souls tormented and ripped to shreds in battles as they go at each other like mad dogs. Some of that horror is communicated

---

[6]In conjunction with improved health measurements, we can expect overall reductions in poverty to lead to improved funding for animal welfare organizations. For example, Kinder World [405], In Defense of Animals [406], People for the Ethical Treatment of Animals [407], the Animal Legal Defense Fund [408], and others may be enlisted in the effort to determine the welfare of animals on any given land parcel.

[7]False reports could be discouraged by various means, such as requiring reporters to post bonds.

[8]See the Animal Clock [410] for details on the obscene number of animals suffering on factory farms.

in movies like *Apocalypse Now* [413] and *Saving Private Ryan* [414], and in the miniseries *The Pacific* [415]. All among us who have experienced the horror will truly understand the magnitude of this gift.

Free entropy money also will massively reduce wastage of our life energies by eliminating wars, thereby ending the diversion of our economic output to war matériel. As President Eisenhower reminded us in his farewell speech, the world in arms is wasting the sweat of its laborers and the genius of its scientists [269].

The reason the evaporation of governmental institutions will eliminate wars is simple and was discovered long ago by our Anglo-Saxon ancestors and others: peace is more profitable, and more pleasant, than violence. Remedies available to achieve peace even in the presence of disputes are well known to us today, thanks to the customary law traditions developed by those Anglo-Saxon ancestors [144, 145]. Those people knew peaceful conflict resolution causes less economic disruption and other problems than violent conflict resolution. They discovered how to accomplish it in peer-to-peer fashion once the Roman brute squads left Britannia in the 400s.

Without government brute squads stealing their money and offering some of it back if they'll kill strangers, no one will be willing to risk their lives in this manner. Without government brute squads, we'll converge on peaceful means of resolving conflicts, even with strangers in far-off lands. We'll be too busy making love and money to make war.

The benefits of free entropy money don't end with escaping *from* some very awful things—they also enable our escape *to* our science-fiction future.

The change to using entropy removed from land parcels as money will result in predictable interest rates, reduced commodity price volatility, reduced regulation-induced barriers to entry, probable elimination of IP statutes, and more spending money in more hands. These changes will lead to improved business conditions, leading to an explosion of products and services, improving everyone's wealth and cash flow even more, improving business conditions more, and so on. Thanks to these improvements, we expect more and more products and services to emerge that help people increase their lifespans, beautify our world, and explore our universe. In an example of an infrastructure improvement that would aid all efforts to improve our world, the synergy between improved business conditions and evaporated governments could result in the development of plentiful, safe, low-cost thorium-derived[9] electrical power [416].

Previously unimaginable benefits will be the gift of our new money. Cancer, cardiovascular disease, pneumonia, road injuries, suicides—we expect the elimination of all these and more. Improvements in the state of the art in medical technology can be expected to restore those with disfiguring scars and missing limbs [368, 417] to their previous bodily perfection, and to cure previously incurable diseases. Those same advancements in medical technology can also be expected to remove the effects of physical aging, restoring skin, organs, and musculoskeletal systems to their youthful and beautiful glory. Everyone's health will be better, and we'll all even get to look better as the state of the art in medical and health science continues its relentless advance (hopefully supercharged by the elimination of IP statutes). Everyone's wealth will be greater, and prices will decline and remain at low levels as the state of the art in automation technology continues its relentless advance (also hopefully supercharged by the elimination of IP statutes).

In addition to all these physical benefits, free entropy money will make our world socially more pleasant in multiple ways. First, in a world in which we're paid to make our living lands healthy, we'll have a financial incentive to help our neighbors keep their parcels healthy too. We'll have this incentive because the health of every land parcel is, in the end, interdependent with the health of its neighbors [418]. Second, this landowner unifying effect may help people relearn how to share. In a world with the morally deficient statutory laws [390] superseded by organically discovered customary laws, some may return to systems for sharing commons. For one of many examples of the possibilities [121, 419, 420], people may revive customary procedures for communal lands similar to those used in England prior to the Enclosure Movement [144, 199].[10]

---

[9]Thorium is a naturally occurring radioactive metal, similar to uranium. Thorium is widely available, and thorium fission reactors can operate at a substantially reduced cost relative to uranium and produce radioactive waste with a substantially lower half-life.

[10]Enclosure has been the transfer of commonly held land to "those who wanted to establish ownership for their own private gain" [p. 19 of 199]. It is known as enclosure because the newly privatized lands become "enclosed" by fences and other barriers on their boundaries. The assumption of a tragedy of the commons has been used by numerous neocolonial development agencies to justify various

Even better, if we imagine a future in which the health of the humans on the parcel contributes to its measured entropy removal rate, parcel owners will likely welcome healthy visitors to their land. These visitors may improve the parcel owners' measured entropy removal rates during the times when those healthy people are on their land. We can also imagine mechanized contracts automatically paying nonowners on parcels for any health improvements they make to the property while they're on it.

Free entropy money may help people get along with each other in other ways, too. In a world with the morally deficient statutory laws superseded by organically discovered customary laws, people will be able to know better what behavior of theirs will and won't be tolerated by others. This improved knowledge will be a direct result of their ability to purchase higher-quality dispute resolution than available with existing statutory legal systems [384, 388, 421].

If we get moving on this lifesaving change to our US dollars fast enough, they may save our beautiful world from a planetary-life-destroying apocalypse. In 2032 we'll pass directly through the Taurid meteor swarm, a field of large debris believed to be the remnants of comet 2P/Encke [422]. The Tunguska event of 1908, leveling nearly a thousand square miles of Siberian forest, the ice age of the Younger Dryas period of 11,000 BC, and many other catastrophes may have been caused by that swarm. A direct hit from a mile-wide fragment could make the planet ring like a bell and produce earthquakes and volcanoes pulverizing every square foot of land. A direct hit in an ocean could also wipe out all the lands in the world as miles-high tsunamis washed over, leaving them buried in hundreds of feet of mud [38:50 of 423]. Based on the number of past planetary wipeouts likely due to the Taurid swarm, the chance of this happening the next time we pass through it, or the time after that, isn't nearly as small as we need it to be. If we manage to switch over quickly to free entropy-type US dollars and therefore quickly and substantially reduce poverty, private companies may get funded to purchase the world's intercontinental ballistic missile (ICBM) atom bomb fleet and upgrade it for asteroid (and comet) defense. In our newly wealthier world, funding may also be raised to put a telescope similar to the James Webb Space Telescope (JWST) [424], but specialized for exploration of our solar system, at one

---

privatization schemes [p. 18 of 199].

of the LaGrange points to help us find those problematic rocks. While we're at it, spotting and deflecting asteroids and comets, we could also take advantage of the situation and deflect some of the mineral rich rocks into earth orbit for mining purposes.

Speaking of catastrophes, our new US dollars have the potential to save us from our sun, too. Our sun routinely produces large, fast-moving bursts of plasma, called coronal mass ejections (CME), with large bursts striking the earth around once every 500 years. Most recently, the earth absorbed a particularly large burst of coronal plasma in the geomagnetic storm of 1859 known as the Carrington Event. The main effects to life on the earth from the 1859 storm were interruptions in telegraph service, but it could be much different today, wiping out computer memories, electrical power, and satellites. The risk of such a destruction of our electrical devices is serious, with a 4 percent chance of a Carrington-magnitude CME every year during a solar maximum, which occurs every eleven years. In other words, we're playing Russian roulette several years in a row every eleven years, with a 4 percent chance of losing during each of those years [352]. In addition to saving us from the impact of a Taurid swarm fragment, the planetary wealth improvements resulting from free entropy money could fund geomagnetic storm preparations, including CME early warning systems and automated post-detection equipment shutdowns.

Free entropy money will help everyone live longer, healthier, and wealthier lives. As these realities sink in, people's time preferences can be expected to shift to longer and longer times, causing planning and execution of improvements to our planet to arrive at science-fiction levels. We, humanity, will have become a race executing plans lasting over centuries, millennia, and longer.

16. FINAL DESTINY

A FTER the concept of a natural death has itself died a well-deserved death, and poverty, crime, and environmental degradation are but distant, nightmarish memories, our new money, along with our non-monetary products and services, will continue to evolve. Your health will improve continuously in a continuously healthier and happier world, and previously unimaginable good things will become almost routine—here is where the evolution of free entropy money will automatically guide us to an excellent science-fiction future. We can expect our bodies to improve, our machines to improve, and the bodies of our animal and plant brethren to improve.

For one possible example of improvements to our bodies, an outcome like the one obtained by the captain of the starship in *Mutineers' Moon* [425] might come true for anyone who wants it (to the extent it isn't forbidden by the laws of our physical reality). In this story, the captain-to-be had to undergo an enhancement procedure before taking command of the ship, and after the procedure, he was *really* enhanced. He could discriminate scents as well as a good chemistry lab, and see individual dust motes as well as choose which part of the light spectrum he would use to see them. He could lift crazy heavy weights, snap a baseball bat barehanded, and subsist on the oxygen reservoir in his abdomen for up to five hours.

In an example of improvements to our machines, those of us so inclined may be able to do things like explore our planet and our universe. For example, no known laws of physics prevent us from turning science-fiction author Donald Moffitt's vision, from his books *The Genesis Quest* [426] and *Second Genesis* [427], into a reality. He envisioned traveling the universe at near light speed in a semi-sentient Dyson tree [428] powered by a Bussard ramjet[1] [429].

---

[1] A ramjet is a type of jet engine using the relative speed between the engine and its surroundings to compress air prior to the addition of fuel and ignition. Bussard ramjets, proposed by physicist Robert Bussard in 1960, use the same principle, except in outer space. A Bussard ramjet uses a magnetic funnel to collect interstellar hydrogen for a propulsion-producing fusion reactor.

Instead of being packed in a crowded tin can, the passengers traveled on a tree hundreds of miles in diameter, housing millions of people. Much like the earth, the Dyson trees were comfortable homes, with a steady one-earth gravity force provided by the ramjet. In Moffitt's stories, the passengers had discovered a so-called immortality virus and lived in perfect health. Accelerating at one gravity, the ship's speed got so close to light speed that time dilation effects caused their journey from the Whirlpool galaxy to the Milky Way galaxy to take just five hundred years of their subjective time, and they had fun doing it in their giant tree house.

Figure 16.1. *Uplift candidates? (Beluga whale photograph courtesy of Yuan Yue on Unsplash, bonobo courtesy of Adèle on Unsplash.)*

Dreaming of improvements to the bodies of our animal friends, the possibilities get even wilder. For example, in the reality envisioned by David Brin in his uplift universe [430], sentient races uplift other races into sentience using selective breeding and biology modification techniques. There's no reason such a thing couldn't happen here, with humans uplifting other species into sentience (Figure 16.1). Imagine living on a planet with eight billion potential human friends, and now add to that possible friends from other species. It may not be out of the realm of possibility your future best friend is a beluga whale, odd as that sounds here in our legacy world.

The overall, long-term benefits of free entropy money are beauty and fun. The world will get more beautiful, and we'll all get more beautiful, inside and out. And we'll have fun, possibly traveling the universe with our new sentient animal friends. Do we have enough good reasons to transition to free entropy money? The reader, the author, and our friends and families may get to live fantastically beautiful and long lives while exploring the universe in a giant tree house, a kind of Ewok village [431] at near light speed. Best of all, think of the things to happen that are beyond our ability to even guess [432, 433]. All we know is they will be good because we engineered our money to make them that way (see requirement E1 in Appendix C).

We, the People, of Spaceship Earth are presented with the golden opportunity to usher in our science-fiction future. The only question is: what are we waiting for?

Part III.

Mechanizing Our Escape

17. A REQUEST FOR PROPOSAL

FREE entropy money will fix everything for us automatically, but how? How do we get a metaphorical entropy money printing press into the hands of every parcel owner? How do we deal with competitors who claim to have a better printing press? How can the printing presses be made transparent and reliable, so users will trust the money? How do We, the People, of these fifty states repeal our national tax and legal tender statutes? How do we abandon our current energy-type US dollars, consisting of energy removed from land as measured by gold, in which we're now bankrupt? How do we adopt entropy-type US dollars, consisting of entropy removed from land as measured by oxygen? How do we settle our gold bankruptcy?

These are all great questions, but we need not worry—it's all going to be easier than any of us might think. We, the People, are going to be able to make this happen through the expedient of an administrative action. As the sovereign of this land, We, the People, are vested with a tremendous amount of power. We have the power to take an administrative action which will get a metaphorical entropy money printing press into the hands of every parcel owner, along with additional administrative actions answering the remaining questions.

The actions proposed here will answer the previous questions, in the form of an easy and profitable way to use our legacy energy-type US dollars to adopt our new and improved entropy-type US dollars. How to use our energy-type US dollars this way becomes obvious when we step back and review our situation.

We're the lucky beneficiaries of two life-altering facts about our existence here on Spaceship Earth: (1) as we now know, we can use free entropy money to escape quickly to our science-fiction future; and (2) our US dollars aren't immutable artifacts. Those dollars are nothing more than human-manufactured products, in the form of gold coins that are used as money, and have evolved over time the same as other products.[1] They're both etymologically and numismatically derived from the old Bohemian Joachimsthalers, and the collective known as We, the People, of these united States intentionally has changed their element once and their weight multiple times. They've changed from being both 371 4/16 grains, or 1/1.2929 of a Troy ounce of silver and (247 4/8)/10 grains, or 1/19.3939 of a Troy ounce of gold [p. 130 of 185, **CHAP. XVI**, Sec. 9 of 187], to both 1/1.2929 of a Troy ounce of silver and 232/10 grains, or 1/20.6897 of a Troy ounce of gold [p. 131 of 185, **CHAP. XCV**, Sec. 1 of 188], to 25 8/10 grains, or 1/20.672 of a Troy ounce of gold [**CHAP. 41**, Sec. 1 of 320], to 1/35 [SEC. 12 of 3], to 1/38 [SEC. 2 of 179], and to 1/42.2222 [180] of a Troy ounce of gold (Figure 17.1). Even their name has changed, from thaler to daler to dollar. In effect, the collective has also changed the dollars from physical ledger entries, in the form of coins and paper notes, to electronic ledger entries, which are records of claims to coins and paper notes. Changing them to electronic ledger entries tracking produced oxygen is the logical next step on their evolutionary journey. We have precedent for changing our US dollars and a motive to change them again.

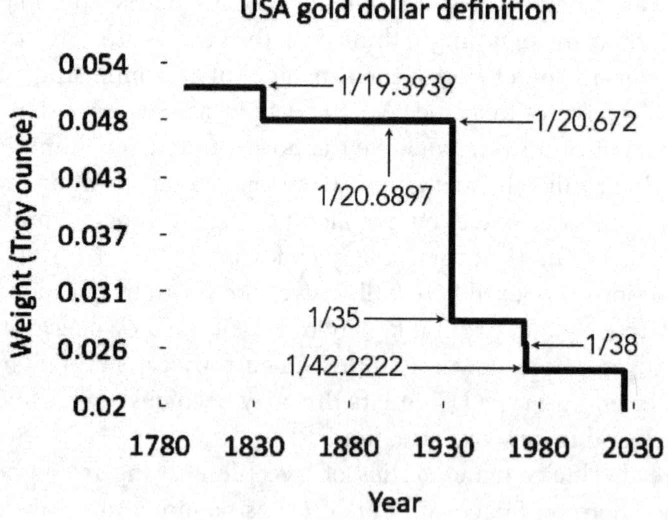

Figure 17.1. *Shrinking US dollar.*

If we change our US dollars from what they are, a form of energy money, to what we want them to be, a form of entropy money, we won't

---

[1]A simplified history of our US dollars is included in Appendix B.

be doing anything new in principle as we already have a long history of changing our money. We now know changing them to entropy money and freeing them will make all our Christmases come true at once.

Again, how? We, the People, need to eliminate the ill effects of our paper money by settling our bankruptcy and migrating to a new and improved replacement, which, according to our design analysis, should consist of a fixed quantity of entropy removed from a given land parcel by its living creatures. We also need a way to do it without doing it because "We" are a 270 million member committee, also known as We, the People, of the United States of America.[2] "We" are the sovereign controlling the production of US dollars, but "We" can't do anything other than make decisions. As described in the introduction, we need to think like the owners of the production of US dollars we are. This is where another life-altering fact helps us out—the collective of We, the People, has a well-used system in place to acquire a diverse set of things, including roads, buildings, and aircraft carriers.

All the collective has to do to obtain our desired new kind of US dollars is the same thing it always does: cheat with money by hiring the job out. Doing this won't be any different in principle than remodeling your kitchen. If you want to remodel your kitchen but aren't able to do it yourself, you might contact some contractors and invite them to submit bids. Some of the contractors might then visit you in your kitchen to get your requirements, and subsequently submit bids. The collective We, the People, does the same thing when it wants to purchase something. When the collective decides to acquire, say, an aircraft carrier, it does the equivalent of what you did when you contacted the remodeling contractors—it delivers what is called a request for proposal (RFP) to various defense contractors. Interested contractors may respond with proposals to construct an aircraft carrier meeting the requirements included in the RFP.

Nothing prevents the collective from doing the same thing to obtain entropy-type US dollars, which are also human-manufactured prod-ucts. It can issue an RFP similar to the one included in Appendix C. This RFP can use orthodox engineering methods by including a formal requirement set, an example of which is also included in Appendix C. Some of the key things to note in these suggested formal requirements

---

[2]If we want to view it through the paradigm that originally produced the federal government of these united States, we can think of ourselves as fifty committees of millions of members each.

are that our new US dollars must do good, and to do good they must reduce poverty, crime, and environmental degradation. The rest of the requirements follow to satisfy those. Importantly for profiting from our escape, as will be seen shortly, one of the requirements specifies our entropy-type US dollars be tracked on a fork from the decentralized autonomous ledger (DAL) maintained by the decentralized autonomous network (DAN) known as the digital cash (https://www.dash.org/) network.[3]

The purpose of choosing the digital cash DAL for our escape is to provide us the crucial reliability benefits of bitcoin while eliminating its deficiencies.[4] The DAL units currently referred to as bitcoins technically should be called prototype bitcoins because, while they've proved the concept of a DAL beautifully and proven to be a good store of value (SOV), they are mostly useless as a means of exchange (MOE), being slow, expensive, and difficult to use.[5] The prototype bitcoin DAL can be compared to a prototype of a car that is complete, except without an interior. The car may go, stop, and turn perfectly, but it's useless if it can't carry passengers. Prototype bitcoin has the equivalent problem. Users have been able to transfer ledger entries reliably to each other for over a dozen years, but it isn't suitable for retail use and thus can't be part of our escape plan.

A version of bitcoin with the metaphorical interior installed can, however. The "digital cash" version of bitcoin, under development since 2014, will fill the bill because it *is* bitcoin, except with the metaphorical interior installed. It will be referred to here as *retail* bitcoin to emphasize that relationship. It is fast, with less than one-second transaction confirmation times; inexpensive, with sub-penny transaction costs; and easy to use, with protocol-level encrypted usernames [435–437]. It is a market-proven, turnkey [438], payments-focused solution for monetary transactions that is optionally fungible, scalable to credit card levels of throughput [1:33 of 439], and as easy to use as PayPal [435–437].

---

[3]The name "digital cash" refers to the electronic cash mentioned in the bitcoin white paper [434].

[4]In the long run, our newly free markets for money may converge on other DALs. In the near term, however, bitcoin competitors are in the prototype stage of development and do not meet the reliability requirement E15 (Appendix C) as well as digital cash.

[5]Although third-party tools make the prototype bitcoin ledger easier to use, they cost the user the decentralization safety and reliability benefits he or she was hoping to obtain by using a DAL.

Its developers have kept its proof of work (POW)[6] software identical
to prototype bitcoin, so it has the proven reliability of the prototype
bitcoin network, by orders of magnitude the most stress-tested DAN
in existence. The network's highly reliable prototype bitcoin code has
been augmented with 51 percent attack[7] protection,[8] and it comes
complete with self-governance in the form of the world's oldest decentralized autonomous organization (DAO). Furthermore, it's well suited
for use both as a MOE, including suitability for point-of-sale (POS) retail
transactions,[9] and as a SOV [435, 441–444]. In another benefit, *retail* bitcoin improves on the divisibility and portability attributes of electronic
claims to paper claims (dollar bills) to gold (dollars), which themselves
are improvements in those two categories over gold itself [ch. 8 of 192],
without sacrificing scarcity.

Important other requirements in this set are that the owner of the
parcel from which entropy was removed owns those US dollars initially,
and our new and improved US dollars must exist in a free monetary
environment. Most of our requirements will be met by the supplier of
the DAL tracking our new and improved US dollars, and the collective
can cause the new money to meet the free monetary environment
requirement by repealing its federal government tax and legal tender
statutes.

For the rest of our description of how to adopt free entropy money,
let us assume We, the People, have chosen a supplier who responded
to our RFP with a proposal that includes the requirements M1 through
M7 in Appendix C. Importantly for describing our escape route, these
requirements specify a new US dollar consists of a certain mass of
oxygen produced by a living plant, and thus we will refer to our new
and improved entropy-type US dollars as oxygen dollars, or oxygen US

---

[6]Proof of work means network software operators must pay, in the form of consumed
electrical power, to be paid in the coin of the realm. Combined with mining difficulty
adjustment algorithms in the network software, it has the effect of rate limiting the
introduction of new "coins" into circulation.

[7]A 51 percent attack is occurring when one entity controls more than half of the
processing power running the network. A successful attack, which has never
happened on either the prototype or *retail* bitcoin networks, would allow the entity
to rewrite history and wrongfully transfer ledger units into its own ledger entry.

[8]51 percent attacks are a threat to some DANs [440]; however, the reality is prototype
bitcoin has well demonstrated the invulnerability of a large network of peers to
such attacks, and *retail* bitcoin is even less vulnerable.

[9]*Retail* bitcoin comes complete with a decentralized application interface (DAPI),
enabling easy integration into merchant accounting software.

dollars.[10] We'll refer to our legacy US dollars as gold dollars, or gold US dollars. Gold US dollars can be thought of as a type of energy money, while oxygen US dollars can be thought of as a type of entropy money (Table 11.1).

Issuing such an RFP will take care of the problem of obtaining our new and improved entropy-type US dollars, but how do we make the switch from gold dollars to oxygen dollars, and how do we pull off the trick of repealing our tax and legal tender statutes? These sound like tall orders, but filling them will be easier than one might think. We can both make the switch and repeal those problematic statutes with a simple administrative action that takes advantage of our wise decision to track our new US dollars on a fork from the *retail* bitcoin ledger. Thanks to this decision, we'll all be paid well to make the switch, even before we make the switch. After the administrative action, we'll make the switch at our leisure, while also repealing our tax and legal tender statutes. We can accomplish all this by using the *retail* bitcoin network to instigate a type of short squeeze.

---

[10]A fixed weight of oxygen could be a particular instance of an entropy-type US dollar, in the same way a fixed weight of gold is a particular instance of an energy-type US dollar. For example, another instance of an energy-type US dollar could be, and has been, a fixed weight of silver, and an instance of an entropy-type US dollar other than oxygen could be a fixed weight of carbon dioxide.

18. A BIG SHORT SQUEEZE

A short squeeze can happen when someone sells something short, thinking the price is going to decrease, but the price increases instead. Selling short is done by putting up collateral to borrow something, then selling it. If the price goes down as you hoped, you buy it back for less than your sell price, repay the loan with interest, and pocket the difference for your profit. However, if the price goes up instead, you have to make a choice—you can either put up more collateral and gamble the price will eventually decrease to less than your sell price, or you can take your lumps and buy at higher than your sell price and return it to the lender, with interest.

When the price goes up too much, more and more short sellers will buy, causing the price to run up more, causing more short sellers to buy, causing the price to run up even more. This kind of event is known as a short squeeze because the shorts are getting squeezed out of the trade by the rising price. Two examples of short squeezes, anticipating the results We, the People, can achieve when we unstoppably transfer monetary value from the center to the periphery, can be found in the GameStop short squeeze of 2021 and the gold short squeeze of 1999.

Coordinated action: the GameStop short squeeze of 2021. In the months leading up to 2021, some of the Wall Street big money did their due diligence, and subsequently took large short positions in GameStop. In a contrary move, some smaller Wall Street money, plus some retail traders and various others, did their own due diligence and came to a different conclusion, that GameStop prices weren't as high as the big money thought. These smaller players managed to combine forces among anonymous strangers to use some of the big money's short positions against them by entering a massive wave of long positions[1] in GameStop. This caused a short squeeze for several of the big money shops, leading to the smaller money taking a substantial sum from the big money in the resulting price run-up [445–447].

---

[1]In other words, they purchased a lot of shares.

Looking into the abyss: the gold short squeeze of 1999.   In another, less well-known example, a short squeeze in gold happened in 1999. Several trading houses, including AIG International Ltd. and NM Rothschild & Sons Ltd. [448], had large short positions in gold and were caught off guard when the first Washington Agreement on Gold, limiting gold sales by the signatories, was announced in September of 1999. Within days the dollar *bill*/gold ratio jumped from $265/ounce to almost $330/ounce, forcing those trading houses to cover their short positions, driving the price even higher while driving themselves out of business.

Thanks to a conversation a few years later between Eddie George, Governor of the Bank of England, and Nicholas J. Morrell, CEO of Lonmin Plc, in front of three witnesses, we know certain things about this gold short squeeze that weren't revealed publicly at the time. Mr. George told Mr. Morrell:

> We looked into the abyss if the gold price rose further. A further rise would have taken down one or several trading houses, which might have taken down all the rest in their wake.
>
> Therefore at any price, at any cost, the central banks had to quell the gold price, manage it. It was very difficult to get the gold price under control but we have now succeeded. The US Fed was very active in getting the gold price down. So was the U.K.

According to the Banque de France 1999 Annual Report, the Bank of Russia was also active in getting the price down, though it may just have been taking advantage of the higher price [448, 449].

In this 1999 short squeeze, We, the People, of the fifty states sold gold from our hoard onto the open market to quell the price. According to the governor of the Bank of England, it was to save some trading houses. Mr. George forgot to mention another reason the gold price needed quelling, however—the money masters of the world were afraid of becoming poor. If the price of gold had continued to run away, it might have gone to 10,000, 50,000, or even 100,000 or more US dollar *bills* per ounce of gold and stayed there due to the large number of dollar *bills* in circulation relative to the amount of gold. The market dollar *bill*/ounce ratio was only in the triple digits, with much room to increase before reaching par with the extant world dollar *bill*/ounce of gold ratio. If such a runaway had happened, a large amount of the financial spending power in the world would have transferred *from* the holders of paper claims on gold *to* the holders of gold.

We the People's short squeeze: cheating the cheater. We, the People, can use the same technique used by the GameStop longs to initiate what effectively will be a short squeeze on everyone who is not long on *retail* bitcoin. We can do this by the expedient of coordinating among each other to enter a massive wave of long positions in *retail* bitcoin. In both examples of short squeezes, the longs overwhelmed the shorts, causing price runaways. The same opportunity, to both cause and take advantage of a price runaway, stares us in the face. This is because very few of us individuals, families, and companies own *retail* bitcoin. It's as if we have short positions, in which we don't own any, but we don't have loans to pay back.

We can take our bankrupt US paper dollar *bills* for a swim right into the abyss with a simple administrative action. All we need do to make this happen is have our federal government purchase a two-year budget supply worth of *retail* bitcoin. Nothing is required other than deciding to do it and communicating that decision to our agents in the federal government treasury. We want this buy to happen for the same reason the money masters of the universe didn't want a similar thing to happen with gold back in 1999—it will make them poorer and us richer.

This wealth transfer will happen because all of us will know the buy is going to happen before it happens and will therefore front run. Front-running is what you do when you're sure the price of something is going to change, in either direction. In other words, if you know in advance sellers or buyers are on the way, you get in line in front of them. Every one of us with two nickels to rub together is going to front run our federal government treasury, and every one of us who participates will benefit financially.

Having our federal government treasury purchase the two-year budget supply, along with requiring our new oxygen US dollars be tracked on a fork from the *retail* bitcoin ledger, will accomplish multiple ends simultaneously.

Front run. First, our treasury buy of *retail* bitcoin will cause a massive transfer of spending power from the center to the periphery, moving market capitalization from the holders of paper claims on gold US dollars to the holders of *retail* bitcoin ledger units. If the treasurer of the federal government is going to purchase a two-year budget supply of something, it will be common knowledge since it is We, the People, who will have given her that instruction. Therefore, everyone on the planet will know, in advance, when and how much the treasury of the federal government of these united States is going to purchase. We'll all be well aware this purchase of a two-year budget supply worth of *retail* bitcoin, amounting to around $14 trillion as of the mid-2020s, will make the dollar *bill/retail* bitcoin ratio shoot to the moon, so we'll all be forced to buy first and take advantage of the price run-up.

All of us who didn't own any *retail* bitcoin before the buy will be forced to buy it before our federal government does, in the same way the short sellers in the GameStop and gold short squeezes were forced to buy. Buyers of *retail* bitcoin won't have loans to make good on, but their dilemma will be basically the same as the one faced by the shorts. The short sellers didn't own any of the GameStop shares or gold ounces because they borrowed some and then sold them, and the *retail* bitcoin buyers don't yet own any because of whatever the reason. In other words, they both don't own any shares or ounces or ledger units because reasons—the important part is they don't own any. The to-be buyers of *retail* bitcoin will have to either buy or get poor as they watch everyone except themselves get rich. As this understanding gets into more and more heads, the dollar *bill/retail* bitcoin ratio will increase faster and faster, the same as the GameStop and gold prices during their run-ups.

The progression will be that individuals and families will front run first. Then companies, charity organizations, and tribes will front run, then city, county, state, prefecture, province, and national governments, approximately in that order. Our front-running will happen in this order because individuals are more nimble in their decision-making and execution than groups, and smaller groups more so than bigger groups. Thanks to this order of front-running, from individuals and smaller groups to bigger groups, there will be a sudden, massive transfer of spending power from institutions to individuals and families. Even the few people who are happy with the way things are will be forced to participate as the dollar *bill/retail* bitcoin ratio runs away. To not participate will be to become poor. As the dollar *bill/retail* bitcoin ratio increases dramatically, all parties who bought prior to the federal government will find their financial situation greatly improved by the time the buying is complete. The sooner these people bought, the more their financial situations will have improved. This front run will be irresistible, a force of nature. It will, in effect, be a run on our gold US dollar bank at Fort Knox. In this run, the bank has stiffed its customers and closed its doors, so the customers are going to dump their bank paper in exchange for another asset, and the bank paper will become worthless. Every one of us will end up in the line to dump our paper, and the financially smaller and weaker will benefit the most [222].

Some will be concerned wealthy people might get even wealthier thanks to the front run, negating any positive effects to the financially smaller and weaker. This concern is misplaced, however, even though the rich almost certainly will get richer in the front run. We all want the financially big and strong to benefit from the front run since that practically guarantees none of them will have an incentive to block our efforts to redesign our US dollars, and thus none of them will attempt to block our efforts. We want them to benefit even more so because their US dollar *bills* flowing into *retail* bitcoin will raise the US dollar *bill*/*retail* bitcoin ratio further, benefiting earlier adopters. We can expect smaller investors to adopt earlier than large investors, and thus benefit more, because large investors are typically more conservative. In this case, most larger investors will probably wait and see a little before jumping in with both feet. In the meantime, while they're waiting and seeing, the ongoing price run-up will be benefiting the smallest and weakest the most.

Another reason not to be concerned if some wealthy people grow even wealthier from the front run is the poor will benefit more than the rich because they have the least. The front-running will have little impact on the rich because they already effectively have infinite money. They aren't going to buy up all the food and rent all the apartments, and probably won't even buy more yachts—they already have everything they need. The change this front run makes in people's lives is mainly going to be for regular people, and the more difficult their living situation the more positively it will impact them. The worst off in our society, those about to fall over the cliff of financial catastrophe, and those who've already fallen and are living in a van down by the river, will benefit the most because it only takes a little money to help them out a lot. Thanks to this front run, many or most of our less well-off will finally be able to afford both shelter and food, rather than only one or the other, or neither.

As word about the possibility of this massively positive change to our money and our world spreads, along with the possibility of transferring massive spending power from the financially big and strong to the small and weak, individuals in their private capacities will front run before they have their companies do it because they'll take care of themselves and their families first. The way it will work is individuals will discover the plan and quietly front run in their off-hours, to take care of their families, then get together with their bosses and make plans for the company do it. The employees and owners of every company and institution on the planet will front run before their company or institution does. The employees and owners of JP Morgan Chase & Co. will front run before their company does. The employees and owners of BlackRock, Inc. will front run before their company does. The employees of every governmental organization on the planet will front run before their employer does.

The employees of our federal government will front run the buy. Hunter Biden and the big guy will front run. The secretary of state will front run. The chief of the Joint Chiefs of Staff will front run. They and many other federal government bureaucrats will probably retire instantly since most of them have bountiful supplies of US dollar *bills* with which to front run. They may be able to improve their financial situations enough to kick it on a Caribbean island instead of doing dreary government work.

The employees of the central governments of the Russian Federation, the Ukraine, the Netherlands, China, North Korea, South Korea, Israel, Zimbabwe, Brazil, South Africa, England, Japan, Vietnam, Thailand, New Zealand, and Kenya will all front run, and many will retire from government work. The mayors, city council members, and other employees of New York City, Seattle, Tokyo, Istanbul, Moscow in Idaho, Moscow in Russia, Johannesburg, London, Rome, and Sampit in Borneo will also front run, and many too will retire.

The governors and other employees of the governments of Texas, Delaware, Florida, Chihuahua in Mexico, the Nunavut territory of Canada, and Fukuoka in Japan will front run too. As a result, the spending power of every person on the earth relative to every organization will improve dramatically. The spending power of companies will increase relative to the governments of cities, whose spending power will increase relative to the governments of states, and the governments of states relative to those of nation-states, and the governments of other nation-states relative to our federal government of these fifty states. Every governmental organization on the planet will probably lose many employees who suddenly don't need their bureaucratic paycheck and want to participate in the new entropy money economy.

Tax and borrowing jubilee. Second, at the time the *retail* bitcoin buy is completed, our federal government will have all the money it needs for two years and won't need to acquire any more during that time. This means as soon as our federal government treasurer has completed the collective's buy, we can declare a two-year tax and borrowing jubilee.[2]

The tax and borrowing jubilee here means our federal government will have a two-year budget supply worth of savings, so none of us individuals will need to supply it with budget money for two years. Hence it can stop borrowing and taxing for those two years—our own kind of jubilee.

Retained value, convenient payments. Third, after our treasurer has completed the two-year budget supply purchase, we can also require the treasury to begin paying federal government bills directly with our two-year supply of *retail* bitcoin. Upon completion of the two-year buy, the dollar *bill*/*retail* bitcoin price ratio will have become approximately constant due to the large financial inertia it will have obtained.[3] Therefore, paying in *retail* bitcoin will have become equivalent to paying in US dollar *bills*, through the ratio. If we choose to do this, the market dollar *bill*/*retail* bitcoin ratio will not drop every time

---

[2]The Jubilee, a Jewish economic tradition, was used to prevent wealth disparity-induced violent revolutions. As described in Chapter 25 of the Old Testament book of Leviticus, in the forty-ninth year of a fifty-year period all debts would be wiped out and collateral property returned. In the same spirit, Israelites are commanded to cancel their fellows' debts at the end of every seven years in Deuteronomy 15.

Partial debt jubilees have been performed by kings on a regular basis since Hammurabi of Babylon and before, also to avert violent revolutions caused by extreme concentrations of wealth. Babylonian kings were known to forgive all consumer debts upon taking power. Similarly, in 594 B.C. Athens, supreme archon Solon devalued the currency to reduce debtors' burdens, ended imprisonment for debts, canceled arrears for taxes and mortgage interest, and established a graduated income tax in which the rich paid twelve times the rate of the poor [ch. 19 of 192].

[3]There will still be some amount of minute-to-minute and day-to-day price variation as speculators trade, but these variations will have become tiny relative to the newly large dollar *bill*/*retail* bitcoin ratio.

the government pays a bill since the treasurer will not be purchasing US dollar *bills* to pay our federal government bills.

Paying our federal government bills with *retail* bitcoin will benefit everyone because the value of their *retail* bitcoin holdings will not be dropping as the treasurer sells, so they too won't need to purchase US dollar *bills*. If the federal government begins paying its bills with *retail* bitcoin, combined with the two-year federal tax jubilee, the way will be cleared for everyone to pay with *retail* bitcoin, benefiting from the convenience and reduced transaction costs that will prevail. We'll all breathe a sigh of relief knowing the two to three percent credit card percentage charge on transactions [223], and twenty five dollar wire service fees to (slowly) transfer money between banks, have become things of the past. Any time we need to pay someone any amount, it will cost less than a penny and be done in a second.

Get paid to hold *retail* bitcoin. Fourth, if the collective manages to purchase more than a thousand units on the *retail* bitcoin ledger, it will be afforded the opportunity to be paid to operate what are known as master nodes. A *retail* bitcoin master node is an executable, or computer program, anyone can run. The *retail* bitcoin master node executables provide speed, fungibility, and ease-of-use services to the network, putting the interior in the prototype bitcoin car, to use that analogy. Anyone who proves to the network they control 1,000 units of *retail* bitcoin ledger entries can get paid by the network to run one of the master node executables converting slow, expensive, hard-to-use prototype bitcoin into fast, inexpensive, easy-to-use *retail* bitcoin.

For every 1,000 units of the *retail* bitcoin decentralized autonomous ledger (DAL) We, the People, own, we can pay a vendor to operate a master node, paying us around five percent annually during the time when we hold the 1,000 units and run the executable. Operating master nodes will also afford us the opportunity to vote on how to spend a budget, which amounts to ten percent of the mining payout,[4] which

---

[4]Mining, for the *retail* bitcoin and prototype bitcoin networks, is how the ledger is secured from double spending and how it pays for electrical power and hardware to run the network software. Anyone who wishes to participate is incentivized to spend money on electricity and computer hardware by being paid with new ledger units. These new ledger units are said to have been "mined." It isn't possible to "mine" new ledger units without consuming electrical power, and the more electrical power consumed, the better chance a computer owner has of getting

will have a very large value after the price run-up caused by the buying spree.

Newly minted wealthy philanthropists. Fifth, another benefit to be obtained from this buy may be a new supply of wealthy philanthropists, those who benefited substantially from the dollar *bill/retail* bitcoin ratio run-up. This fortunate crowd may add to the charitable contributions already being made by existing philanthropic organizations. We can expect many deserving charities to benefit from our treasury's buy, enhancing the services they provide and helping them help more people.

We can expect substantially increased donations to human, animal, and nature charitable organizations. The Rainforest Action Network, The Nature Conservancy, Conservation Northwest, the Turtle Island Restoration Network, and the International Anti-Poaching Foundation, to name a few of the author's favorites, and many others might receive substantially increased donations. The help these organizations provide our living world should quickly and dramatically improve. Garbage will commence being cleaned out of our oceans, lakes, and rivers right away, dioxins and hormone-altering chemicals will commence being removed from our living world, animal populations will begin recovering, and more greenhouse gases will be removed from the atmosphere. We're going to save the planet we've spent so long killing.

We can also expect a great acceleration in the destruction of the world child molester network as mentioned in Chapter 15, as charitable

---

some of the newly produced ledger units. Would-be cheaters can't get new bitcoin ledger entries without running the network software and by doing so help secure the ledger from double spending, thus making them not cheaters. The more "miners" running the network software the harder it is to cheat, and the network adjusts the difficulty of mining to maximize the number of miners. Every few minutes, the network reconciles a new version of the ledger and adds a certain number of new units to a semi-random ledger entry owned by the owner of one of the "mining" machines consuming electrical power, thus making it profitable for computer owners to contribute to the network. This method of securing the ledger from double spending is known as proof of work (POW). For the *retail* bitcoin ledger, forty five percent of these new units are added to the ledger entries of miners, forty five percent are added to the ledger entries of master node operators, and ten percent are used for budget proposals. Budget proposals are voted for or against by master node operators, who have "skin in the game" since they own a thousand ledger units per master node.

donations to molester hunters pour in from the suddenly larger group of wealthy philanthropists.

Finally, in an unexpected benefit that's as-of-yet on almost no one's radar, the work of our new philanthropists will enable humanity to witness the founding of Project Salamander (Chapter 27) to regrow human limbs [368], and subsequently fix almost everything else that might ail a person. Practically every one of us will gain relief from our pains and commence becoming healthier, and then even healthier.

Two-year window of opportunity to drown our legacy US dollars. Sixth, by purchasing a two-year supply of *retail* bitcoin, we will have taken our paper US dollar *bills* for a swim in the abyss and bought ourselves a two-year window of opportunity to drown them. Taking our paper US dollar *bills* for a swim in the abyss will be accomplished by using them to purchase the two-year supply of *retail* bitcoin and, in effect, using *retail* bitcoin as our national money for two years or less. We can drown them by using those two years to settle our bankruptcy in gold and engineer a new kind of US dollars by way of the request for proposal (RFP), then adopt these excellent new dollars.

At the time we adopt our new oxygen US dollars, each of us will own the same number of units on the new oxygen dollar ledger as we do on the *retail* bitcoin ledger, some of which we'll all own now due to our front-running. Thanks to our wise decision to use *retail* bitcoin to take our paper US dollar *bills* for a swim in the abyss, and the requirement that our new oxygen US dollars be tracked on a fork from the *retail* bitcoin ledger, we'll all get a head start in our new monetary age.

19. FUNDING, MEASURING, SETTLING AND EXECUTING

WE'RE planning to purchase a two-year federal government budget supply worth of *retail* bitcoin, but haven't yet discussed where we'll get the money. Again we're in luck, and it won't be difficult. All we have to do is a little more of what we're already doing and have been doing for a long time, which is sell bonds. We can sell a special bond run called, say, Escape bonds, onto the primary market with our metaphorical left hand and purchase them from the secondary market with our metaphorical right hand. It won't be a problem to purchase as many of these bonds as needed from the secondary market because as we found in Chapter 4, our metaphorical right hand, also known as the Federal Reserve System, is controlled by the collective.

If the current, as of late 2025, US debt amounts to around $38 trillion, and if the annual budget need is $7 trillion, borrowing a two-year budget supply amounts to only about a 37 percent increase in the debt.[1] Once we've successfully transitioned to oxygen US dollars, the debt will be paid in its entirety, in nominal US dollars, because debt service is part of our $7 trillion yearly budget. We won't need to worry about any bureaucrats getting bright ideas about borrowing again since any such moves will be punished by the market in our new monetary era of free, as in free to compete, money.

Obtaining entropy money data

---

[1]To be clear, our federal government debt is going to increase by $14 trillion no matter what we do. We have the choice to either let it continue growing the old way, on its way to infinity, or bump it up this one last time knowing it finally will be repaid.

Issuing an RFP and choosing a responsive proposal won't help us much unless it's possible to obtain the needed oxygen production rate measurements. Once again we're in luck because as mentioned in Chapter 10, land parcel respiration rate data is readily available.[2] It's possible the first version of the new money could use oxygen production rate estimates obtained simply by doing the equivalent of counting green pixels on a satellite photograph of your parcel. This won't be a perfect measurement of ecosystem services, but that's okay because there won't ever be a perfect measurement. All we need to do is put on our engineer hats and get close enough. When we've repealed tax and legal tender statutes, the estimates will improve over time thanks to people trying to earn business with better monetary mousetraps. For example, oxygen production rate measurements can be modified to pay parcel owners to have biodiverse ecosystems (Figure 14.2), or perhaps bioproductive ecosystems, or maybe a norm of the two. Machine learning techniques could aid in the production of biodiversity, bioproductivity, and other such estimates [451].

Recording entropy money data

Obtaining measurements of mined entropy isn't enough—it must be recorded in a useful way. We want to record this information on a DAL, and again we're in luck because it is becoming increasingly common to track real-world assets on DALs. Examples of DAL real-world asset tracking include the Polymath ledger to track securities, the Novem Gold, Digix Gold, and GoldMint ledgers [452] to track gold ownership, and the Mattereum ledger [453], which aims to track various forms of real property on a DAL using what are known as Ricardian Contracts [454].

---

[2]Land parcel respiration rate data can be provided by projects such as the Forest Inventory and Analysis program in the USA, LiDAR remote sensing [290], the FLuorescence EXplorer [294, 296–301, 308], eddy covariance flux towers [291], and others [p. 399 of 132]. Also available is the data used by Planet.com and Google Earth. Google Earth uses the Earth Engine Data Catalog [450], which includes data from the NASA Landsat Program, Copernicus Sentinel Program, MOD09GA MODIS/Terra Surface Reflectance Daily L2G, MCD43A4 MODIS Terra+Aqua Nadir BRDF-Adjusted Reflectance, ETOPO1 1 Arc-Minute Global Relief Model, Land Water Mask Derived from MODIS and SRTM L3, and Hansen Global Forest Change v1.2.

The goal of the Mattereum project is to decrease the consumption of raw materials by allowing people to include trustable provenance with items for sale, thus increasing their sale prices. The intent is to provide people with financial incentives to take care of their property, and not throw it away, because they can sell it for a higher price with provenance than without. In an example of this technique, Captain Kirk, also known as William Shatner, has been using the Mattereum network to establish the provenance of memorabilia from the *Star Trek* television series, improving sale prices by giving people real value in the form of trustable information about the goods they're buying. The methods used by the Mattereum project and others can be used to track mined entropy.

We also need to associate the entropy removal data with parcel owners to complete the positive feedback loop putting our human financial and living biological worlds in harmony with each other. Again we're in luck, and won't need to invent anything new to safely accomplish this task. This safety will be obtained with the use of decentralized networks of autonomous machines living on the Internet since these networks eliminate any need for the public to trust individuals or groups. Several DAL projects, such as Civic [455] and BrightID [456], are already in operation, enabling people to establish digital identities safely. These techniques can be expanded relatively easily to establish digital identities for parcels, and correlate owners and parcels using data available from sources such as county recorder parcel ownership databases.

The technology and data either exist or easily can be made to exist to pay landowners reliably for ecosystem services.

Settling our bankruptcy

Since we have more paper claims to our dollars in circulation than there are dollars, with no realistic hope of acquiring enough dollars to cover the paper and with the serious problems being caused by the shortage and by the gold itself, we need to settle our bankruptcy.

One of the tasks we'll be able to complete during our two-year window of opportunity is to settle our bankruptcy in gold US dollars. We'll be able to accomplish this by offering up the gold in Fort Knox at a rate discounting the dollar *bills* in circulation appropriate to their excess number.

The settlement will consist of an offer from the collective of We, the People, to redeem dollar *bills* at the appropriate discounted rate. Everyone will be afforded the opportunity to present their dollar *bills* to our federal government treasurer in exchange for dollars at that discounted rate. The treasurer would redeem one gold US dollar for every 1,992.56 US dollar *bills* presented, assuming a gold US dollar is defined by the full faith and credit of We, the People as 1/20.672 ounces of gold per the Gold Standard Act of 1900 [320, 457], there are 7,413.446 tonnes of gold in the vault at Fort Knox [181], and 22 trillion dollar *bills* in circulation [458]. Equivalently, one ounce of gold would be redeemed for every 84,130.36 US dollar *bills* presented. Using these assumptions about dollars and *bills*, dollar *bill* holders will receive a 99.975 percent haircut in this settlement from the 1/20.672 ounces per bill promised by We, the People, in 1900. More details of this calculation are presented in the simplified history of our US dollars in Appendix B.

A variation on this action could be to open up the gold trading window to accept trades both ways, at least in the remaining time during which US dollars are still defined as a fixed weight of gold. This could be done by opening up the gold trading window and redefining, for the duration, a gold US dollar as 1/84,130.36 of an ounce of gold. Such a temporary opening for trades could aid people who desired to purchase *retail* bitcoin with dollar *bills* in getting a fair deal for their gold. After we adopt the new and improved oxygen US dollars, the gold trade window could revert to purchasing only dollar *bills* in exchange for gold. Informed opinions on the best way to settle our bankruptcy while switching to our new and improved oxygen US dollars could prove valuable.

Execute with memorandums of agreement

We can put this all together by communicating to each other our desire to purchase the two-year budget supply worth of *retail* bitcoin, along with our other escape steps. We can accomplish this with two memorandums of agreement (MOA).[3] Every one of us politically competent

---

[3]A memorandum of agreement is a memorandum signed by all of us, where our signatures communicate to our political peers we agree to the contents of the memorandum. For example, if the MOA says something to the effect of "Dear Mrs.

individuals can choose to sign these memorandums, which will communicate to our political peers our desire for the administrative actions detailed in the memos to take place.

The first MOA could read something like:

I, State Your Name [459], from [Hawaii, Alaska, California, Oregon, Washington, Idaho, Nevada, Arizona, Utah, Montana, Wyoming, Colorado, New Mexico, Texas, Oklahoma, Kansas, Nebraska, South Dakota, North Dakota, Minnesota, Iowa, Missouri, Arkansas, Louisiana, Mississippi, Tennessee, Illinois, Wisconsin, Michigan, Indiana, Ohio, Kentucky, Alabama, Georgia, Florida, South Carolina, North Carolina, Virginia, West Virginia, Maryland, Delaware, Pennsylvania, New Jersey, Connecticut, New York, Rhode Island, Massachusetts, New Hampshire, Vermont, or Maine],[4][5] in joining my fellows of these fifty united States of America to eliminate now and forever the scourges of poverty, crime, and environmental degradation from our beautiful world, do hereby instruct my secretary of the treasury, my treasurer, my president, and my representatives in the Congress of the federal government of these

Treasurer: Please sell this many bonds and use the proceeds to purchase that many *retail* bitcoin ledger entries," all signatories are communicating to their political peers they want Mrs. Treasurer to take that action.

[4]Signaling our wishes on a state-by-state basis, according to the residence of the signer, would be a way of following the precedent of doing things by states rather than by the totality of the individuals of all the states. This is the precedent that created the federal government in the first place, when in 1788 the ninth of the thirteen states ratified the Constitution. It is also the system used in presidential elections in which the states choose the president of the central government, with each state getting a number of votes (electoral votes) proportionate to its population size. That being said, if we decide instead to sign the MOA as a unitary national group, that works too—whatever it takes to get our treasurer's buying started.

[5]As an aside, taking this action of engineering new US dollars would be a way of respecting the wishes of the people of the original thirteen states, who did not want a strong national government. Those people had instructed their delegates to the Constitutional Convention in Philadelphia to keep, but improve, the Articles of Confederation. In the Articles, they had created a weak national government without the power of the sword or the purse, considered a federal government in the language of the time. These wise ancestors of ours were "the true radical liberals and torchbearers of the American Revolution and supporters of real decentralized federalism" [p. 42 of 207], who wanted a group of sovereign united states in the common noun sense, not a unitary United States in the proper noun sense. They had fought and died to rid themselves of the unitary government of King George not even a decade before being saddled with another one when the Constitution was ratified.

united States, to execute the following, hereafter known as The Plan:

1. Issue a special bond run, called Escape bonds.
2. Use the proceeds from the Escape bonds to purchase *retail* bitcoin, also known as digital cash (https://www.dash.org/), until the accumulated US dollar *bill* value of these purchases is sufficient to pay the bills of the federal government of these united States of America for a period of two years,[6] given the present budget. Continue selling Escape bonds until the two-year budget supply worth of *retail* bitcoin has been acquired.
3. Purchase Escape bonds as needed from the secondary market using funds from the Federal Reserve System.
4. Initiate, for the federal government of these fifty united States of America, a two-year tax and borrowing jubilee immediately upon acquisition of a two-year supply of *retail* bitcoin.
5. Starting immediately after the two-year budget supply of *retail* bitcoin has been accumulated, pay all the bills of the federal government of these united States of America directly using *retail* bitcoin. Make the payments in amounts delivering equivalent market value as if the payments had been made in US dollar *bills*, through the extant free market dollar *bill*/*retail* bitcoin ratio.
6. Operate as many master nodes on the *retail* bitcoin network as possible.
7. Publicly issue the attached request for proposal (Appendix C) for new and improved entropy-type US dollars.
8. During any time when *retail* bitcoin master nodes are being operated, vote on *retail* bitcoin budget proposals according to further instructions from We, the People, of these united States of America.
9. Settle the bankruptcy in gold US dollars of the federal government of these united States of America upon obtaining a two-year supply of *retail* bitcoin.

My digital signature on this memorandum of agreement is to be considered valid when 90 percent[7] of my political peers in (indicate

---

[6]The reasoning behind the idea to buy a two-year supply of *retail* bitcoin is two years should be enough time to develop and adopt our new oxygen US dollars, whereas one year might be a little short, and three years seems like a long time.

[7]Why 90 percent? Because it is a conservative number—the fact is more than 99.999

your state) have also signed it. I desire my secretary of the treasury, my treasurer, my president, and my representatives in the Congress of the federal government of these united States, as appropriate, to execute The Plan upon receiving this memorandum of agreement from each of the fifty states.

Signed,

State Your Name

Today

Making the signature on the vote dependent on political peers also signing is intended to make the final vote happen all at once and thereby give a binary signal to the treasurer and other representatives. If the number of people voting for the initiative simply gradually increased as more people heard about the campaign and voted, the treasurer would not have an unambiguous way of knowing when to commence issuing bonds and purchasing *retail* bitcoin DAL units. Should she act when 51 percent of the people of each state say so, or 75 percent, or 90 percent? If no one in each state signs until 90 percent have indicated their intention to sign, such an ambiguity for our treasurer is removed.

Execute signing of the MOA

Nothing prevents an existing business from enabling We, the People, of these united States to sign an MOA with each other. For example, nothing prevents Google Earth engineers from adding functionality to their product. They could modify it so land parcel ownership and residence databases are used to allow citizens of the states to securely identify themselves as one of We, the People, of their state. The services of decentralized autonomous networks like Civic or BrightID could be enlisted to help individuals safely and reliably identify themselves.

Nothing prevents Google Earth engineers from altering their product so it can allow each one of us to prove to the algorithm we are who we say we are and live where we say we live, and communicate to our fellows in our state, and to our fellows in the other states, our desire to transition to the new money by, say, clicking on our home. A click could amount to signing the MOA, publicly stating the signer's desire

---

percent of us want this to happen. An incomplete list of the constituencies who want it is provided in Chapter 25.

for our treasurer to issue the Escape bond run, spend the raised US dollar *bills* on *retail* bitcoin, and issue an RFP, operate master nodes, pay bills with *retail* bitcoin, and await further instructions for budget proposal votes. Trustable polling could be enabled by decentralized solutions such as Blockchain Voting Machines, Follow My Vote, Inc., and TIVI [460].

A list of some of the benefits of the collective's purchase of a two-year budget supply of *retail* bitcoin are:

1) Dramatic reduction in poverty due to value transfer from the collective We, the People, of the United States to us individuals, tribes, companies, and all the other governmental organizations in the world.
2) Immediate start of a two-year federal government tax jubilee for We, the People, of the United States.
3) Immediate start of a two-year federal government borrowing jubilee for We, the People, of the United States.
4) Lowered costs of payment for our federal government and for all us individuals, companies, and so on.
5) Elimination of our federal government revenuer employees' payroll expenses.
6) Elimination of our tax compliance expenses.
7) Income from any *retail* bitcoin master nodes the collective We, the People, of the United States acquire.
8) More wealthy philanthropists donating to deserving charities.
9) Two-year window of opportunity to settle our gold US dollars bankruptcy and adopt new and improved entropy-type US dollars.

The final MOA, to choose our new US dollars

Once the requirements of the first MOA have been fulfilled, the collective We, the People, of these fifty United states of America are possibly getting paid to operate master nodes, and we individuals are enjoying our tax jubilee and our newly improved financial situations, it will be easy to use similar mechanics to vote on *retail* bitcoin budget proposals. After a budget proposal for our new entropy money has been approved, we can politically choose to adopt oxygen US dollars with another MOA. The MOA to adopt oxygen US dollars could read something like:

I, State Your Name, from (indicate your state), in the interest of eliminating the scourges of poverty, crime, and environmental degradation from the earth, do hereby declare that the official US dollars of the United States of America each consist of 30 grams of oxygen[8] that have been produced by living green plants. I instruct my treasurer[9] of the United States of America, first, to provide federal government land ownership data to the oxygen US dollar decentralized autonomous network that has been produced by Mint[10] in response to our RFP for a US dollar replacement and begin exclusively using our oxygen US dollar proceeds from our national lands to satisfy all federal government financial obligations, and second, to:

1. Repeal all tax statutes of the federal government of the United States of America.
2. Two years after today's date, on which our US dollars were changed from 1/42.22 of an ounce of gold to 30 grams of oxygen, repeal all legal tender statutes of the federal government of the United States of America.
3. Repeal all IP statutes of the federal government of the United States of America.

My digital signature on this memorandum of agreement is to be considered valid when 90 percent of my political peers in (indicate your state) have also signed it. I instruct my secretary of the treasury, my treasurer, my president, and my representatives in the Congress of the federal government of the United States, as appropriate, to execute these steps upon receiving this memorandum of agreement from each of the fifty states.

Signed,

State Your Name

---

[8] Or whatever the correct number is of oxygen, or carbon, or carbon dioxide, as we see fit.

[9] Or president, or congressmen and congresswomen, or whoever's job this is.

[10] Or whatever the name of the company is whose DAN We, the People, choose to track our new and improved oxygen US dollars. This company is the one whose response to our RFP we are choosing to produce the network that tracks our new and improved money.

Today

And just like that, we'll be out. Our physical world will appear unchanged when we first step out, but everything will begin materially improving rapidly, all without anyone knowing exactly how it's being done. We will have begun literally buying our way out of trouble.

20. MECHANIZING: SUMMARY

THE escape options for the collective We, the People, of the United States of America are constrained by the fact that we are, in effect, a very large committee, or fifty very large committees, consisting of the around 270 million or so of us politically competent peers. The only things we can do are come together to make administrative decisions, and to our great fortune, it turns out administrative decisions are all we need. In answer to our questions of how:

How does one get a metaphorical entropy money printing press into the hands of every parcel owner?   We, the People, instruct our employees in the federal government of these fifty states to issue an RFP for new and improved entropy-type US dollars, then instruct them as to which responsive proposal to choose. We furnish these instructions by means of MOAs.

How does one deal with competitors claiming to have a better printing press?   We give our employees two further instructions, to repeal federal government tax and legal tender statutes. That way, decisions about competitors will be made by the giant parallel computing machine consisting of each of us individuals, the most powerful computing machines in the known universe, freely making economic deals with one another and thereby discovering prices.

How can the printing presses be made to be transparent and reliable, so users will trust the money?   In the same way we deal with competitors, by making the new entropy-type US dollars free as in free speech. When users of money are free to vote with their feet, untrustable money will be weeded out automatically, without any direct action needed by the collective We the People. All we need do is make the money free.

How do We, the People, of these fifty states repeal our national tax and legal tender statutes? By signing an MOA requiring our agent employees in the federal government to do that. The MOA gives all federal government agents (including elected officials) instructions for their official duties.

How do we abandon our current gold US dollars and adopt entropy US dollars? We buy ourselves a two-year window of opportunity by signing an MOA instructing our federal government treasurer to purchase a two-year federal government budget outlay supply worth of *retail* bitcoin. During that window, we engineer our new and improved entropy-type US dollars by instructing our treasurer to issue an RFP. Then, we adopt them by instructing our treasurer to sign up for an account with the decentralized autonomous network that will mint our new and improved entropy-type US dollars, and instructing other employees to define them as our new and improved US dollars.

How do we settle our bankruptcy in our gold US dollars? We settle by signing an MOA instructing our treasurer to offer our creditors a haircut. We'll instruct her to do this by offering to redeem our US dollar *bills* for dollars at the appropriate discount.

Not only can We, the People, take administrative actions leading to a settlement of our bankruptcy and adoption of a new world reserve money, but we can cause ourselves to be remunerated economically for our efforts. We can be paid to make the change, and paid a regular fee thereafter. Best of all, the mechanics of manufacturing our new and improved entropy-type US dollars are straightforward. These new US dollars will be much easier to manufacture than many other artifacts, such as automobiles, cell phones, etc.

We'll be paid well

The switch to our new and improved entropy-type US dollars can be created by the political expedient of all of us members of the giant committee(s) agreeing with each other to have the collective borrow some money, buy some magic internet money (MIM), initiate a tax jubilee, and vote to choose which new and improved entropy-type US dollars to adopt.

Borrowing and buying is part of our poverty reduction program. By the time 90 percent of us have voted to borrow, buy, and vote, all of us individuals will have had the opportunity to front run the collective. It will be an easy way to transfer significant real value from collectives to individuals, giving us a head start on our larger poverty reduction program. This front run by the members of the collective also works perfectly for the collective itself because it needs a high-quality means of exchange (MOE) and a stable store of value (SOV). The collective will obtain a high-quality MOE simply by purchasing *retail* bitcoin, which has all the features needed for efficient market exchanges. It will get a stable SOV thanks to the large financial inertia obtained when the USD/*retail* bitcoin ratio shoots to the moon, thanks in turn to the combined buying of individuals and collectives.

The effect we individuals will have by front-running the collective is to drive the price up before the collective can complete step two of The Plan. This works well for both individuals and the collective because we individuals need the poverty relief we'll get by front-running, and the collective needs a high-quality, stable SOV. It will get this, thanks to the massive long position acquired as a result of the two-year federal government budget supply purchase and the preceding front-running. The SOV will be so stable we'll get to save federal government money by paying the collective's bills with its newly acquired *retail* bitcoin, avoiding the middleman previously needed to transfer fraudulent receipts for gold.

Another benefit to be obtained from this monetary transition is we may get to vote on how to spend a lot of money after we've transitioned to our new and improved entropy-type US dollars. This is because, per our requirements, it will be a fork from *retail* bitcoin, and therefore will have master nodes and a budget. If the collective can acquire enough of our new and improved entropy-type US dollars to operate master nodes, we political peers in these fifty states will get to vote for projects further improving our new and improved entropy-type US dollars. Our votes will count.

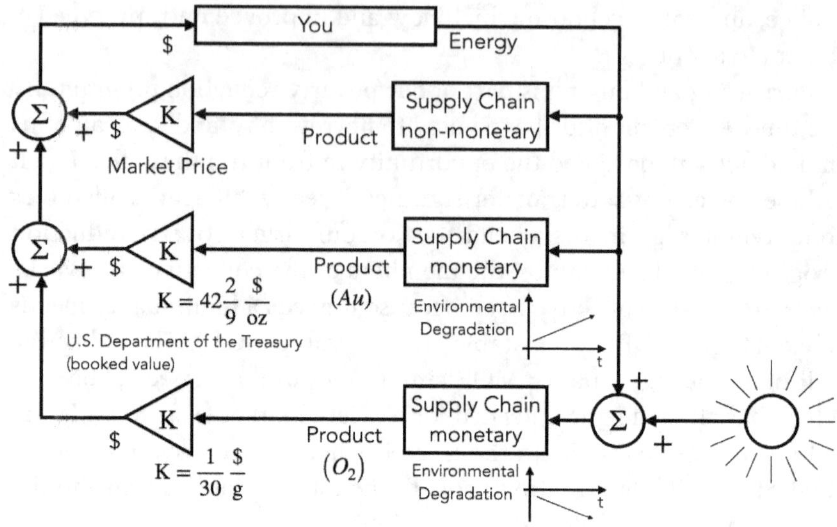

$$K = 42\frac{2}{9}\frac{\$}{oz}$$

$$K = \frac{1}{30}\frac{\$}{g}$$

Figure 20.1. *A new way to earn money.*

We'll get a new way to earn money

A successful transition to our new and improved oxygen US dollars will add tools to everyone's money-earning toolkit (Figures 20.1 and 12.1).[1][2] Any person expending energy to obtain money ("You," in Figure 20.1) can participate in supply chains producing either non-monetary or monetary products. Previously, the only monetary product supply chains available to participate in produced gold coins and bars (counting only the world's dominant money, gold). Our oxygen US dollars will add a new monetary supply chain, available to any parcel owner. In this new monetary supply chain, energy outputs from the owner and the sun are energy inputs to the parcel. These inputs either help the living beings do work or hinder them, such as if the owner covers the parcel with buildings and asphalt. With oxygen US dollars, the living beings on the parcel can be thought of as part of a monetary supply chain, and their output, the ecosystem service of produced oxygen, can

---

[1] See the example gain calculation of Equation 12.3 for a derivation of the dollars/gram of O_2 ratio in Figure 20.1.

[2] The gold monetary supply chain in Figure 20.1 shows the semi-official definition (the amount kept on our treasury books for every ounce of gold in the vault at Fort Knox) of gold US dollars rather than the number of dollar *bills* one might be able to purchase for a given amount of gold on the open market.

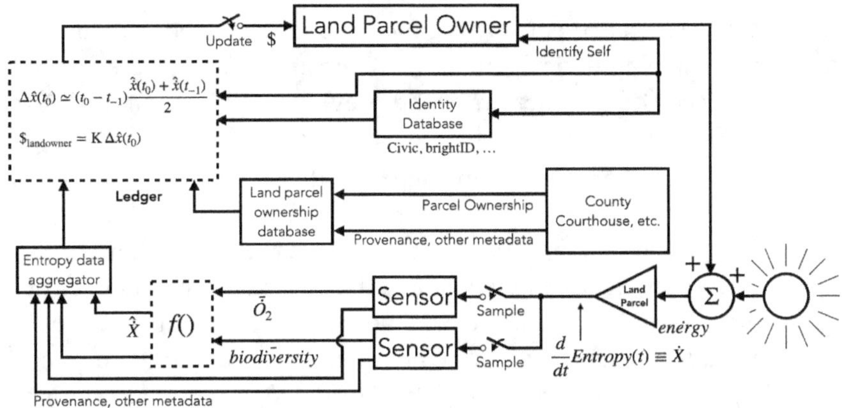

Figure 20.2. *Implementation.*

be measured and converted into a US dollar ledger entry spendable by the owner of the parcel. Every parcel owner, including political groups such as nation-states, prefectures, provinces, states, counties, and local municipalities, will get a new way to earn money.

Implementation is straightforward

In a possible implementation architecture for this new way for parcel owners to earn money, the owner and the sun supply energy to living creatures on a given land parcel, enabling the creatures to remove entropy at some rate $\frac{d}{dt}Entropy(t)$, or $\dot{X}$ (Figure 20.2).[3] Satellite, and/or aircraft-based sensors, and/or ground-based sensors, such as eddy covariance towers or manual inspections, measure the oxygen production rate of the parcel. Mechanical sensors or human surveys may measure parcel biodiversity, and other sensors may measure other parcel states. These measurements can be combined using some function $f()$ to produce an estimate of $\hat{X}$, the entropy removal rate.[4] This estimate will have dimensions of mass per time, at least for this first incarnation of entropy money, which will use produced oxygen as a proxy for mined

---

[3] The dot above X changes the symbol's meaning from X to the rate of change of X with respect to time.

[4] The hat above the $\dot{X}$ means this is an estimate of entropy removal rate, not true entropy removal rate. Here, bars are used for sensor measurements, and hat is used for the synthesized entropy removal rate estimate.

entropy. The estimated entropy removal rate is associated with an individual parcel and numerically integrated into an estimate of the amount removed since the production of the previous entropy removal rate estimate. Finally, the estimated removed entropy is converted through $K\left(\frac{\$}{\text{mass}}\right)$ into a dollar amount and added to the ledger entry controlled by the entity that has proved to the network it's the lawful owner of the parcel. Mined entropy rate and parcel ownership data are made valuable through the use of metadata such as affidavits and indemnities against falsified data from sensor operators. Cryptographic techniques can be used to preserve parcel owner anonymity, and dynamics can be added to the numerical integration of entropy removal rate into entropy removed. In an example of adding dynamics to the numerical integration, a lead term could be added by a smart contract to pay a parcel owner to plant trees after a clear-cut. Such a lead term would make replanting more likely by increasing cash flow to the owner once he's taken the action but not yet obtained results. Things like wildlife habitat certifications could be used for validation purposes in the smart contract.

One possible economic organization of this loop is for the entropy removal rate estimate $\hat{X}$ and its associated parcel ownership data to be produced by data processing companies, who would sell the data to a decentralized autonomous network (DAN). The parcel owner could identify itself to the DAN, so the appropriate number of new and improved entropy-type US dollars are added to its ledger entry. The data processor(s), the identity databases, and the operators of DAN instances could be paid with a percentage of the parcel owner payout. Operators of DAN instances could also have their income supplemented in the conventional way, with proof of work (POW)-based addition of new ledger units and transaction fees. Raw data providers who operate the oxygen rate, biodiversity, and other sensors could in turn be paid by the data processor(s) if they are different business entities.

If multiple data processors submit entropy removal rate data to the ledger operator, the operator must choose the ones to be paid by the network, and how much. Possible methods of choosing include, but are not limited to, consideration of the five most recent entropy removal rate estimates submitted for each parcel, per their time stamps.[5]

---

[5]To ensure competition in measurement data, the network could reject data if fewer than a given number of companies were providing it.

The operator could preferentially choose those including certain data, such as, for example, biodiversity and/or bioproductivity. It could also preferentially choose entropy removal rate estimates with no less than a certain provenance standard, and suitable indemnities against false information. If $\hat{t}_0$ is the time stamp of the most recent entropy removal rate estimate submitted, $\hat{t}_{-1}$ is the next most recent, and so on, a vector of times can be tracked:

$$[\hat{t}_{-4}, \hat{t}_{-3}, \hat{t}_{-2}, \hat{t}_{-1}, \hat{t}_0]. \tag{20.1}$$

If the data processors are providing estimates $\hat{X}$ of the rate of entropy removal from the land parcel, a vector of rate estimates at those times also can be tracked:

$$\underline{\hat{X}}(t) = [\hat{X}(\hat{t}_{-4}), \hat{X}(\hat{t}_{-3}), \hat{X}(\hat{t}_{-2}), \hat{X}(\hat{t}_{-1}), \hat{X}(\hat{t}_0)]. \tag{20.2}$$

The DAN can process estimates with, for example, norm operations on the vector of entropy removal rate estimates. For example, a median or a root mean square (RMS) norm could be used, with percentages awarded based on closeness to the chosen value. Such methods would be used to provide network-enhancing incentives so, in the absence of knowledge of a competitor's activities, the most profitable strategy for entropy removal rate estimate providers is to measure as close as possible to truth. Special algorithms and manual checks could be used to adjust the vector operator in the event of sudden changes to parcel entropy removal rates, such as if a forest is clear-cut or a food crop harvested.

What to do with this new idea

We now know we want to adopt new and improved entropy-type US dollars, and we know how to do it, and furthermore how to get paid to do it. We even know the basic implementation details, including economic incentives for the people who mechanize these new US dollars. We'll buy ourselves a two-year window of opportunity, issue an RFP for our new, improved US dollars during that window, and vote on responsive proposals. We know why we want to do it and how to make it happen, but there is still a remaining question: Who does what? What exactly is each of us supposed to do to make this happen?

Part IV.

What Is to Be Done?

21. IS IT POSSIBLE TO UNITE TO DO THIS?

I N 1902, the monster Vladimir Lenin authored the political pamphlet *What Is to Be Done?* [461]. The pamphlet was arguably the foundation document ushering in 70 years of murder and mayhem in the crime syndicate known as the USSR. Rummel and others estimate a death toll of around 60 million innocents during the syndicate's lifetime [241–245]. We political peers here in these fifty states are a very lucky group of people because we have the opportunity to answer Lenin's question with actions that, rather than leading us into hell, waltz us right out of it.

Before assigning jobs, though, let us address the elephant in the living room: Is it even possible to take these administrative actions? Based on the present analysis, this group of us who control the production of the world's reserve money, our US dollars, is presented with the opportunity to cooperate to get paid to transform our living world into a paradise planet. But is that seemingly excellent opportunity real? Many would doubt this chance to escape is even a possibility since pretty much all of us need to agree to do it, and we all can't seem to agree on anything. In spite of our doubts, however, the fact is we're the lucky beneficiaries of ancestors who bequeathed to us the ability intentionally to come together politically, and innovate solutions to seemingly intractable problems. This escape is something we really can do, and right now would be a wonderful time to take full advantage of that fact.

We humans and our ancestors

We know it is indeed possible for us to come together in the subject endeavor by examining our evolutionary history, in which our ancestors successfully made what some would call an impossible transition: they changed their societies from despotic[1] organizations to ones arranged around egalitarian[2] principles. We know our direct ancestors lived in despotic societies because our closest relatives in the animal kingdom, the three major ape groups from Africa (chimpanzees, bonobos, and gorillas), live in despotic societies, which means their common ancestors almost certainly did too. Because we humans share a common ancestor with them, as recently as six million years ago for our closest ape relatives, chimpanzees and bonobos [462], we know our distant human ancestors also lived in despotic societies since they too were descendants of those same despotism-plagued shared ancestors [p. 4 of 463].

However, cultural evolution can and did occur. From studies of the last of the modern immediate-return societies, such as the Mbuti pygmies of Zaire [464, 465], the !Kung bushmen (San) of Botswana and Namibia [466–469], the Pandaram and Paliyan of South India [470, 471], the Batek Negritos of Malaysia [472–474], and the Hadza of Tanzania [475–478], we know our more recent ancestors had transitioned to living in not merely non-despotic societies, but fully and assertively egalitarian ones. Instead of the chains of subservience and domination characteristic of despotic societies, individuals in these immediate-return societies lived in a near-ideal state of equality. Equality was achieved through direct individual access to resources, direct individual access to means of coercion and mobility, procedures that prevent saving and accumulation and impose sharing, and mechanisms allowing goods to circulate without making individuals dependent on others [479]. Our hunter-gatherer ancestors actively enforced their core values of equality, autonomy, and sharing [480] by means of social sanctioning [481, 482].

Transition from despotism to egalitarianism

The sequence of events, from the common ancestors to our distant, but distinctly human ancestors, appears to be something like the following: As these distant ancestors, still living in despotic societies, gradually became our more recent hunter-gatherer ancestors, their abilities to think and communicate their thoughts improved—this was because

---

[1]A despotic society is one in which a few have power over many.

[2]An egalitarian society is one in which none have power over others.

they were molded by selection pressure for groups with individuals better at cooperating. This selection pressure caused social and physical changes.

The physical changes included changes in their breathing and eating apparatus to allow for complex sounds, and thus the communication of complex thoughts, and changes to their brains, allowing them to think complex thoughts. The ability to think complex thoughts, combined with improving communication capabilities and the ongoing nuisance of despotism, resulted in many experimental political arrangements [483] and eventually led to a political solution to the despotism [463]. The solution took the form of an implicit contract between members of society to the effect that everyone is their own boss and therefore others can't boss them around, nor can they boss others around. This implicit contract resulted in social systems in which the many dominate any few who show signs of getting too big for their britches, referred to by Christopher Boehm as reverse dominance hierarchies [482].

By no later than around a hundred thousand years ago, our ancestors had completed the transition from despotic societies to what Richard Lee calls "fierce" egalitarianism [484–486]. Fierce egalitarianism means in these societies there is no tolerance for anyone putting on airs or acting like a "big man." Among the !Kung bushmen of the Kalahari Desert region, part of the mechanism keeping the society egalitarian is hunters use arrows owned by others and agree the owner of the arrow, not the hunter, owns the kill. Another part of the mechanism is when a hunter returns from a hunt looking dejected, as if he has failed, the people are happy because they know he scored something big. Any who come back bragging about their big kill will be ridiculed mercilessly and quickly learn to be more humble.

Multiple anthropologists have discovered this fierceness the hard way. In one example, an anthropologist living with Indians in the Hudson Bay area tried to protect them by chewing out some whites she believed were taking advantage of the locals. Afterwords, she was confused and hurt when people became less friendly to her. Finally, someone told her she was too aggressive and had made them uncomfortable. In the Kalahari Desert region in southern Africa, an anthropologist who had been living with some !Kung bushmen bought a big ox to celebrate with the people when he was about to leave because he liked them so much. He was confused, then, when they got angry with him. He finally got someone to explain they perceived he was being aggressive, as if to make them owe him. In another example from North America, a lady told an anthropologist they had to have a hair trigger for putting down people who get full of themselves, especially young men. She pointed out those are the most dangerous people in their society, and could kill someone if not kept in check.

For our purpose of escaping from the unholy trinity of poverty, crime, and environmental degradation to our science-fiction future, what this all means is our ancestors have shown us the way with precedents. We don't have to invent anything new to come together politically and find an innovative solution to our big problems. Our ancestors did it, and humanity in general is good at political experimentation thanks to hundreds of thousands of years of practice with innovative organizational arrangements [483]. Our natural tendency is to work together peacefully to survive [487]; therefore, we know for a fact making this change is something we really can do. We're born with the ability to devise novel solutions to difficult problems [488]—given the state of our early twenty-first-century world, now would be a good time for a novel approach.

A wildly unanticipated direction

As journalist Caitlin Johnstone informs us, "If there's anything that might work it's going to come from a wildly unanticipated direction, from way outside the failed mental processes which have accompanied us to this point" [150]. Free entropy money would certainly fit that description. While it's true humanity has never engineered a world-saving money, it was also true our ancestors had never engineered aggressively egalitarian processes, until they did. They developed those processes simply because they didn't like how things were, and they used their brains, mouths, and ears to find a way to live with one another never before seen in our world. We modern people can choose to engineer this world-saving money, the likes of which has never been seen, in the same way our ancestors chose to engineer "fierce" egalitarianism.

We can do this, and thankfully, for most of us, our jobs will be small and easy, political in nature. Some of us will have additional jobs, to do the work to obtain the necessary data and close the feedback loop between our human financial world and our biological living world.

We have the opportunity to come together as a team and make this lifesaving change to our world reserve money happen.

There will be two general categories of jobs we can do to make this change to our world reserve US dollars happen. Political jobs, in which we participate in the administrative aspect of this project, and the jobs involving real work, including programming computers and obtaining data.

22. POLITICAL JOBS

OF the political jobs, several will be common to us all, involving signing MOAs and front-running. There will be many other political jobs as well, depending on who you are and how you are connected to others.

Jobs we'll all do

Three easy political jobs will need to be completed by us all, or maybe only 90 percent of us all, to make this dream a reality.

The first job will be signing the MOA instructing our federal government employees to take the steps of borrowing legacy US dollar *bills* and buying *retail* bitcoin, beginning the tax jubilee after we've acquired a two-year supply worth of *retail* bitcoin, and issuing an RFP.

The second job will be for individuals and groups to front run the collective by buying *retail* bitcoin.

The third job will be to sign an MOA indicating our preference for proposals for the new money in response to our RFP.

What you can do right now

Further political jobs must be done beforehand, basically amounting to spreading the word. Are you employed on the Google Earth engineering team? Get your teammates to read this book, then you'll all know what to do. Do you know someone who knows someone who knows someone on the Google Earth engineering team? Get them this book, so they can pass it on to the team. It's the same for the *retail* bitcoin, also known as digital cash, development team members. The sooner we can get to branching[1] the *retail* bitcoin code, designing the architecture for our

---

[1] Branching means making a copy of some patterns and modifying the copy, so there are two different patterns afterward. This can apply to documents written in human languages like English as well as computer code. In the example of *retail* bitcoin, it means making a copy of the *retail* bitcoin software package and modifying the

new oxygen US dollars, and obtaining land ownership and respiration rate data, the better.

Do you know anyone, such as yourself, who uses US dollars, or for that matter pretty much any so-called fiat[2] money? Maybe someone you know is headed for trouble right now with the never-ending price hikes of almost everything. Make them read this book. Anyone in trouble, or who cares about those in trouble, definitely wants a new world reserve money with a reduced inflation tax, along with an easy way to park monetary value in a place where it gains value over time. Those being harmed by our runaway prices could be saved by this chance to participate in the most massive commodity price run-up ever.

Maybe you know someone worried about global warming or planetary health in general. Make them read this book. They'll want new and improved US dollars to pay the people who supply us all with breathable air and drinkable water while simultaneously removing greenhouse gases from our atmosphere.

Maybe you know someone who knows someone who . . . who knows Catherine Austin Fitts. See if you can get Escape to her—she understands money, and will definitely know what to do.

Maybe you or someone you know is concerned about animal cruelty and wants it to end. Make them read this book. We all desperately want a new kind of money paying parcel owners less, or even charging them, if they are cruel to the animals on their parcel. We all want to end fur farms, dog and cat meat markets, overcrowded stockyards, caged chicken warehouses, most slaughterhouses, etc.

Maybe you or someone you know is sickened nigh unto death by the never-ending wars in this world, with the never-ending slaughter of innocents. Make them read this book. We have a real chance to end all this right now—eliminating coercive tax-subsidized governments means no more mass slaughter of innocents. Here, the claim is not made that worldwide murder and mayhem will end instantly upon the adoption of free entropy money. The claim instead made is the mass slaughters

---

copy so it meets the requirements set out in We the People's request for proposal. On one side of the branch will be the original *retail* bitcoin software, and on the other will be the new, improved oxygen US dollar software. This process is also referred to as forking.

[2]Most, or all, paper government money can be referred to as fiat money, as in "By fiat of the king," because it is forced on people with tax and legal tender statutes.

from government wars will end fast, practically overnight, with smaller-scale murders and mayhem following and gradually disappearing from our world.

How about your own mortality? Do you know anyone who isn't done yet, who wants more time to get the things done that need to get done? Perhaps you know someone who wants their loved ones to live longer and healthier. Make them read this book. They want a new money that pays for the health of the creatures on the various land parcels, and also is free to evolve so it pays for the health of us humans. They'll also want the improved monetary environment in which the strategies for engineered negligible senescence (SENS) organization [364] will exist, helping them help us all live longer and healthier.

Are you a marketing guru? Do you have a presence on the inter-webs? You know what to do. Can you get through to any good science-fiction writers who may be able to do something with these ideas? Or an economist who can improve on some of the explanations? Ask them to read this book. Perhaps someone asks you why the dollar *bills/retail* bitcoin ratio suddenly began running away a couple of days ago, increasing by 500 percent in that short time. Tell them to read this book.

Perhaps you know a video producer. You know what to do—ask the producer to read this book, and they'll know what to do. Whoever you are, you can help make all our Christmases come true at once.

23. TECHNICAL AND BUSINESS JOBS

IN addition to the political jobs we all can do, several technical and business jobs must be done by a few of our specialists to make good on our escape. To begin with, people are needed to develop the software and obtain the data needed to close the feedback loop between our human financial and living biological worlds. For example, sensors are needed to provide land parcel health measurements, and software is needed to process them. Software is also needed to enable the ledger to associate parcel health measurements with parcel owners (Figure 20.2), and business-oriented people are needed to assemble and manage companies to complete these software and data collection jobs.

Remote-sensing and biology specialists are needed to manufacture and operate entropy removal sensors. Economics and game theory specialists are needed to design a DAN for recording our new oxygen dollars. Specialists who can access databases correlating land ownership and individual identities are needed. Programmers are needed to produce a website and application(s) for landowners to verify their identity and land ownership information. Programmers and software architects are needed to implement the DAL and hosting DAN for tracking oxygen US dollars. While we're at it, if some of our best and brightest would like to get together and develop a DAN, or enhance the capabilities of an existing one, to track land ownership and thus eliminate the need for county recorders—that would be terrific. Since DANs already track real-world items, such as gold, securities, and Star Trek memorabilia, we know this is possible.

If the MOA signatures are to be submitted through the Google Earth application, Google Earth engineers will be needed to modify it. These engineers will be needed to add functionality to their product so each of us can identify ourselves as one of We, the People, of these fifty united States of America, then sign the MOA. Specialists who can access the land parcel ownership and individual identity databases to identify parcel owners are needed for this effort.

Contract law and English language experts are needed to finalize the language of our RFP and MOAs. Finally, engineers with expertise and experience developing formal requirements are needed to review the requirement set to be included with our RFP (Appendix C).

Organize it all with no central planner

Do we need someone to be the brains behind the operation, to put it all together? No—the beautiful part about putting this all together, with actual people completing actual tasks, is it can all be accomplished without a central planner or particular leader, in the same way number two wood pencils are manufactured without one. Everyone has their own unique set of talents and experiences, and their own unique social and professional circles filled with family, friends, and colleagues. Since the goal of adopting a world-saving money is shared by practically every one of us, but yet to be known to every one of us at the time of writing, word is likely to spread quickly. As mentioned above, for most of us, getting the word out may be one of the main ways we help make this come to pass, along with our political jobs of signing MOAs and participating in the front run.

As more and more of us become aware a couple of simple administrative actions can launch us quickly on our way to a paradise planet, those who can do certain technical and business jobs will naturally seek each other out to form synergistic teams. These teams may get financial support from some of our legacy wealthy philanthropists, or possibly governmental institutions, and may be able to swing it by participating in the front run. All will know what we can do once we've grasped the concept our legacy gold US dollars are not written in stone and can be changed, like they've already been changed in the past, and we can make it happen with easy administrative actions.

Speaking of getting the word out, there may be a significant factor giving us an advantage, bigger than most of us yet know.

Word may get out by nonmaterial means

Our journey, from only a few desiring this fix to our legacy gold US dollars to practically every one of us wanting it so much we're willing to do what it takes to make it happen, is likely to proceed in a geometric-like sequence. In such a sequence, it would happen slowly at first, then faster and faster. With luck, though, we're going to commence front-running and relieving our financial distress even faster than that—faster than anyone thinks possible.

This escape will be due partly to the usual talking, passing around books, and seeking one another out we're all familiar with. Additionally, we may get help from direct mind-to-mind communication, according to data biologists and others have been accumulating. Anecdotal evidence from hundreds of thousands of reports, along with empirical evidence from many thousands of controlled experiments, has revealed anomalies in our world that appear to contradict the precepts of a strictly material reality [489, 490]. People guessing when they're being stared at more accurately than they should, correctly guessing coin flips of a person seated behind them more often than they should, correctly guessing playing cards far more than random chance, and correctly guessing who's calling on the phone too often to be explained by our standard physical models are just the tip of this seemingly paranormal iceberg. Rats even appear to learn mazes faster after rats thousands of miles away learned the maze—examples of these phenomena are diverse and numerous.

When we speak with others about money, we almost never discuss what we're using as money; instead we speak of dollars, or Benjamins ($100 *bills*), or Jacksons ($20 *bills*), and how many we have or want. Speaking with most of us about what we're using as money is kind of like speaking with a fish about what it's swimming in—it simply isn't thought about much. However, in the near future, as more and more of us come to understand there's a way to fix everything by fixing our US dollars, more and more of us will begin thinking about what we're using as money. We'll get these thoughts by traditional communication methods, and may also be aided by extrasensory means. One way or the other, we'll gradually all come to know fixing our money is the right and obvious thing to do, and we'll dream it together and make it a reality [491]. Working together, we can achieve the impossible and escape: *from* poverty, crime, and environmental degradation, *to* a beautiful science-fiction future.

Part V.

Conclusion

24. NEAR-TERM RESULTS

WHAT should we expect immediately after the change if this all goes down per our plan? Imagine we pulled it off—our metaphorical left hand sold the Escape bond run and raised two years worth of federal government budget in *retail* bitcoin, and our metaphorical right hand purchased as many of the bonds as necessary from the secondary market with newly printed Federal Reserve Notes. Imagine our two-year tax jubilee had begun, and the collective was about to settle its gold US dollars bankruptcy. What has changed for us?

At this point, poverty, crime, and environmental degradation have already been reduced significantly. Poverty is reduced because all or most of us individuals have increased our financial wealth dramatically relative to companies and governments by front-running them in the *retail* bitcoin buy. Poverty is also reduced by the universal basic income resulting from the two-year tax jubilee as our money is no longer being paid to the federal government revenuers. Further, poverty in the form of our wasted time is reduced because We, the People, let our federal government revenuers go, causing us all to breathe a collective sigh of relief. No longer will we be forced to do tax planning to keep our own hard-earned money. No longer will we all have to stress every January until April, not wanting to fill out the hated tax forms but knowing they'll get even more of our hard-earned money if we don't. Poverty in the form of liability exposure has now been reduced as we are no longer forced to fund trespasses against others. Environmental degradation has been reduced by restoring to us all our deserved protection of the law, reducing harm to people who otherwise would have been hurt without that protection.

All of us lucky enough to have paying jobs will be experiencing the miracle of substantial pay raises as the collective no longer skims off the top of our individual wages before we even see them. All of us lucky enough to be self-employed will be experiencing that same miracle, plus the miracle of relief from filling out forms and sending our pound of flesh to the revenuers every three months. Many of us will get to stop spending our hard-earned money on tax accountants. Those of us not lucky enough to have jobs previously could see our luck change when oxygen US dollars begin entering circulation economically closer to us, giving us better chances at getting pieces of the action.

All of us who own shares of companies will be experiencing the miracle of increased dividends as our companies benefit from cost reductions due to the reduced paperwork requirements and elimination of national taxes. All of us retail consumers will be experiencing the miracle of reduced prices as federal tax burdens are removed from supply chains. Many of us not lucky enough to have paying jobs will also be seeing our luck change as jobs to support the new entropy money economy spring into existence. Finally, shrinking poverty rates will cause crime rates to likewise shrink as the poverty motive for crime disappears.

Environmental degradation will begin its exit from our lives as landowners everywhere begin plotting and scheming to make their parcels healthier, so they can be paid more. This will cause poverty rates to shrink even more, thanks to the economic niches opening up for people to get a piece of that action by aiding them in these pursuits. For one example of many, the market for arborists and foresters will be growing, to provide tree health advice to parcel owners.

Imagining further, two years after we've officially adopted our new and improved free entropy-type US dollars and repealed our legal tender statutes, our money has become truly free to evolve and serve our needs better and better. Since our national forests, parks, and monuments are now officially supplying the entire budget needs of our federal government, we all get to heave another sigh of relief as it sinks in that those federal government revenuers are out of our lives forever. Because debt service is part of the budget and our federal government no longer needs to borrow money to meet its budget needs, our federal debt has is now shrinking, on its way to zero. Our reward for making the effort to fix our world reserve money has been to remove our federal government revenuers and moneylenders from our lives.

Thanks to the money produced by our state, county, and local parks, we also get to reduce our state, county, and local taxes. All the rest of us in the world get government tax reductions too, all prefectures, provinces, states, counties, and cities. Our finances and our mental health will have improved thanks to the removal of revenuers and the more equitable introduction of the new money into circulation. On the morning of the day our new and improved entropy-type US dollars officially come into being, we'll all be filled with the relief of having stepped out of our prison. It will be like we are standing outside the prison walls, with the big, wide, beautiful world beckoning. We'll know the world has started getting better, and we all now get to help actively, unimpeded by parasites.

We'll feel a deep, soul-wrenching relief as we think about all the bad things now being discriminated against economically thanks to our new and improving money, and the beauty of our living world now returning. We'll feel this relief not only for ourselves, but for our fellow beings too. All of us with injuries, physical or psychological scars, and diseases will know we're actively on our way to healing. We'll know all we have to do to improve our world is use price information to cooperate, and our money has commenced making us rich and thin.

Our living world will be getting steadily healthier, we'll all be getting steadily healthier, and the injustices in our world will be disappearing. Naturally, this will make us happier and more outgoing, with more happy topics to discuss with our fellows. For the first time in a long while, we'll all have some time to spend enjoying one another. In yet another benefit, we'll get to spend this new free time with one another using one of our special gifts: the art of dialogue [492, 493]. Dialogue, in which you suspend your assumptions, neither attack nor defend, and in which truth is the goal, is humanity's special gift. As more and more of us get the time, and by chatting with others naturally engage in this art, more and more of our problems will be solved as these dialogues yield real fruits.

Maybe we'll get to a point where prices are low enough to enable us all to take as much vacation as we need. Maybe a person could take more than one-day or one-week vacations and instead take vacations lasting months, years, or even decades, or whatever—whatever a body needs. We'll get to play, carefree for a while, and there'll always be someone to take up the slack while we're away, thanks to matched labor supply and demand feedback loops, thanks in turn to the elimination of money supply from non-monetary supply and demand computations. While we're resting, maybe we'll think of new things for our old jobs. Maybe we'll decide to retrain from time to time, do something new, and combine it with our previous knowledge.

Maybe, as time goes on, each of us will achieve his or her full potential mental power, knowledge, and wisdom. Can you imagine eight billion wealthy genius polymaths animating a price discovery machine that actively discriminates against poor health? Can you imagine eight billion of the most powerful computing devices in the known universe tightly connected in a massively parallel configuration? The sky's the limit.

25. THIS ESCAPE ROUTE IS REAL

REVIEWING our current situation, we have practically everything we need to escape poverty, crime, and environmental degradation, right at our fingertips.

We have land health or ecosystem service data—take a look at the images presented on Google Earth, and imagine counting green pixels on those images with parcel boundaries overlaid on them. We're almost certainly only a few hundred lines of software away from utilizing those images' data sources to estimate oxygen production rates by parcel, with improved data from FLuorescence EXplorer-type satellites [304] already beginning in 2026. We also have land parcel ownership data, again with only a relatively small amount of computer code needed to associate it with parcel oxygen production rates.

We have over a dozen years of experience in the production, operation, and maintenance of decentralized autonomous networks (DANs) enabling users to transfer electronic ledger units reliably among one another, without a need to trust human intermediaries. We now also have many years of experience interfacing these electronic ledgers with the physical world, enabling ownership transfer of things like gold, real estate, securities, and retail goods securely, with no need to trust anyone not to cheat. Again, we're almost certainly just a few hundred lines of software away from interfacing a version of the most reliable DAN available, *retail* bitcoin, with land parcel owners and oxygen production.

Software technology to identify individuals reliably is already well developed, and our Google Earth engineers are almost certainly only a few hundred lines of code away from enhancing their product to allow individuals to persuade an algorithm they are who they say they are, and live where they say they live, and sign MOAs. We now have something close to the text of our MOAs, we have something close to the final text of an RFP, including a set of formal requirements, and we have the basis for computations for use by a DAN to convert oxygen production rates into parcel owner spendable US dollar ledger entries. We have precedent to change our US dollars and a great need to do it now and save as many lives as possible. Working together, this proposed change is something the team can accomplish practically overnight.

In addition to possessing all the technical tools we need, we're privileged to be part of a political group capable of mustering 90 percent support to make a lifesaving change to its money. When you first hear the number 90 percent, the task may seem impossible, making attempting it a waste of time. The fact is maybe it's impossible and maybe it isn't, and it doesn't much matter which—the alternative to fixing things at the deep, fundamental level of our money is too awful to contemplate. We simply must fix our US dollars. Eliminating excuses, it's easy to do.

It's apparently possible for so many of us to agree, at least on some topics. More than 90 percent of us certainly can agree we all need our most precious resource, breathable air [494], and we all agree none of us is getting younger. In a way, pretty much every one of us agree agreeing is impossible. Here in the mid-2020s, 90 percent of us probably agree 90 percent of us can't agree on anything. To be fair, at the time of writing, during the time when we all agree we can't all agree, it does seem daunting, even impossible.

That being said, more than a century ago the White Queen of Lewis Carroll's *Through the Looking Glass* explained impossible isn't as scary as it sounds:

> Alice laughed. "There's no use trying," she said. "One can't believe impossible things."
> "I daresay you haven't had much practice," said the Queen. "When I was your age, I always did it for half an hour a day. Why, sometimes I've believed as many as six impossible things before breakfast. There goes the shawl again!" [495]

And where is it written the weak can't come together to dominate the powerful? As recounted in Chapter 21, our ancestors did it. At least one modern journalist understands that combined into the royal We, we can choose anything we like:

> The only thing keeping the powerful powerful, keeping money operating the way it operates, and keeping government running the way it runs is the stories we all agree to tell each other about those things. If everyone collectively decided today that poker

chips are the new currency[1] and Kim Kardashian is the Supreme
Ruler of the Entire World, those stories would be the new reality, and tomorrow we'd all be doing whatever Empress Kim
commands and Las Vegas would be the new Wall Street. [496]

By 90 percent of us signing the MOAs, we're collectively going to
decide free entropy money is the type of our new US dollars, and each
one of us is the Supreme Ruler of our own lives. Tomorrow, we'll be
doing whatever We Ourselves command, and old-growth forests will
be the new gold mines.

For any to whom messing around with the world's reserve
money seems daft, regardless of the strong arguments for doing it, think about where we are and who among us wants
this.

Where we are, if even a fraction of the literature is correct, is on
a dying planet swirling around the drain of a totalitarian nightmare
world government, with a few Übermensch dominating a great mass of
poverty-stricken, wailing souls [497]. If we're smart and set aside our
egos, what once seemed crazy may be worth a second look.

Who wants this money is pretty much every constituency out there.
We know 90 percent is a conservative number because free entropy-type
US dollars meet so many needs:

- They meet the needs of us all by eliminating concentrated power.
  People can't cause trouble for others without controlling the
  levers of power. If there's no concentrated power, individuals or
  groups can't cause problems for the rest of us, no matter what they
  say or do—they won't have the ability; it simply won't be possible.
  As the Ellen Ripley character said in *Aliens* after proposing to
  "nuke the entire site from orbit," it's the only way to be sure [498].
  Similarly, as Daniel Quinn observed, a king without an army is
  just a windbag in fancy clothes. Compared to our troubled legacy
  world, in a world free from concentrated power we'll have better

[1]As pointed out by Alden, it isn't quite this easy to change monies—things used
as money have to be scarce or they can't be used as money. If everyone started
using poker chips as money one day, smart entrepreneurs might figure out how
to mass produce them at low cost, which could cause their purchasing power to
drop substantially [ch. 3 of 192]. In any case, Johnstone's point about humans'
psychological ability to switch from one medium of exchange or store of value to
another remains.

security, better dispute resolution, better roads, and better social harmony.

- They meet the needs of us all by eliminating the mass surveillance and control to be enabled by central bank digital currencies (CBDCs) [192, 499, 500].
- They meet the needs of us all by eliminating USA federal government revenuers.
- They meet the needs of us all by making our world worth money both dead and alive [130], and thus healthier [501].
- They meet the needs of those concerned about the side-effects of solar radiation blocking, or geo-engineering. If our compulsory governmental organizations evaporate as is hoped, people will still be free to spray solar radiation blocking mixtures into the atmosphere [502], and manipulate weather by electro-magnetic means such as the High-frequency Active Auroral Research Program (HAARP) antennae [502], but other people will be free to sue them for damages. Those concerned enough to add feedforward to the feedback loop implemented by our Anglo-Saxon customary law traditions could also act. For one possibility, air-traffic controllers could refuse to grant flight clearance to airplanes not inspected by companies they trust, to verify the airplane can't spray. Companies underwriting personal liability insurance policies for air-traffic controllers might do such inspection work themselves, to reduce the risk of personal injury lawsuits from those harmed by any such spraying and weather manipulation. In another possible feedforward, a money could be produced that economically penalized those who pollute others' air, such as by spraying harmful mixtures into the atmosphere to block the sun.
- They meet the needs of us all by making us all wealthy.
- They meet the needs of poor people by making us all wealthy.
- They meet the needs of hungry people by eliminating wars, which, by destroying agricultural and food distribution systems, are the most obvious creators of hunger[503].
- They meet the needs of hungry people by getting more money into more hands, thus eliminating the main cause of hunger: lack of money to buy food. Vijay Prashad reported that each of us eight billion on the earth consumes about a tonne of food per year, while eleven billion tonnes of food are produced—thus, no-one

should go hungry. "If you want to end hunger, you must end poverty" [503].

- They meet the needs of hungry people by making agriculture both more productive and less biologically harmful, for example by the use of regenerative agriculture to improve soil quality [504, ch. 2 of 342]. Farmers who use ecosystem-friendly techniques may be able to produce much more food per hectare than their ecosystem-harmful competition [147, 505, 506, ch. 2 of 342, ch. 24 of 340], while effecting a steady growth in soil fertility [ch. 2 of 342]. Entropy money gives farmers additional incentive to use these techniques by paying them for the additional ecosystem services their lands provide as they adopt sustainable agriculture methods to increase productivity. Entropy money could also incentivize farmers to practice agroforestry, growing their crops among trees rather than in treeless monocrop fields. It could also incentivize farmers to grow trees that themselves provide human food, including olives, coconuts, pistachios, walnuts, cashews, chestnuts, almonds, avocados, pine seeds, hazel seeds, and many, many more [pp. 386 - 392 of 132, ch. 2 of 342].

- They meet the needs of people concerned about global warming by removing greenhouse gases from our atmosphere [147, 286, 288, 340–342, 373, 375–377, 501, 504, 507–512].

- They meet the needs of those concerned about global warming by causing healthier forests, resulting in more cloud cover [351] and therefore reduced heat retention in the earth's atmosphere [513].

- They meet the needs of people who use money by making our money(s) stable, predictable, valuable, scarce, divisible, portable, and ethical.[2]

- They meet the needs of people concerned about overpopulation. In a truly free world, entrepreneurs concerned about overpopulation may invent a take-it-and-forget-it contraceptive, as envisioned by Russ Finley in *Poison Darts* [514]. This would be a reversible contraceptive, taken once to activate. Once a person has taken the contraceptive, they would have to take a positive

---

[2]In the conclusion of *Broken Money*, Lyn Alden concludes ". . . open-source decentralized money that empowers individuals, that is permissionless to use, and that allows for a more borderless flow of value, is both powerful and ethical" [ch. 30 of 192].

action, such as ingesting a temporary antidote, to be fertile, eliminating unwanted pregnancies. Entrepreneurs in a truly free world may produce many other inventions helping people coordinate among each other to have children only when it makes sense for their financial situations [515]. Such coordination of human action would be enabled by the useful price signals produced by free markets. The truly free world engendered by free entropy-type US dollars will also enable the elimination of harsh authoritarian population control measures used in the past [515].

- They meet the needs of people who want to see our capital resources used well. In our new world, elemental gold and paper receipts for it will no longer be the commonly used units of account. In our legacy world, there is a conflict between the need for people to conduct commerce remotely and the use of these physical forms of money. Banks and credit card companies filled the resulting economic niche by enabling remote commerce with the use of electronic or paper claims to paper claims to gold. In our new world, digital gold (*retail* bitcoin) and records of oxygen US dollars will be inherently electronic in nature and thus well suited for both face-to-face and remote commerce, replacing banks in that economic niche. The buildings and real estate previously consumed by the banking industry will be freed up for better uses.

- They meet the needs of those cautious about trying something new by hedging our bets, by eliminating the collective's monopoly on the production of money. This is what Hayek recommended [516].

- They meet the needs of those cautious about trying something new by building on the precedent of changing our US dollars. We, the People, of the United States, in our capacity as a collective, have done this multiple times already. We changed them from silver to gold, and from 1/19.3939 of a Troy ounce of gold [**CHAP. XVI**, Sec. 9 of 187] to 1/20.6897 of an ounce [185, **CHAP. XCV**, Sec. 1 of 188], then to 1/20.672 (25.8 grains of gold nine-tenths pure) [**CHAP. 41**, Sec. 1 of 320, 457], to 1/35 (15 5/21 grains of gold nine-tenths pure) [3, 517, 518], to 1/38 [Sec. 2 of 179], and finally to 1/42.2222 [180–184] of an ounce. Now, for our escape, we'll change them to 30 grams of oxygen, or some mass of another measurable element or molecule, such as carbon or

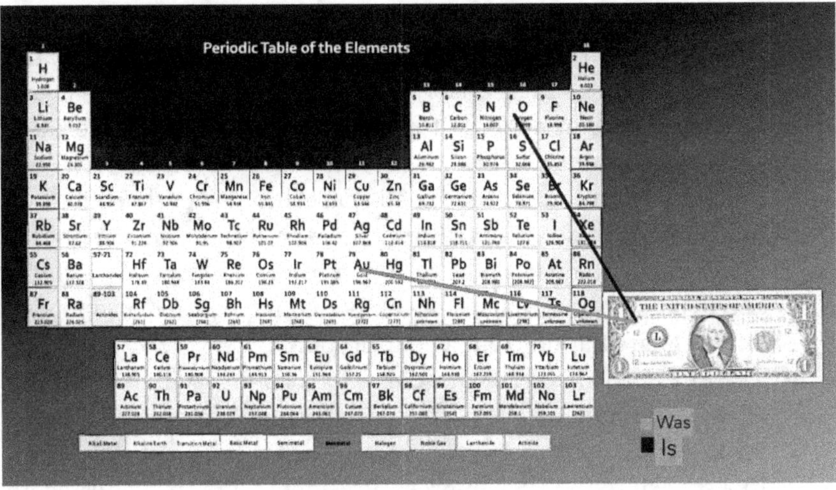

Figure 25.1. *From gold to oxygen. (Graphic thanks to shadoweddimples at Fiverr.)*

carbon dioxide. In the past, paper US dollar *bills* were a type of pointer to a fixed weight of gold. Now, the ledger entries tracking our new entropy-type US dollars will be the digital equivalent of US dollar *bills*, and will be a type of pointer to a fixed weight of oxygen produced by living green plants (Figure 25.1). The concept is the same, but our oxygen US dollars will use a digital ledger, in which each dollar is tracked as a number on the virtual ledger, whereas our legacy gold US dollars use a kind of physical ledger, in which each gold US dollar is tracked in the form of a paper note. Finally, we will be secure in the knowledge these digital ledger entries will not exist in excess of the US dollars our living lands have produced because the DAN controlling the ledger will be incapable of doing such a thing.

- They meet the needs of those cautious about trying something new by building on the precedent of using a nation's fiat money to acquire a stable store of value. The people and the central banks of China and other countries have been doing this for years, by abandoning both their own fiat money and US dollar bills in favor of gold [519].
- They meet the needs of those cautious about trying something new by building on the precedent of monetizing an atmospheric

gas. We have already done this in the form of carbon tax credits, which, in effect, pay people to remove carbon dioxide from the atmosphere. It can reasonably be argued oxygen money is equivalent to a carbon tax credit because both are part of the same carbon dioxide to oxygen to carbon dioxide cycle of plant and animal respiration on this small spaceship. Properly calibrated oxygen money is an improvement over carbon tax credits because it gets the federal government revenuers out of our lives, and bypasses the problems of compound interest-induced money entering circulation from a central source.

- They meet the needs of those cautious about trying something new by building on the precedent of monetizing energy. Taxes on energy usage have been proposed and voted on at least twice. In a speech to the US Congress, President Clinton suggested an energy tax, which he described as a BTU tax [3:28 of 520], to tax consumed energy. The 2018 ballot of the State of Washington asked voters if they wanted to implement an energy tax [521], also to tax consumed energy. Similarly, our new entropy-type US dollars monetize entropy, which is consumed energy. President Clinton suggested, and Washington voters were asked to decide on, a way of paying people not to consume energy. Entropy money will effectively do the same thing, by paying people to produce energy in the form of healthy living beings.

- They meet the needs of those cautious about trying something new by building on the precedent of paying landowners for ecosystem services [313]. Our new entropy money is an improved version of previous environmental degradation reduction schemes involving ecosystem service payment to landowners [110, 143]. It is also a superior and possibly synergistic version of the latest attempt to reduce environmental degradation by monetizing ecosystem services using carbon tax credits, tourism, and sustainable agriculture, to be accomplished with a new investment vehicle called a Natural Asset Company (NAC) [120, 278].

- They meet the needs of those cautious about trying something new by building on the precedent of printing new money. All things used as money must be "printed," or manufactured, to make them scarce and fungible. For a long time, individuals have been printing money by manufacturing blocks of salt, bags of rice, barrels of whiskey, packs of cigarettes, and so on, and also by minting copper, nickel, silver and gold coins. Various polities have been printing paper money for as long as three millennia [p. 52 of 191], typically taking the form of claims on silver or gold coins, which themselves were "printed." Taking the step of using entropy mined from the ground as money and measuring and tracking it is, in principle, identical to what people already do with gold. With the legacy practice of using entropy added to land as money, people remove gold from the parcel, measure it, store it, and trade paper claims of ownership to it, or electronic claims to paper claims. With the new practice of using entropy mined from land as money, our living world removes entropy from the land, companies measure it but don't store it, and people trade the numerical results of the measurements. We'll do two things differently with the new money: First, we won't store the oxygen—instead, we'll let it flow into the atmosphere for us animals to enjoy. Second, we'll invert the direction of the energy flow—from gold, removing energy from the land, to oxygen, adding energy to the land in the form of healthy living beings.

- They meet the needs of people who need money because everyone will be able to participate in the front run. For many of us, it will mean we finally get to spend some quality time with our family and doing things we think need doing. Some of us will get to donate more to the charities of our choice.

- They meet the needs of those who cannot spend a lot of time creating this black swan event. For most of us, improving our money in this way will be as fast and easy as a few online button clicks.

- They meet the needs of people who don't trust others to do the right thing. The fundamental argument supporting the expected success of making such a change to our money is it requires no one to be a saint for it to work. Phrased in evolutionary biology terms, the new monetary paradigm will be evolutionarily stable, meaning it will function well in the presence of defectors. In this case, defectors would be people who try to get all the money. All anyone will need to do in the new monetary regime is what they already do: continue to work to get enough money to pay the bills. The harder they work to get money, the better the system works. When concentrated power is eliminated, and the only honest way to get money is to satisfy the wants of others, and destroying our living world doesn't pay as well as in the before time, working harder to get money benefits us all.

- They meet the needs of us all by helping US dollars continue their world domination [522]. If everyone signs up for accounts, US dollars will enter circulation almost everywhere, which will be convenient both for us in the States and for everyone else. With US dollars entering circulation everywhere, nearly everyone on the planet will probably begin trading directly using US dollars. For example, if the people of India repeal their central government tax and legal tender statutes, they'll be able to accept payment in US dollars instead of rupees from people in other countries, and spend those US dollars anywhere on Earth. This outcome will help us all increase our real wealth because all of us on the planet will get increased access to a stable and widely used monetary product. By doing this, we will have continued the work of the attendees of the July 1944 conference held in Bretton Woods, New Hampshire [321–323], who endeavored to decrease the world's strife and increase its prosperity with a trustworthy, high-quality money.

- They meet the needs of people who want the *retail* bitcoin DAL to be used widely. They meet the needs of the *retail* bitcoin network masternode operators whose ambition is to be a wealthy philanthropist.

- They meet the needs of people who want to be good, not evil. According to Kaplan [523], no one successfully has contradicted Peter Singer's conclusion that if you spend your money on luxuries rather than on helping others who are dying, such as from famine, you are objectively committing an evil act [524]. The rationale is the same as if you choose not to rescue a drowning child in a pond while walking by on your way to a meeting because your clothes might get dirty. These new and improved entropy-type US dollars, and the financial wealth transfer accomplished in the front run, are going to result in a new group of wealthy philanthropists, and most all of us are going to end up with at least a little extra cash we can use for charity. Thanks to that, many of the innocent poor among us will finally get some much-needed help. There's also going to be a flood of money headed toward charities protecting children, animals, and our wild living world. As noted previously, other money headed toward poverty-stricken people will come in the form of more jobs. Using Singer's unassailable logic, We, the People, of these fifty states are morally obligated to fix our US dollars in this way.

- They meet the needs of people who dream of a Star Trek utopia where the need for money has vanished. As interpersonal communications capabilities increase in quantity and quality globally, and as prices hold steady, with more and more dropping, economies may gradually drift toward gift economy status. Moneys-in-use could drift from commodity monies toward credit monies [ch. 6 of 192]. In the long run, things used as money could possibly be commodities highly useful to others, with utility for their value as gifts, or perhaps in times and places vanishing altogether as people link up tighter and tighter.
- They meet the needs of people with youngsters, for whom the good of those youngsters is the alpha and the omega, by gifting us all a beautiful and healthy living world.
- They meet the needs of people who want their loved ones in the armies to come home. If our new entropy money meets expectations of causing compulsory governments to evaporate, the soldiers will finally come home.
- They meet the needs of people who enjoy working with others to solve problems as reductions in poverty and concomitant increases in free time gift us more time to engage in our natural, problem-solving talent of dialogue [492, 493].
- They meet the spiritual needs of us all to live in a world without cruelty and suffering, but instead with health, happiness, love, and joy. They meet the needs of us all to be happy and healthy on a paradise planet.

The one thing we all need, but don't all yet have at the time of writing is, of course, the understanding we already have practically everything we need to acquire a new, world-saving money, and we really, really want it.

26. FURTHER READING

Many readers will have serious questions about some of the events postulated to happen in humanity's future, especially the part where "revenuer" is no longer a job category. They're encouraged to visit the frequently asked questions (FAQ) at http://www.projectsalamander.org/ for answers and more information. Spreadsheets showing entropy money payout calculations, and our federal government Treasury department gold holdings can also be found on that page.

For those who would like to see how the numbers work when assets and liabilities are added to our books like particle anti-particle pairs, an accounting book-style presentation of the arithmetic used to justify borrowing with the left hand while printing with the right is included in Appendix A. For those interested in learning more about how we got to this point in our history with our problematic gold US dollars, a simplified version of the story is presented in Appendix B. A first cut at a formal set of requirements for the RFP we'll instruct our treasurer to deliver can be found in Appendix C. More details about the concepts of entropy and energy are presented in Appendix D, and a short note on universal basic income (UBI) is found in Appendix E.

Readers are also encouraged to read the referenced books and articles. If you only have time for one article, it should be "Regrowing Human Limbs" [368], from the April issue of the *Scientific American* magazine, also discussed in Chapter 27. The article will make you eager to witness further advancements in the state of the art in medical technology. If you have time for a book or two, you'll have a great time reading Donald Moffitt's *The Genesis Quest* [426] and *Second Genesis* [427]. Moffitt's inspiring tale will move your eyes from your feet to the horizon, taking in the long-range picture. Plus, it's a great story about the goodness we humans have when working together, aided by the art of dialogue. Speaking of the art of dialogue, you'll feel invigorated with a sense of hope and awe at the true potential of humanity's problem-solving ability if you read David Bohm's *Thought as a System* [492] and *On Creativity* [493]. If you want a thorough and easy-to-read explanation of the origin and evolution of money, the problems we're caused by government, or fiat, money, and an educated exposition of the hope and promise of humanity's latest technological advances in money, you can't do better than Lyn Alden's 2023 *Broken Money* [192], cited copiously in the present work. Finally, if you're interested in the book making anything other than free entropy money not an option if we truly want a healthy, happy world, you'll feel like the scales have fallen from your eyes after reading Jörg G. Hülsmann's *The Ethics of Money Production* [185].

27. MAKE IT SO

By this point, the reader has learned some very interesting things about her or his world. In a nutshell, we've learned We, the People, of theUnited States of America have a big money problem we can easily fix. Our gold US dollars, which are also the de facto reserve money of the world, are causing big problems, but can be fixed easily with a couple of administrative actions. Administrative actions are something the group of us really can do, and conveniently. We've also learned a certain easy action by our treasurer will launch us all on the way to a bright and happy science-fiction future, amazingly even before she takes the action. We even know what our jobs are, and we're highly motivated to do them since we personally, along with everyone we care about, will benefit greatly.

As we've discussed, the main job for most of us is to get the idea of free entropy-type US dollars into the "air," so to speak. We may not even need any extensive advertising campaigns—word of mouth might work fine, and could be fast. For all we know, a whisper campaign might get us out in only a month or two. We already have sufficient land health data, and we probably need only a few hundred lines of software to connect it with parcel ownership data. This task should prove easy for our programmer geniuses to accomplish in the timeframe of a couple of years.

All we have to do is quietly make the change to new and life-saving world reserve US dollars—there's not a lot to talk about as once one gets the idea, what to do becomes obvious and why to do it even more obvious. As it gets into the air, it may spread even faster thanks to extrasensory information transmission [489, 490]. It will also happen faster and faster as people begin checking the dollar *bill/retail* bitcoin (https://www.dash.org/) ratio and notice it beginning its inevitable rocket ride to the moon. As this happens, those of us who can do certain specific jobs, including building decentralized autonomous networks and obtaining data, are naturally going to seek one another out and engage in serious, productive discussions.

What makes this idea a winner, for We, the People, to use our national treasury to purchase a two-year supply of *retail* bitcoin and for us individuals to front run the collective, is the movement toward replacing our legacy gold US dollars with oxygen US dollars quickly will become unstoppable, in the most literal meaning of that term. This is because, as the earliest risk-takers take the plunge and risk some of their US dollar *bills* by purchasing *retail* bitcoin ledger units, they will acquire "skin in the game," with all that implies. The earliest risk-takers will take this plunge, probably with small amounts of legacy US dollar *bills* so they can afford to lose them, because they'll know they themselves are going to be the ones initiating the dollar *bill/retail* bitcoin runaway. They'll also take this risk because they will benefit the most, and the sooner they acquire their units the more they'll benefit. They'll likely act quickly since they'll know time isn't their friend at the beginning of the front run—here in the before-time *retail* bitcoin ledger units are thinly traded and attractively priced. They'll know it will take only a relatively small amount of buying pressure to set the dollar *bill/retail* bitcoin ratio on a run.

At that point, these earliest risk-takers will have acquired a strong financial incentive to spread this idea, that We the People can fix everything by fixing our US dollars, and therefore will spread it. As they do, the dollar *bill/retail* bitcoin ratio will commence shooting up faster. This effect will be especially pronounced at the beginning of the process, before *retail* bitcoin's trading volume and market capitalization have increased much. It will quickly become even more pronounced as *retail* bitcoin sellers exit markets once they learn our treasurer is going to purchase a two-year budget supply worth. Understanding a massive price run-up is on the way, these sellers will refuse to sell at low prices, driving the price up more. As the dollar *bill/retail* bitcoin ratio continues to shoot up, it will attract more attention, with people asking, "Why?" Those early movers will answer that we're going to fix everything by fixing our US dollars, and we're going to use the most reliable, retail-ready, and decentralized digital cash available, *retail* bitcoin, as the bridge to our new, world-saving version of US dollars. Oh, and here's a book (*Escape*), 'splainin' the concept in more detail.

What will attract even more of us then, faster and faster, is that the plan isn't for our national treasury to purchase the *retail* bitcoin and later sell it, but to purchase it and use it directly to pay our national bills. This will attract even more people because it will make *retail* bitcoin the perfect investment. Individuals won't need to trade some US dollar *bills* for *retail* bitcoin units and then nervously wait for the dollar *bill/retail* bitcoin ratio to get large enough for them to purchase US dollar *bills* for a profit, and hope not to miss the timing (said technique known as greater fool theory). Instead, all any of us will need to do is purchase the *retail* bitcoin, then relax and enjoy our new and improved financial situations. We'll know we'll be able to spend our *retail* bitcoin units directly and it will be convenient and easy because everyone else will be doing it, too. Importantly, we'll know the value appreciation we experience with our *retail* bitcoin will be lasting, so we won't need to stress over it. We'll be even more relaxed because a two-year tax jubilee will commence as soon as the national treasury acquires a two-year supply of *retail* bitcoin, so we'll never again have to purchase those evil Federal Reserve Notes. We'll know prices in terms of our new digital cash (*retail* bitcoin) will tend to decrease over time, not run away, encouraging saving rather than consumption [253].

Finally, the personal health benefits of this idea make it irresistible. The to-be-founded Project Salamander to regrow human limbs, mentioned in Chapter 18, is the ember that will become the flame of our escape. This is because of its explosive and almost unimaginable benefits, to every one of us on the planet. With the discovery that adult human fibroblasts, important in wound healing, retain spatial memory the same as do salamander fibroblasts, the time of regrowing human limbs may be near. Ken Muneoka, Manjong Han, and David M. Gardiner, in the April 2008 issue of the *Scientific American* magazine article entitled "Regrowing Human Limbs" [368], estimated we may be only a decade or two away from human body part regeneration, and the mid-2020s is in the middle of that forecast. Considering the possibility of massive funding from our new "front run" wealthy philanthropists, we can predict almost all human suffering may be on the way to ending, practically overnight.

Use your imagination and think of the possibilities. If the gifted and dedicated researchers among us solve the problem of regrowing human limbs, is there anything that can't be done to improve human bodies? Heart trouble, aging joints, scarring, cancer and incurable diseases, hair loss, wrinkles, etc. would be repaired cell by cell, similar to when we grew after conception, and it gets better. There are very few of us who don't have a thing or two they need to fix, and not one of us doesn't know others who need this, that, or the other thing fixed. As soon as our *retail* bitcoin two-year budget supply purchase is complete, and even before, thanks to our front-running, the countdown toward all these people we care about getting fixed will commence, and it won't be a long countdown. It may be measured in single-digit years for many or most of us.

If you're afflicted with that voice in your head whispering you don't deserve this, tell it to stifle. You deserve it. Your precious babies deserve it. Your spouse deserves it, and your parents, brothers, sisters, aunts and uncles, nieces and nephews, cousins, grandparents, grandchildren, friends, colleagues—every one of them deserves it and you know it. Do it for them if not for yourself, and send the voice to limbo. And remember, even if our new, improved US dollars fail, it's no problem because we'll have made our money free as in free speech—we won't care. We will have already settled up our gold US dollar bankruptcy, we'll already be using a perfectly good form of gold, digital gold (*retail* bitcoin), and the field will be open to competitors. It's not a question of "How could we do this?" but "How could we not?" Keep in mind engineering this lifesaving money will be much easier than engineering mass-produced pocket-sized supercomputers, and much easier than accomplishing Flash Gordon-style rocket tail landings.

By making this change, the quality of products used as money is going to improve faster and faster, even before we've all signed the first MOA. Our finances will improve dramatically almost instantly, as soon as very many of us start speaking with one another and deciding, yes, let's do this. All we're proposing here is to be honorable by correcting our books and adding our living world to them, where it belongs.

The last word: In the 1987 movie *Wall Street* [525], big money wheeler and dealer Gordon Gekko taught us greed is good and re-minded us how so. Many of us have had it beat into our heads that greed is a sin; in fact, it's considered one of the seven deadly sins in Christian teachings. But like many things, it isn't that simple. As with the other deadly sins, greed is a sin only to the extent it's an abuse, or an excessive version, of your natural passion. Gordon Gekko correctly pointed out it's good to be greedy for a better life, for more money for you and your family, and for more knowledge—these things make our world a good and improving place. The only constraint on our greed is we shouldn't trespass against others while working to improve the lives of ourselves and our loved ones.

In conclusion dear reader, embrace your greed. You stand on the precipice of a dramatic improvement in your family's finances. You stand on the precipice of a change to your money that will turn our entire world economy into a health-maximizing optimization machine (Figure 27.1), working through We, the People, of the earth to turn our beautiful world into the paradise it's meant to be. You now know what is to be done. The time has come to pass this book on to the next person and get to work. Go team!

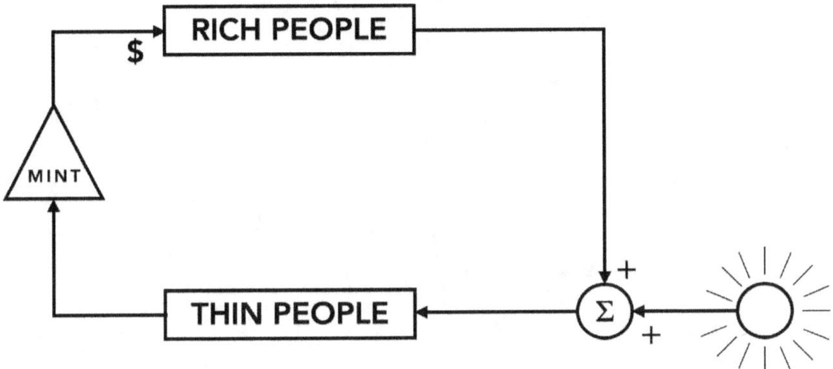

Figure 27.1. *Harmony.*

Part VI.

Appendices

A. BORROWING WITH LEFT HAND, PRINTING WITH RIGHT

THE progenitors of the 1913 Federal Reserve Act, which created a central bank with the power to print legal tender notes, knew users of US dollars would reject centrally produced paper money because of the almost-certain-to-result price inflation. Central banks had already been attempted in the new Republic, but We the People had dissolved each of them, and the bill's sponsors knew their latest attempt would also fail unless the voters didn't understand what was happening. Therefore, they endeavored to conceal their actions. To devise a plan to create yet another money-printing central bank, six[1] or seven[2] people, who between them represented a fourth of the financial wealth of the entire world, met in secret at the Jekyll Island resort in Georgia in 1910 [193, 526]. Their purpose, in which they succeeded, was to print paper money on an industrial scale with the plebs none the wiser.

That fateful 1910 gathering led to the Federal Reserve Act, signed into statutory law by President Wilson on the 23rd of December, 1913 [216]. The statute set up a system in which We, the People, of the United States would sell debt notes onto the open market, and certain banks owned by the progenitors of the act would purchase some of those notes.[3] Some of the notes purchased by the progenitors' banks in turn would be marked up in price and sold back to We the People's new central bank, which would pay for them with newly printed paper money known as Federal Reserve Notes.

---

[1]Nelson Aldrich, A. Piatt Andrew, Henry Davison, Arthur Shelton, Frank Vanderlip, Paul Warburg [526].

[2]Nelson W. Aldrich, Abraham Piatt Andrew, Frank A. Vanderlip, Henry P. Davison, Charles D. Norton, Benjamin Strong, Paul M. Warburg [193].

[3]This was merely the newest version of Alexander Hamilton's plan to pay central government debt by borrowing more money [207, 527].

The department of the federal government printing the new money and buying back the debt, the new central bank, was to be known as the Federal Reserve System. This so-called banking system would masquerade as independent, but in practice would be a new department of the federal government, bringing with it a new tax [211, 215–217].

The inflation tax

The new federal government department had inflicted on us a cruel hidden tax known as the inflation tax [211]. Here, a simple example of this tax's mechanics is presented (Figure A.1, which is a bookkeeping-specific version of Figure 4.1). We show the accounting details of a system printing paper money in the shadows, with few aware of its existence. In this example, We, the People, (WTP) sell a $1.00 IOU, or

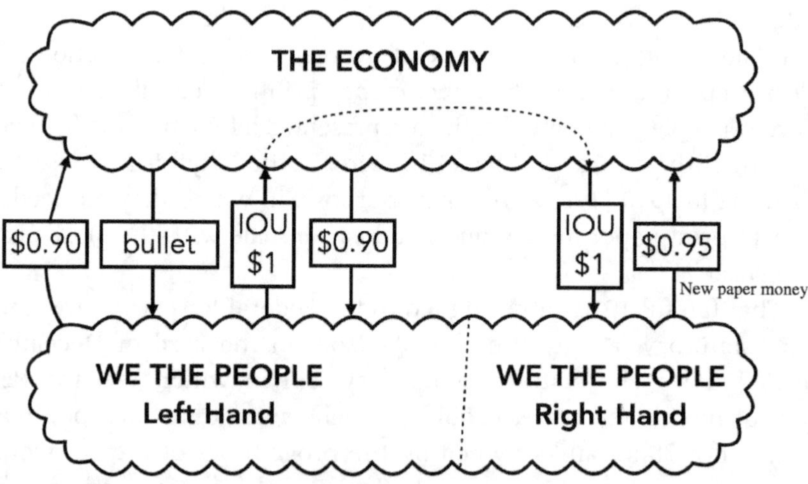

Figure A.1. *Sell IOUs and buy them back with new money.*

bond, for $0.90 on the open market and use the $0.90 to buy a bullet. Behind the scenes, WTP print $0.95 and buy back the bond with it. The $0.05 difference between the $0.90 WTP received out in the open, on the primary market, for the bond and the $0.95 worth of new paper WTP spent to buy it back on the secondary market is profit to the banks that purchased it on the primary market. These banks are the ones owned by the progenitors of the Federal Reserve Act back in the day, and the $0.05 profit is how WTP cut them in on this laundering operation.

Table A.1. *We, the People, (Left Hand)*

Date	Description	Out	In	Bal.	Economy + WTP Bal.
	initial balance			1.00	2.00
today	sell bond		0.90	1.90	2.00
tomorrow				1.90	2.95
next day				1.90	2.95
next day	buy bullet	0.90		1.00	2.95
+30 years	buy bond	1.00		0.00	2.95
next day				0.00	2.00
next day	receive profit		0.05	0.05	2.00

Tables A.1, A.2, and A.3 show the details of the out-in-the-open accounting book of WTP, referred to as the left hand of WTP and abbreviated as WTPLH, along with the hidden book of the central bank, referred to here as the right hand of WTP and abbreviated as WTPRH, as well as the book of the remainder of the economy, referred to as TE, The Economy.

The account of WTPLH initially has a value of $1.00, WTPRH starts at $0.00, and TE also starts with $1.00. The total balance of both hands of WTP, along with TE, is $2.00.

On the first day, today, WTPLH sells a 30-year $1.00 bond for $0.90 on the open market, giving it a balance of $1.90. TE in turn buys the bond for $0.90, leaving a balance of $0.10. No action was taken by WTPRH, and the total balance of WTP and TE remains $2.00.

Tomorrow, WTPRH prints $0.95, increasing the total balance of WTP and TE to $2.95. The creators of the Federal Reserve Banking System scheme justified this money supply inflation by promising to shred the new money later to keep the accounts correct. It gave them a fig leaf to stand behind for their claim they weren't printing any new money because the new money was matched by a negative entry in their books. When the new money returns, it and the negative book entry cancel each other out, like a particle-antiparticle pair spontaneously popping into existence and then annihilating each other, keeping the books at zero. They could say the printing was simply an emergency intervention to get some extra money into circulation. The story is the new money will flow temporarily into TE to help new businesses start. Once the new businesses are on their feet, the new money can be withdrawn from TE, with none the wiser.

As demonstrated in this example, in which the total amount of money in circulation starts at $2.00, grows to $2.95, then shrinks back to its original amount of $2.00 at the end, it can actually work this way. The problem is it can only work this way if WTP does what it can't do: pay off our old debt without acquiring new.

The next day, WTPRH uses the new $0.95 to purchase the $1.00 bond from TE. As a result, the balance of WTPRH decreases back to $0.00 while the new money enters the book of TE, giving it a balance of $1.05, with the total of WTP and TE balance remaining at $2.95.

Table A.2. *We, the People (Right Hand)*

Date	Description	Out	In	Bal.	Economy + WTP Bal.
	initial balance			0.00	2.00
today				0.00	2.00
tomorrow	print		0.95	0.95	2.95
next day	buy bond	0.95		0.00	2.95
next day				0.00	2.95
+30 years	sell bond		1.00	1.00	2.95
next day	shred	0.95		0.05	2.00
next day	transfer profit	0.05		0.00	2.00

The day after that, WTPLH uses the $0.90 in proceeds from the bond sale to buy a bullet from TE, giving it a balance of $1.00. Since TE sold the bullet, its balance increased by $0.90 to $1.95. Total balance remains $2.95.

Thirty years later, with no other economic activity, WTPLH buys the $1.00 bond from WTPRH. This causes the balance of WTPLH to decrease to $0.00, while the balance of WTPRH increases to $1.00. Total balance remains $2.95.

The next day, WTPRH shreds $0.95 of the $1.00 paid to it by WTPLH, to conserve mass and energy, so to speak, decreasing the total balance of WTP and TE back to $2.00.

Finally, on the last day, WTPRH transfers the profit of $0.05 back to WTPLH. The end result is WTP paid $0.95 for a $0.90 bullet. The $0.95 was transferred to TE, which paid for it with $0.90 of production transferred from whatever else it would have produced to the production of the bullet [137]. The collective used tax and legal tender statutes to force its members to produce a bullet instead of what they might have preferred to produce, such as shelter or food or recreation. The economy ended up with more money and different economic output than might have been chosen freely by market actors, as astutely observed by President Eisenhower [269].

Table A.3. *The Economy*

Date	Description	Out	In	Bal.	Economy + WTP Bal.
	initial balance			1.00	2.00
today	buy bond	0.90		0.10	2.00
tomorrow				0.10	2.95
next day	sell bond		0.95	1.05	2.95
next day	sell bullet		0.90	1.95	2.95
+30 years				1.95	2.95
next day				1.95	2.00
next day				1.95	2.00

This scheme would achieve the advertised result of not permanently increasing the money supply if it worked this way in practice. The amount of money in circulation increases, hopefully helping businesses produce and sell products and services, and is then removed from circulation. In the meantime, WTP pay \$0.95 in thirty years for a bullet today (conjuring memories of Wimpy in the Popeye cartoon offering a quarter Tuesday for a hamburger today), then getting its \$0.95 back from TE by taxing it.

However, the reality is it takes place in the shadows for a good reason—WTP haven't been paying off the loans with money from Our account. Instead, We've been buying back the old bonds with the proceeds from new bonds, resulting in the bullet-manufacturing, bullet-buying, bullet-shooting, compound-interest situation that's ruining everything. Consistent with that dynamic, Stockman reported central bank balance sheets worldwide in the mid-2020s are around \$22 trillion larger than in 2000 [528]. Fractional reserve processes have multiplied those trillions into quadrillions on the world's financial books.

B. A SIMPLIFIED HISTORY OF OUR US DOLLARS

WHY does money exist? What is it? As described in Chapter 10, money exists because it allows people to make deals in two steps, avoiding the need for coincidences of wants. It gives us a way to accept something we don't want in exchange for our valuable product or service, only because we know its market price in thing(s) we do want [p. 39 of 191].

Money enables its users to compare apples to oranges conveniently; for example, if apples and oranges are priced in terms of US dollars, one can know how many apples an orange will cost by comparing the ratios of dollars to apples and oranges—dollars/apple and dollars/orange. If they are priced in cigarettes, one can compare the ratios of cigarettes to apples and oranges—cigarettes/apple and cigarettes/orange. No matter what you are using as money, it drops out of the fractions when making the comparisons, so you end up knowing the price of oranges in apples or apples in oranges:

$$\frac{\frac{\text{cigarettes}}{\text{orange}}}{\frac{\text{cigarettes}}{\text{apple}}} = \frac{\text{cigarettes}}{\text{orange}}\frac{\text{apples}}{\text{cigarette}} = \frac{\text{apples}}{\text{orange}}.$$

If anything will suffice as the common numerator, why do we normally use gold US dollars, in the form of US dollar *bills*, rather than cigarettes, or blocks of salt, or barrels of whiskey, or whatever? Comparing gold coins to cigarettes, for example, gold coins are more durable and less usable for non-monetary purposes, and thus there are a fairly constant number in circulation, and they weigh less than cigarettes relative to what they can purchase.[1] However, in various times and places people have used other things as money, such as cans of mackerel, sea shells, bags of rice, or barrels of whiskey. Those products are rarely

---

[1]It would take a large weight and volume of cigarettes to purchase a nice suit, which typically can be had in exchange for a one ounce gold coin, occupying little space and only weighing an ounce.

used as money anymore because gold coins are better for monetary purposes. The psychological ability of people to switch from using one thing to another as money is the crux of our escape possibility.

In certain times and places, you could possibly persuade someone to part with something of value, say, twenty bushels of wheat, for a block of salt he didn't want and only accepted because he thought he could later unload it in exchange for something he did want. But not anymore. It's the same for barrels of whiskey, cattle, bags of rice, bags of nails, etc. Once upon a time, these commodities had a quality in the minds of others allowing for their use as money, but not anymore. This answers the question "What is money?" Money is a quality of a thing it can acquire and then lose, depending on human actions. As time passes, various items acquire and then lose this quality, which could be referred to as moneyness. In various times and places, many things have been used as money and have therefore had moneyness. The most popular modern items with this property are US dollar *bills*.

For a made-up example of moneyness, imagine Bob has a Ford, Alice has two Dodges, and Tom has a Chevy. Initially, none of the cars has moneyness; they're just cars, human-manufactured artifacts used to transport people and things from here to there. But then each of the parties acquires certain wants, and one of them acquires valuable information. Imagine Bob wants the Chevy, but Tom doesn't want the Ford; he wants Alice's two Dodges. Alice wants the Ford, and to everyone's good fortune, knows what Bob and Tom want. So she gives Tom her Dodges in exchange for his Chevy, then gives Bob the Chevy in exchange for the Ford she wanted. The Chevy acquired moneyness, and you could say it *was* money, for the purposes of this deal. You could compute the market price of Fords in Dodges using their prices in Chevys. For example, in this two-part deal, the prices in Chevys were 0.5 Chevys/Dodge, and 1 Chevy/Ford, and the Dodges/Ford price was 2.

In general, Chevys don't make great money and don't get used as money very often; nevertheless, that property the Chevy acquired for the two-part deal helped three people improve their lots, even though no trading pair of them had a coincidence of wants. Everyone got what they wanted, thanks to the miracle of moneyness.

In another example of moneyness, the author is a trillionaire, in dollars. This is not an exaggeration—he personally owns a 10-, a 50-, and a 100-trillion-dollar note. . . dollars Zimbabwe, that is. In a case of lost moneyness, the entire $160,000,000,000,000 worth of Zimbabwe notes was purchased more than a decade ago for about $4 worth of US notes. However, when those Zimbabwe notes were first introduced they had moneyness, for at least a few weeks or days, because people were using them as money by purchasing things like shelter and food with them. These days you could bring all three notes to a grocery store in Zimbabwe and probably not even get a candy bar.

Things used as money acquire economic demand due to their utility in facilitating deals in the absence of a coincidence of wants. Money, or moneyness, is a property or quality a product acquires by being used as money. Our US dollars are a case in point.

History of money and our US dollars.   The widespread practice of using certain things as money may have first emerged in concert with the use of those things in the customary law tradition of "wergild," or "man price." This tradition has been used in some tribal societies to prevent blood feuds by assigning prices to be paid to victims or their families by the perpetrators in cases of injury [529–531]. Wampum was used for this purpose by North American Indians [532–535], and gold in the form of Roman solidi (~4.5g gold coins) [536, 537], and grain or silver in the form of shekels was used for wergild in medieval Europe and the Middle East [538–540].

The late Philip Grierson, Professor of Numismatics at Cambridge University, speculated wergild in less populous societies was initially denominated directly in valuable things like chickens or cows, and later indirectly, through ratios of commodities, such as grain or precious metals. Commodities were probably settled on due to their monetarily desirable characteristics, including scarcity, durability, and fungibility, though people at the time may not have been explicitly thinking of the properties good money should have. The change from direct to indirect wergild may have been the birth of the idea of moneyness: various quantities of the same commodity standing in for everything else—a new mental model had entered the world. With the option of indirect wergild, if society had found payment of a cow to the victim of your trespass would prevent a blood feud, and had decided paying 20 shekels of grain was the same as paying a cow, you could either pay the victim of your trespass a cow, or shekels in lieu of the cow.

Grierson speculated that, as societies grew large enough to result in people regularly interacting economically with strangers, the practice of paying wergild in various quantities of the same commodity made it natural to also use the wergild commodities in deals with strangers. The practice of using intermediaries with exact market prices to make deals didn't exist in smaller societies where everyone was friends and neighbors. Trades in these smaller societies usually took place with the same friendly, gift-economy type barter exchanges used between many neighbors to this day, typically something along the lines of "You helped me build my house so I'd like to repay the favor by helping you harvest," or the everyday informal social accounting people do to track who the producers are and who the slackers are [ch. 1 of 192].[2] Wergild practices, in contrast, needed more exact prices to satisfy both perpetrators and victims in cases of trespass, where relationships between parties were less friendly. After the advent of the agricultural revolution and its resulting high population densities caused by surplus food production, along with high division of labor-type products enabled by those extra people, who now could produce things other than food thanks to the agricultural surplus, gift and barter exchanges became less possible. Gift exchanges with strangers suffered from the risk of defection, and barter became difficult because coincidences of wants between market participants became fewer and further between—there was too much variety of economic output [ch. 2 of 192]. Concurrent with these factors, exchanges between strangers using wergild commodities were natural starting points for the development of market prices denominated in monetary intermediaries [541].

Once the concept of establishing market prices in terms of things people don't want for the things they do had been established in the human psyche, many things were found to fill the role of monetary intermediary. This included, as noted elsewhere, such diverse items as cows, sheep, gems, salt, skins, shells, nails, tobacco, whiskey, cigarettes, cotton, rice, canned mackerel, copper, nickel, silver, and gold. The more people accept things they don't want in exchange for their valuable products or services, the more others are likely to take a chance by

---

[2]Lyn Alden has unified the credit theory of money with the commodity theory in what she calls the ledger theory of money. In *Broken Money*, she explained that both credit and commodities are forms of ledger entries; one virtual, the other physical [ch. 4 of 192]. Credits and commodities are ways for humans to work together with others with whom they have varying relationships, from family, to friends, to acquaintances, and even strangers, without cheating or being cheated. For those closer, such as friends and family, memory works fine, if needed at all. For those less close, like strangers, with their associated risk of defection, liquid commodities are typically the best bet.

accepting those same things, that they also don't want.[3] Things people accept even though they don't want them can acquire value because they've acquired value, converging on a Schelling point [543].

A Schelling point is a type of equilibrium achieved when people make the same guess about what others will guess in the absence of communication between them. A Schelling point can be arrived at when you correctly guess what another person expects you to expect from them. For example, what if you have to meet someone in New York City on a certain day, but don't know when or where? When and where might the other person expect you to expect them to go? If, for example, you both guess Grand Central Station at noon, you've arrived at a Schelling point. In Seattle, one might guess the pig at the public market at noon, while in London, England, perhaps Trafalgar Square at noon. In the case of moneyness, products used as money gain monetary popularity due to characteristics causing them to have a monetary value over and above their utility value [ch. 2 of 192], causing people to save them for a rainy day, increasing their supply relative to consumption (stock to flow ratio). This makes their supply more constant and thus increases their utility as money, causing people to save them more, making their supply more constant, . . . , in a feedback loop resulting in a real-world tautology in which certain products are used as money because they're used as money. Another way of thinking about this effect is from the point of view of an individual—if everyone else is using, say, gold coins as money, he or she pretty much also has to use gold coins as money. When in Rome, do as the Romans do.

By the twentieth century, gold effectively had won the monetary arms race worldwide, due to its superior scarcity, durability, fungibility, divisibility, portability, beauty, ease of use, and lack of industrial demand. Monetary gold here in these fifty states exists in the form of US dollars. Where did these US dollars come from?

Origins of our US dollars: Joachimsthaler to dollar. Before gold dollars, there were silver thalers. In 1517, in the kingdom of Bohemia,[4]

---

[3]While this process has often been accelerated by governmental intervention, through tax and legal tender rules [542, ch. 8 of 192], it is also known to work organically. The use of cigarettes or canned mackerel in prisons, and rare commodities in massively multiplayer video games such as *Diablo II* [ch. 2 of 192], are well known examples of the organic adoption of human-manufactured artifacts as money.

[4]Northwestern Czechia in the early twenty-first century.

near the town of Sankt Joachimsthal [544], or Jáchymov [545], or Joachim's Thal [193], the Counts von Šlik, one of the wealthiest noble families in Bohemia, first minted the coins known as Joachimsthalers.[5] "Thaler" means "of the thal," or "dell," or "dale" in German, and "valley" in English [546], so the coins' names mean "of Joachim's Valley."[6] No one at the time knew the products of the von Šlik's silver mines would lead to the world's money of moneys. They thought they were merely mining a metal from which they could manufacture products—silver coins, in this case—intended for use as money. The Counts von Šlik, who owned the land, struck coins with the silver and spent them into circulation, in the process paying off their debts to the Nuremberg bankers [547]. They were printing money in the form of silver coins called Joachimsthalers, eventually commonly referred to as thalers.

Although some may gasp at the idea of printing money, the world did not end in a hyperinflationary runaway, even though money was being printed. Why not? Because the rate of printing was constrained by the physical limitations of getting ore out of the ground, refining it, and striking coins, and because the total amount printed was constrained economically. The coins had a rate-limited, hard monetary policy. Total coin production was constrained by decreasing profits as the number of coins in circulation increased, eventually nearing zero. Instead of causing poverty due to a great excess of them forcibly being spent into circulation from a central point as is the case with modern US dollar *bills*, the coins reduced poverty by letting people freely choose to use them, thus constraining their temporal monetary policy.

As time went on, thalers were produced from various mines. The silver content of the coins was reliable, and they were therefore trusted by their users, greasing the skids of commerce by removing the need for scales to weigh silver. When dealing with thalers, the amount of silver could be quickly ascertained by weighing the coin with one's hand, chinking it on the table to see if it sounded right, and visually inspecting the engravings. The thalers were honest money, and by manufacturing and spending them into circulation the von Šliks were reducing poverty.

---

[5]According to Cantelon, Joachimsthalers were first minted in 1519 [p. 41 of 191].

[6]There was an earlier version of silver coins called Guldengroschen, mass-produced starting in 1486 by Sigismund, then Archduke of Tirol, from silver deposits discovered in Schwaz [546].

Thaler, to daler, to dollar.   Due to their reliable silver content, thalers circulated around the continent, and to the English colonies in the New World. The coins remained mostly the same, but the name changed as local rulers renamed them in their own languages. They were called "tolars" in Slovenia [546], "Reichsthalers" in Germany, "rigsdalers" in Scandinavia, "rijksdaalders" in Holland, and "talers" in Poland [p. 41 of 191]. The US version was named after the Dutch leeuwendaler, or daler for short [547]. Interestingly, the English colonies in North America did not adopt the dollar from England but from Spain. Under the Spanish monetary reform of 1497, silver *reals* became the Spanish units of account, and became known as Spanish dollars due to their similarity in weight and fineness to thalers [193].

After the English colonists in the thirteen states in North America separated politically from King George in the 1770s, they too began printing money in the form of silver coins named dollars, and those dollars continued to grease the skids of commerce and lift people out of poverty. By the time of the Gold Standard Act of March 14, 1900, the dollars had evolved from 1/1.2929 of a Troy ounce of silver to 1/20.672 of a Troy ounce of gold (twenty-five and eight-tenths grains of gold nine-tenths fine) [**CHAP. 41**, Sec. 1 of 320, 457],[7] but other than that, they had not changed. By governmental definition, these dollars were still a certain weight of a certain material. People were still printing them and using them to obtain shelter, food, and other goods and services.

Although the dollars continued to work well, when the collective took control of them their demise was already baked into the cake, so to speak. When the colonists rebelled against King George, they had decided the collective of them, or the committee, was the sovereign, not the king. With this power in mind, they went about establishing a national government with the ratification of the Constitution, not realizing they had set in motion a machine that always needs more

---

[7]The definition of a US dollar changed from a fixed weight of silver to a fixed weight of gold partly because of gold's superior durability, partly because silver is considered by most to be less beautiful than gold, and partly because it is less scarce than gold. These superior qualities make gold a more desirable monetary asset, resulting in prices in silver of 15 times or more than in gold during the time of the Republic of these fifty states (for example if you can buy a nice suit for an ounce of gold it would cost you 15 ounces or more of silver). Incidentally, this causes silver to have an important disadvantage compared to gold for a spendthrift government—it is more expensive to transport from one fractional-reserve bank to another when attempting to quash systemic bank runs [p. 210 of 185].

money.[8] They had decided it was a good idea to burden themselves with a national government that could print money, with a monopoly on that ability, and then spend it.

At least the people who stood to profit thought it was a good idea. It was speculators in Continentals and land, and artisans in the cities, who made the decision. The majority of the people in the thirteen states didn't want a national government but got it anyway, with the help of a lot of dirty tricks [207]. That wise majority had a good reason for not wanting a national government—they knew, in one way or another, the story of Pharaoh and his money, meaning the story of money and rulers. They knew, as do we, rulers had discovered a long time ago the trick to easy parasitism over a large group of people is to make them use the money they, and they alone, print. This is the reason for the draconian control by the collective over the printing of anything possibly construable as a US dollar. As related in the earlier discussion of tax and legal tender statutes (Chapter 9), rulers have discovered the easy way to make people use their money is to (1) force them to cut the ruler in on their commerce with a percentage (tax them) in terms of the ruler's money; and (2) monopolize dispute resolution services and only uphold contracts written in terms of the ruler's money. Still later, with the founding of the Federal Reserve System in 1913, they figured out how to sneak new money into the system without the people noticing and causing a hyperinflationary runaway by dumping their money.

The following is the version of the story of Pharaoh and his money the author received from a Russian friend, after they'd discussed the topic of money and funny money, causing her to remember it. From the author's notes: "She related the story to Kratos. She said the voluntary slavery story came from the mythology realm. That Pharaoh is not a literal title; it's simply a way to imagine the situation in the example of building a pyramid. But it could be referred to any mythology, Greek or Roman. The point is world democracy comes from daemon Kratiy making it into human life."

    THE LEGEND OF VOLUNTARY SLAVERY "Look," said Pharaoh Kratiy to the priests, "there are long chains of slaves and each of them carries a stone. . . They are guarded by many soldiers. The more slaves, the better for the state—so we always

---

[8]This machine operates through the dynamics of people voting themselves money as described in Chapter 3.

believed. But, the more slaves, the more we have to fear their rebellion. We strengthen the protection. We are compelled to feed our slaves well, otherwise, they will not be able to perform heavy physical work. But they are all the same, lazy and inclined to rebellion". . . "See how slowly they move, and the lazy guard does not drive them with whips and does not hit, even healthy and strong slaves. But, they will move much faster. They will not need a guard. The guards will also become slaves. You can do this like this. Let today, before sunset, the heralds will spread the decree of Pharaoh, which will say: 'With the dawn of the new day, all the slaves are given complete freedom. For every stone delivered to the city, a free person will receive one coin. Coins can be exchanged for food, clothing, housing, a palace in the city and the city itself. From now on you are free people!" In the morning of the next day, the priests and Pharaoh again ascended to the platform of the artificial mountain. The picture, which appeared to their gaze, was amazing. Thousands of people, former slaves, raced with the same stones as before. Losing sweat, many carried two stones. Others, who were one by one, fled, picking up dust. Some guards also dragged stones. People who considered themselves free—because they removed the shackles, sought to get as much as possible coveted coins to build their own happy life. Kratiy spent several months on his site, watching with satisfaction the events below. And the changes were enormous. Some of the slaves joined together in small groups, built carts and, loading up stones, sweating later, pushed these carts. "They still have a lot of adaptations to make," Kratiy thought with satisfaction, "and now internal services have appeared: peddlers of water and food. . . Soon they will choose their chiefs and judges. Let them choose: they, after all, consider themselves free, but the essence—has not changed, they, still, carry stones. . ."

In Russian, democracy is pronounced de mo kratia. That powerful creature that rules the enslaved humans is named de mon kratiy.

Like Pharaoh's slaves, the colonists too had recently experienced a king making them build his "pyramids" by forcing them to use his money (British sterlings in the form of Bank of England notes[9]) to obtain shelter and food, something they were in no mood to experience again. This was in addition to all the other slights, such as being forced to quarter the king's soldiers and submit to arbitrary searches and seizures, all without even the fig leaf of representation in parliament. The colonists rightly wanted to spend their hard-earned money on themselves, and knew a national government exposed them to the danger of national slave money. They knew even a representative government, chained down by a constitution, exposed them to the risk of enslavement through use of the monopoly money trick as theirs soon did. Although the colonist's federal government monopoly money worked pretty well for a while, and in many ways continues to work well in modern times, it wasn't a good idea to have a national government with a money printing monopoly. Even at this late date in the history of our gold US dollars, one can use a relatively attainable number of claims on them, meaning dollar *bills*, to purchase an iPhone or an airplane ride to the ends of the earth; but as we all know, purchasing enough US dollar *bills* to pay rent and buy groceries isn't always easy.

The 1934 Gold Reserve Act. Thanks to our money production monopoly, We, the People, are in over our heads. In 1934, in a step reminiscent of the 270-year, 98 percent decline in the silver content of the Roman *denarius* [551], the collective shrunk each gold US dollar from 1/20.672 of an ounce of gold to 1/35 of an ounce.[10] Through this artifice, the funds available for federal government spending expanded by 100((1/20.672)/(1/35)-1)=69 percent.

Each gold US dollar shrank by 41 percent, in what was effectively a modern bureaucratic coin-clipping exercise (Figure B.1). This coin-clipping exercise began when the people's representatives in Congress

---

[9]When the Rothschilds' bank discovered the Colonies were issuing their own money, called colonial scrip, it caused the English Parliament to pass a bill preventing English colonies from issuing their own money [ch. 11 of 206, p. 98 of 548], subsequently ruining the colonists [549]. Thomas Jefferson reported the colonists wouldn't have thought of separating from the King if not for the money dispute [p. 96 of 550]. Ben Franklin said the colonists wouldn't have sweated the tea tax if only they could have continued using their colonial scrip [p. 99 of 548].

[10]As noted in Chapters 17 and 25, this was in addition to previous coin-clipping, changing a US dollar from 1/19.3939 [**CHAP. XVI**, Sec. 9 of 187] to 1/20.6897 of an ounce of gold [p. 131 of 185, **CHAP. XCV**, Sec. 1 of 188], and subsequently to 1/20.672 [**CHAP. 41**, Sec. 1 of 320, 457] (Figure 17.1).

voted to pass the Gold Reserve Act bill, requiring the new weight of a
US gold dollar to be set at less than 60 percent of its previous weight of
1/20.672 oz. [SEC. 12 of 3]. President Roosevelt completed the exercise
by signing the bill into statutory law on January 30, 1934, then changing
the definition of a US dollar to a 35th of an ounce of gold the following
day, with Proclamation 2072 [183, 517, 518, 552, 553]. This was the
beginning of the end for our venerable gold US dollars.

Figure B.1. *Gold Reserve Act of 1934 and Presidential Proclamation 2072
devalued our gold US dollars by 41 percent, increasing the US dollar
supply by 69 percent. The 1/35 oz. coin on the right side is 59 percent of
the size of the 1/20.672 oz. coin on the left. (Gold coin image courtesy of
WikiImages from Pixabay.)*

Presidential Proclamation 2072 was signed after preparations carried
out the prior year. Only a few months earlier, on April 5 of 1933,
Presidential Executive Order 6102 [183, 554] forced all individuals to
give their gold dollars to the collective[11] for safekeeping, under the
threat of federal criminal indictment, conviction, and incarceration
for 10 years in a federal penitentiary.[12] For each dollar an individual
turned in to the collective's agents in the federal government, he or

---

[11]From Section 2 of Executive Order 6102: "All persons are hereby required to deliver
on or before May 1, 1933, to a Federal Reserve Bank or branch all gold coin, gold
bullion and gold certificates now owned by them."

[12]At that time, the collective also defaulted on its debt by henceforth paying individuals
for their treasury bonds and bills in irredeemable paper money. The holders of those

she was given a receipt, known as a dollar *bill.* Each dollar at that time was defined as 1/20.672 ounces of gold, and each dollar *bill* was a solemn promise from We, the People, of the United States of America the holder owned 1/20.672 of an ounce of gold in a federal government vault. Subsequently, once the federal government had the people's money, President Roosevelt's Proclamation 2072 changed the solemn promise to 1/35 of an ounce, defrauding the people and inflating the circulating supply of US dollar *bills.*

In a single-digit span of months, the collective had set us up for a hyperinflationary runaway by removing the rate limit on money printing, which was determined by how fast gold bullion could be purchased and gold coins minted. Because all the gold dollars were in the vault and circulating by way of promises to the dollars, meaning dollar *bills,* the possible money printing rate was nearly infinite, limited only by the speed of a paper printing press and the psychological ability of users to trust money whose supply was increasing too fast. This paper printing press has been cranked mightily by our federal government agents,[13] so fast the last connection between the dollar *bills* and the dollars was finally broken in 1971. That break has led directly to our present price runaway problem.

We, the People, are bankrupt.   This final rush toward bankruptcy began in July of 1945, when our federal government agents signed the so-called Bretton Woods Agreement with the other 43 allied nation-states who had won the Second World War [321–323]. The treaty stipulated each of these 44 countries would, in effect, use gold as their national money, even though they would be using their own local paper currency. This was accomplished by each of the Bretton Woods signatory central banks "pegging" their national currency to gold, meaning they would buy or sell US dollar *bills* on the open market with their

---

bonds and bills had purchased them in exchange for the promise of redemption in *specie,* meaning gold [555]. Senator Carter Glass told President Roosevelt on April 27 of 1933 his action was worse than anything Ali Baba's forty thieves had done [p. 43 of 191]. He let Roosevelt know he had done a dishonorable thing by causing the federal government to renege on promises to pay in gold coin the widows and orphans to whom it had sold gold bonds [p. 28 of 186].

[13]From Christopher Whalen's book *Inflated*: "Whether one speaks of the WWI and WWII loans to Europe or the bad foreign debts of the largest banks, Washington's tendency in the twentieth century was to paper over the problem with more debt and inflation" [p. 313 of 208].

national currency to maintain a given US dollar *bill*/(national currency) market ratio, within 1 percent of the official peg. They used US dollar *bills* because per the Bretton Woods Agreement, each dollar *bill* was a receipt for a dollar, where a dollar was 1/35 of an ounce of gold, and therefore buying or selling dollar *bills* was equivalent to buying or selling gold. US dollars were used because most of the world's aboveground gold happened to be in these fifty states at the time. Dollar *bills* were preferred over dollars for settling accounts because it is more expensive to transport gold than paper. The other signatory nation-states agreed to use the dollar *bills* only on the condition our US federal government would "defend" them, meaning it would redeem dollar *bills* for dollars on demand, via the so-called gold window.

By maintaining an approximately constant dollar *bill*/(national currency) ratio, each country was in effect, using gold as their national money. The intent was to eliminate one of the causes of those awful world wars by eliminating the ability of countries to cheat each other economically by printing excess paper money. In the Bretton Woods system, if any country printed too much paper, the open market price of gold in its paper would rise, violating its treaty obligation to peg to gold and undoing its attempt to purchase an unfair amount of real goods and services from another country.

The system never had a chance of working because the collectives in the Bretton Woods signatory countries were spendthrifts, so their central banks tended to print more and more of their local paper currency. This made it difficult to maintain their gold pegs, and to make things worse, many of them were papering over their spending problems with loans from the International Monetary Fund (IMF). The collective We, the People, of the United States was not immune to the spendthrift problem, and through its federal government Department of the Treasury was printing more dollar *bills* than there were dollars (Figure B.2) [556].

The collective We, the People, of the United States, and the collectives of Germany, the United Kingdom, Italy, France, Switzerland, the Netherlands, and Belgium [p. 52 of 186], had to coordinate to maintain the gold peg the same as the other countries, except to maintain the US dollar per US dollar *bill* ratio instead of the US dollar *bill* per (some other national currency) ratio. Per the Bretton Woods Agreement, these collectives were obligated to buy and sell US dollars with US dollar *bills* as needed so the gold US dollar per US dollar *bill* ratio produced by open market traders would stay within 1 percent of 1 [part III of 186].

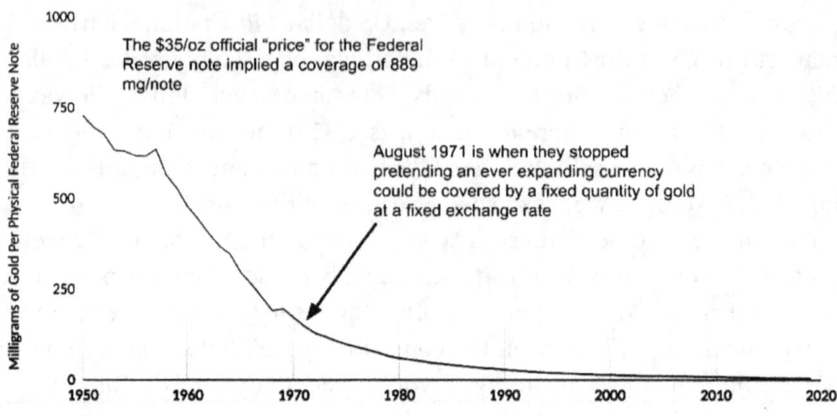

Figure B.2. *Like the Roman denarius. (Plot courtesy of belangp.)*

Because the collective We, the People, of the United States was spending so many US dollar *bills* into circulation, the US dollar per US dollar *bill* ratio wanted to sink and could only be brought back up to par by selling gold US dollars onto the open market. If the treasury didn't sell enough gold US dollars the free market US dollar per US dollar *bill* ratio could sink far enough below 1 to attract currency traders, who would take advantage of the arbitrage opportunity. For example, if the market ratio moved too far below 1, traders might sell US dollar *bills* in exchange for US dollars at the gold window at the price of 1 US dollar per US dollar *bill*, then turn around and buy US dollar *bills* on the open market for a price of less than 1 US dollar per US dollar *bill*. In other words, they would sell dollar *bills* high at the gold window, then buy them low from the market.

At the end of the day, US dollars were leaving We the People's vault, either by selling them in exchange for US dollar *bills* to maintain the gold peg, or by surrendering them to currency traders if not enough were sold. Through those two mechanisms, our out-of-control federal government spending and concurrent dollar *bill* printing was causing gold to flow out of the Fort Knox vault and thus limiting the life span of the Bretton Woods system.

Ironically, part of the reason the collective We, the People, of the United States had such a large spending problem was the Bretton Woods system required the 44 signatory countries to use US dollars, by way of US dollar *bills*, to keep everyone on a gold standard, but for the system to work the other 43 non-USA countries had to get their hands on US

dollars somehow. In an arrangement now known as an exorbitant priv-
ilege, We, the People, of the United States have been getting US dollar
bills to the other 43 Bretton Woods signatory countries by exporting
them in exchange for real goods and services. Those other countries,
in turn, export real goods and services to us in exchange for our paper,
which we increasingly obtain by borrowing, often from the same people
sending us the goods. Economist Robert Triffin identified this dilemma
in 1960, in which the only way for the new global trading system to
work was for the supplier of the world reserve money, We, the People,
to incur large trade deficits, and therefore debt, resulting in monetary
inflation, and therefore price inflation [p. 341 of 208], and therefore the
self-limiting phenomenon of gold exiting the vault.

Thanks to Triffin's dilemma, the Marshall Plan, which resulted in the
collective giving large sums to many of the world's national governments [pp. 21 - 24 of 191], the Korean War, the Vietnam War, President
Johnson's Great Society programs, the space race, and many other programs needing funding, our federal government was sinking into debt
faster and faster, supported by bond sales to the Federal Reserve banks,
who were paying with newly printed Federal Reserve Notes. The excess
paper printing was public knowledge, and as the forties turned into the
fifties and sixties, a run on the bank ensued.

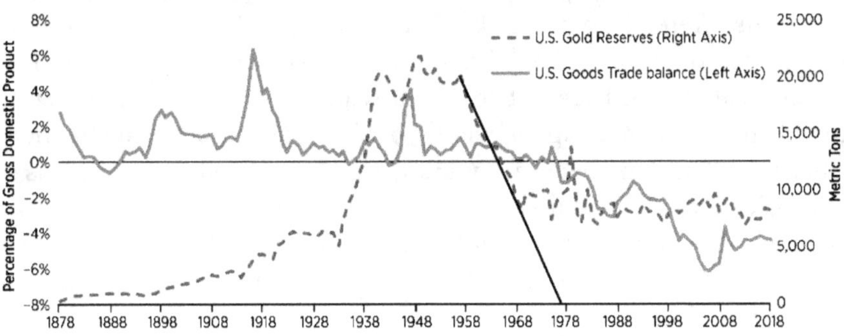

Figure B.3. *Disappearing USA gold hoard. (Plot courtesy of Federal Reserve
Bank of St. Louis.)*

The central banks of the other forty-three Bretton Woods signatory nation-states were making us make good on our promise to "defend" the dollar *bills*. They were putting their dollar *bills* on the counter, and our treasurer was accepting the *bills*, returning their dollars, and thanking them for their business. The other Bretton Woods signatory nation-states were taking their dollars home, meaning our gold was flowing out of the country. The bank run started around 1958,[14] when those central banks began to drain the gold from our vault in earnest (Figure B.3 [557]). The trend was obvious, and something had to be done or the people's treasure would be gone. According to Cantelon, from 1950 to 1971 We the People's gold reserves shrank from 42 percent of the Free World's gold to only 8 percent [p. 9 of 191]. Lips quoted John Exter reporting 13,000 tonnes of gold left our vault during that time [p. 41 of 186].

By 1971, only around 20 percent of the dollar *bills* could be covered. Finally, on the 15th of August, the collective's agent President Nixon "temporarily" suspended redemptions.[15] Nixon said we suspended because of a national emergency, and was telling the truth. If the process had continued until the remaining dollars left the vault, the people in these fifty states might have been excluded from international trade.

In such a case, all would have known we had no money, but instead IOUs for money. One can imagine how a salesman from the Toyota company in Japan might have reacted in such a situation if one of us offered him some US dollar *bills* in exchange for a car—he might say something like, "You want my nice car and you bring me paper? Get out of here!" The world-wide death and turmoil resulting from such a bankruptcy event would have been unspeakably horrific. President Nixon certainly knew that in such a case there was a real risk he would end up hanging by his heels from a lamp post. By saying redemptions were only temporarily suspended, the fiction of the solvency of the collective We, the People, could be maintained, at least for a while.

---

[14]Lips reported the final monetary crisis started in the 1960s when the Federal Reserve Banks succumbed to political pressure from President Kennedy to "get the country moving again" [p. 40 of 186].

[15]President Nixon said the suspension of redemptions was temporary because what else was he supposed to say? We didn't have the money, but we had the guns, so we went easy on the truth. Many decades later, redemptions are still "temporarily" suspended.

In spite of this claim of solvency, however, the collective in fact is not solvent. Due to the collective's ongoing spending problem, many more dollar *bills* have entered circulation since 1971. Market actors have discounted the dollar *bills* relative to dollars so much that in the mid-2020s time frame it costs around 83 US dollar *bills* to buy a US dollar. If a US dollar is 1/42.22 ounces of gold, this is the equivalent of roughly 3,500 dollar *bills* to purchase an ounce of gold. Some have estimated that in a bankruptcy settlement, in which the collective divided the number of dollars in the vault by the number of dollar *bills* outstanding and offered that amount to anyone presenting it dollar *bills*, one's financial haircut might amount to anywhere from 1/300 to 1/3,000 of a dollar redeemed per dollar *bill* presented [194].

Consistent with that estimate, if ~$22 trillion of "broad money" [ch. 15 of 192] is circulating, as indicated by a report on the M2^{16} measure of money supply [458], and we own 7,413.446 tonnes of gold [181], there are 84,130.36 dollar *bills* and electronic claims on them in circulation for every ounce of gold in the vault:

$$\frac{22,000,000,000,000 \text{ dollar } \textit{bills}}{7,413 \text{ tonnes Au} \cdot 2,205\frac{\text{lb}}{\text{tonne}} \cdot 16\frac{\text{oz.}}{\text{lb}}} = 84,130\frac{\text{dollar } \textit{bills}}{\text{oz. Au}}.$$

A smaller haircut estimate can be found by using the Federal Reserve System currency in circulation ("base money" [ch. 15 of 192]) report of ~$2.33T, marked at face value [p. 2 of 558]:

$$\frac{2,325,195,000,000 \text{ dollar } \textit{bills}}{7,413 \text{ tonnes Au} \cdot 2,205\frac{\text{lb}}{\text{tonne}} \cdot 16\frac{\text{oz.}}{\text{lb}}} = 8,910\frac{\text{dollar } \textit{bills}}{\text{oz. Au}}.$$

Now is an excellent time to settle our bankruptcy. If the collective settles its bankruptcy now using M2, or broad money, its creditors will receive only 0.000011886 (1/84,130.36) oz. of gold per dollar *bill* tendered, rather than the amount promised prior to 1934 of 0.048 (1/20.672) oz., a 99.975 percent haircut. Using the Federal Reserve currency in circulation report, or base money, its creditors will receive 0.0001122 (1/8,910.17) oz. of gold per dollar *bill* tendered, for "only" a 99.768 percent haircut. If the collective owns less than 7,413 tonnes of gold [p. 44 of 191], the haircut will be worse, for whatever difference it makes

---

^{16}As noted in the description of Figure 2.1, M2 includes paper dollar bills, coins, savings deposits, and money market funds.

since the haircut is essentially a shave at this point. Referencing the collective's M2 bankruptcy settlement to the original promise of 0.0516 (1/19.3939) oz., and again assuming it owns 7,413 tonnes of gold, will result in a a whopping 99.977 percent haircut for its creditors. We've been kicking this can down the road for many decades now, and as sadly recited in Chapter 1, our situation is dire. Every day We, the People, of these fifty states fail to settle our bankruptcy in gold US dollars and adopt a new and improved version is a another day we get sicker and poorer. Every day we haven't yet adopted our new and improved free entropy US dollars is another day of waiting for our excellent science-fiction future.

C. REQUEST FOR PROPOSAL

THE request for proposal (RFP) from We, the People, might read something like: "Whereas We, the People, of these fifty United States of America endeavor to eliminate global poverty, crime, and environmental degradation quickly and permanently, We hereby request a proposal for the production of money that will achieve that end. It is Our intent for this money to become the latest incarnation of Our US dollars, and to replace Our legacy gold dollars. This money must meet the following requirements:" and then include a formal set of requirements.

Designing and engineering a product and manufacturing it is, in essence, the creation of a prophecy and the deliberate fulfillment of that prophecy by its creator. In other words, engineers and technologists create self-fulfilling prophecies. Engineering and management decide what attributes the to-be-manufactured product should have, which can be thought of as prophecies, and are referred to by engineers as requirements. When the product is built correctly, the prophecy has been fulfilled. In the case of our money, we're going to prophesize the removal of the scourges of poverty, crime, and environmental degradation from our world, and fulfill the prophecy by manufacturing new and improved US dollars that make it happen.

To engineer a high-quality product, a correct, formal set of requirements (prophecies) must be written. Each requirement must have parents, be accompanied by assumptions and rationale, and use the word "shall." Parent requirements are more general than their children, and the purpose of a child requirement is to satisfy its parents. Requirements proceed in tier levels from more general to more specific. Tier 0 is more general than Tier 1, which is more general than Tier 2, and so on.

For example, a commercial airplane manufacturer could choose to produce an airplane competing in the 300–350 seat, 8000 nautical mile (NM) segment; in this case, 300–350 seats, 8000 NM is a Tier 0 level requirement for the yet-to-exist airplane. Thinking in terms of prophecies, it could be said the manufacturer prophesied the existence of a series of airplanes with 300 to 350 seats and a maximum range of 8000 NM. Child requirements become successively more specific, until they finally become specific enough for people to act on them by manufacturing software or hardware. Requirement levels typically do not proceed past Tier 3 since at that level they are usually specific enough to build hardware or software.

The top-level, most general requirement for the proposed entropy money is the money must do good, and to do good it must reduce poverty, crime, and environmental degradation. The following is a proposed formal set of requirements to be issued by We, the People, of the United States of America for our new and improved US dollars. E1 stands for entropy money requirement number 1, and T0 means it is a Tier 0 level requirement, at the top of the requirements tree. All child requirements must aid the money in meeting this parent of the whole tree:

E1 (T0) The money shall do good.

> Assumptions/rationale: Self-evident.
>
> Parent(s): We Spaceship Earthicans.[1]

E2 (T1) The money shall reduce environmental degradation.

> Assumptions/rationale: Reducing environmental degradation is self-evidently good.
>
> Parent(s): E1. The money shall do good.

E3 (T1) The money shall reduce crime.

> Assumptions/rationale:
>
> Reducing crime is self-evidently good.
>
> Reducing crime reduces environmental degradation by reducing damage to people, who are a sacred part of our sacred world, and by freeing their energy previously wasted on defense from their own kind for use in doing good for others, both human and non.
>
> Parent(s): E1. The money shall do good; E2. The money shall reduce environmental degradation.

E4 (T1.5) The money shall reduce poverty.

> Assumptions/rationale:
>
> Reducing poverty is self-evidently good.

---

[1] Thanks to the brilliant writers of *Futurama* for that one.

Reducing poverty reduces environmental degradation by reducing the need for people to work supply chains transforming raw materials into retail goods.

Reducing poverty reduces crime by reducing the poverty motive for crime.

Parent(s): E1. The money shall do good; E2. The money shall reduce environmental degradation; E3. The money shall reduce crime.

E5 (T2) The money shall be scarce.

Assumptions/rationale:

Defining scarcity as the quality of being finite in number, if there were an infinite number of ledger units competing for a scarce, or finite, amount of economic output, all units of economic output would have a price of infinity in those ledger units, and therefore would have no utility in establishing prices, and therefore would not aid in the monetary function of using discovered prices to reduce poverty by enabling the rational allocation of scarce resources. Scarce money, with a finite number of ledger units in circulation, reduces poverty by allowing for the discovery of useful prices, helping people make deals.

Parent(s): E4. The money shall reduce poverty.

E6 (T2) The money shall enter circulation predictably.

Assumptions/rationale:

Predictable entry into circulation aids in the production of predictable prices by reducing price volatility for commodities, including prices of money (interest rates). This improves the success rates of business planning and therefore results in more successful businesses creating income for owners and employees and goods and services for customers, therefore reducing poverty.

Parent(s): E4. The money shall reduce poverty.

E7 (T2) The money shall enter circulation equitably.

Assumptions/rationale:

Equitable entry into circulation reduces poverty by reducing the inflation tax for market participants who are not first receivers of new money.

Parent(s): E4. The money shall reduce poverty.

E8 (T2) The quantity of money in circulation shall be constant. [2]

---

[2]In the present work, we're proposing to use an approximation of the integral of the

Assumptions/rationale:

Keeping the quantity of money in circulation as constant as possible causes the prices of goods and services to become more dependent on the supply of and demand for those goods and services, and less dependent on changes in the quantity of money in circulation. This aids product optimization, which reduces poverty. Poverty is also reduced by shrinking the time, energy, and risk to market participants caused by making money supply-induced price changes and by reacting to money supply-induced price changes made by other market participants.

Parent(s): E4. The money shall reduce poverty.

E9 (T2.0) The money shall be durable.

Assumptions/rationale:

Long shelf life for products used as money reduces poverty by helping users save the fruits of their labor.

Long shelf life for products used as money helps keep the number of ledger units in circulation constant by reducing their numerical shrinkage.

Parent(s): E4. The money shall reduce poverty; E8. The amount of money in circulation shall be constant.

E10 (T2) The money shall be fungible.

Assumptions/rationale:

Fungible money reduces poverty because, if each monetary unit is identical to all the others, the coincidence of wants problem is mitigated. Deals are easier to make if each unit of money can be used without an inspection to ensure face value, which reduces poverty.

Parent(s): E4. The money shall reduce poverty.

E11 (T2) The money shall be divisible.

Assumptions/rationale:

Divisibility in products used as money reduces poverty by increasing the granularity of discovered prices. Increased price

---

last term on the right-hand side of Equation 12.1 as our new and improved, entropy-type US dollars. Since the living beings on land parcels consume low entropy from the sun or deep-sea vents continually, and at an approximately constant rate, the temporal monetary policy of this version of US dollars is for the number of units in circulation to increase linearly, and therefore not meet requirement E8. We can speculate future versions of money may use an approximation of the integral of the term on the left-hand side of the equality, which should result in a monetary policy more closely meeting requirement E8.

granularity increases the ease of making deals by increasing the possibility of making deals fair to all parties. Increasing the ease of making deals makes everyone wealthier.

Parent(s): E4. The money shall reduce poverty.

E12 (T2) The money shall be portable.

Assumptions/rationale:

Portability in products used as money reduces poverty by increasing availability of the money for use in transactions.

Parent(s): E4. The money shall reduce poverty.

E13 (T2) The money shall be easy to use.

Assumptions/rationale:

Ease of use of products used as money reduces poverty by making commerce easier.

Parent(s): E4. The money shall reduce poverty.

E14 (T2) The money shall be popular.

Assumptions/rationale:

Popularity of a product type used as money reduces poverty by enabling the expression of its other monetary properties.

Parent(s): E4. The money shall reduce poverty.

E15 (T2) The money shall be reliable.

Assumptions/rationale:

Reliability of a product designed for use as money reduces poverty by providing assurance to its users their transactions are secure.

Parent(s): E4. The money shall reduce poverty.

E16 (T2) The money shall have low transaction costs.

Assumptions/rationale:

Low transaction costs reduce poverty by reducing costs to users.

Parent(s): E4. The money shall reduce poverty.

E17 (T2) The money shall be not very useful for non-monetary purposes.

Assumptions/rationale:

Products used as money shrink in number less quickly if they are not consumed in non-monetary uses, causing them to remain more constant than otherwise.

Parent(s): E8. The amount of money in circulation shall be constant.

E18 (T2) Each unit of the money shall consist of a fixed quantity of entropy removed from the earth.

Assumptions/rationale:

If something from a land parcel is used as money, people can be expected to voluntarily remove it from the parcel; therefore, if entropy from land parcels is used as money, people can be expected to remove entropy from their parcel(s) voluntarily. Removing entropy from land parcels reduces environmental degradation because the matter and energy in healthy living beings is in a lower entropy arrangement than in less healthy ones.

Paying for the removal of entropy reduces poverty by creating jobs to measure and track the entropy.

Using entropy from the land as money results in a scarce number of ledger units in circulation because the rate of entropy removal from parcels is finite.

Using entropy from the land as money results in predictable entry of new monetary units into circulation because the rate of entropy removed from parcels by the beings living and growing on them is predictable—plant and animal populations are relatively constant, month over month.

Using entropy from land parcels as money causes the total number of units in circulation to increase at an approximately constant rate.

Parent(s): E2. The money shall reduce environmental degradation; E4. The money shall reduce poverty; E5. The money shall be scarce; E6. The money shall enter circulation predictably; E8. The quantity of money in circulation shall be constant.

E19 (T2) The money shall be scaled, at the time of initialization, to provide all of the USA national budget outlay needs from national lands, with the scaling thereafter remaining at the initialized value.

Assumptions/rationale:

Scaling to provide the national budget from national lands reduces environmental degradation by eliminating revenuer-caused stress to the population because it allows for the elimination of federal government revenuers.

Scaling to provide the national budget from national lands reduces environmental degradation by providing all members of We, the People, of the united States of America a non-trivial financial incentive to maintain and improve the health of our national lands.

Scaling to provide the national budget from national lands reduces poverty by freeing up the $409 billion spent every year on "tax compliance" [335] because it allows for the elimination of federal government revenuers.

Parent(s): E2. The money shall reduce environmental degradation; E4. The money shall reduce poverty.

E20 (T2) The money shall exist in a free monetary environment.[3]

Assumptions/rationale:

A free environment enables competition, which continuously improves product quality and reduces product price (but increases product price in the case of money itself) due to users' freedom to substitute, and in addition a free environment eliminates exposure of the money to central points of failure. Improved quality in money will improve its monetary qualities—scarcity, predictable and equitable entry into circulation, constant supply, durability, fungibility, divisibility, portability, ease of use, popularity, reliability, and low transaction cost.

Improvements in entropy money (requirement E18) will increase the accuracy of entropy measurements as well as the benefits to us all produced by entropy data to monetary payout conversions.

Parent(s): E5. The money shall be scarce; E6. The money shall enter circulation predictably; E7. The money shall enter circulation equitably; E8. The quantity of money in circulation shall be constant; E9. The money shall be durable; E10. The money shall be fungible; E11. The money shall be divisible; E12. The money shall be portable; E13. The money shall be easy to use; E14. The money shall be popular; E15. The money shall be reliable; E16. The money shall have low transaction costs; E18. Each unit of the money shall consist of a fixed amount of entropy removed from the earth.

E21 (T2.5) The money shall be the new incarnation of our US dollars.

Assumptions/rationale:

We, the People, of the United States of America are bankrupt in our gold US dollars. This bankruptcy is causing poverty, crime,

---

[3]A waiting period before repealing legal tender statutes will give everyone time to establish a Schelling point [543] for their money before turning it over to the evolutionary process produced by market competition. A Schelling point for money is a real-world tautology in which people use things as money because others are using those things as money. Further discussion of this concept is included in Appendix B.

and environmental degradation. Settling the gold bankruptcy is therefore necessary, but to transition without causing more problems our gold US dollars must be replaced. Taking the logical step of transitioning to new and improved money is most easily accomplished by making the new money into the newest version of our US dollars, which enables popularity.

Parent(s): E14. The money shall be popular.

E22 (T2.5) Anglo-Saxon-American customary law traditions shall apply to the money.

Assumptions/rationale:

The use of entropy as money (requirement E18) is intended to reduce environmental degradation and poverty by creating a positive feedback loop between the health of our living biological and human financial worlds, making what is good for one good for the other. This positive feedback loop is established when the parties who control the parcel and therefore have the power to affect parcel health, the owner(s), are the parties who receive payment for parcel health. In the same way the owner of a land parcel owns any gold mined from it, the application of Anglo-Saxon-American customary law traditions to the money will cause the owner of the parcel to be the owner of any entropy mined from it, maximizing entropy removal rates and therefore minimizing environmental degradation.

Paying landowners for the entropy from their parcels causes new money to enter circulation relatively equitably because everyone is economically relatively close to new money when it enters circulation, in turn because there are many owners of parcels, including individuals, families, tribal organizations, companies, cities, counties, states, provinces, prefectures, and nation-states. Paying land parcel owners for the entropy from their parcel allows We, the People, of these fifty united States of America to eliminate their national taxes by scaling the entropy to cover their entire national budget.

Applying Anglo-Saxon-American customary law traditions to the money is necessary for it to exist in a free monetary environment because those traditions do not proscribe the peaceful transfer of property, including monetary property.

Parent(s): E2. The money shall reduce environmental degradation; E7. The money shall enter circulation equitably; E19. The money shall be scaled, at the time of initialization, to provide all of the USA national budget outlay needs from national lands, with the scaling thereafter remaining at the initialization value; E20. The money shall exist in a free monetary environment.

E23 (T2.5) The money shall be tracked on either a fork of, or a virtual machine operating under, the *retail* bitcoin network, also known as the digital cash (https://www.dash.org/) network.

Assumptions/rationale:

Tracking the money on a fork from *retail* bitcoin reduces poverty by giving the collective of We, the People, of these fifty united States of America incentive to purchase *retail* bitcoin to provoke a front run by everyone else, thus reducing poverty due to the front run and due to owning entropy-type US dollars immediately upon the transition from gold US dollars to entropy-type US dollars.

Durability, fungibility, divisibility, portability, ease of use, reliability, low transaction costs, and uselessness for non-monetary purposes are all provided by using the *retail* bitcoin network software.

Parent(s): E4. The money shall reduce poverty; E9. The money shall be durable; E10. The money shall be fungible; E11. The money shall be divisible; E12. The money shall be portable; E13. The money shall be easy to use; E15. The money shall be reliable; E16. The money shall have low transaction costs; E17. The money shall be not very useful for non-monetary purposes.

Requirements E20 and E21 will be met when the collective We the People's employee/agents in our federal government respond appropriately to our MOAs. Requirement E22 will be met by a politically energized and newly independence-minded populace newly aware of the importance of the protection of law.

Requirements for our new and improved US dollars from responsive proposals. Proposals responding to these requirements from We, the People, could include the following requirements:

M1 (T2.5) The entropy removed from the earth shall be measured.

Assumptions/rationale:

Products intended for use as money must be measured to be scarce in number.

Entropy from land must be measured to use it as money.

Parent(s): E5. The money shall be scarce; E18. The money shall consist of a fixed amount of entropy removed from the earth.

M2 (T2.5) The measurement of entropy obtained shall be tracked in a ledger entry spendable by the lawful owner of the given land parcel.

Assumptions/rationale:

Anglo-Saxon-American customary law traditions protect land ownership, which protects ownership of entropy removed from the parcel. Therefore, it is lawful and proper to credit any removed entropy to the lawful owner of the land parcel.

Parent(s): E22. Anglo-Saxon-American law traditions shall apply to the money; M1. The entropy removed from the earth shall be measured.

M3 (T2.5) The measurement of entropy removed from a land parcel shall be approximated by measurements of the health of the beings living on that parcel.

Assumptions/rationale:

The matter and energy in healthy living beings is in a lower entropy arrangement than that in less healthy ones. Therefore the health of the living beings on the land can be used as a proxy for the entropy of the land.

Parent(s): M1. The entropy removed from the earth shall be measured.

M4 (T2.5) The measurements of the health of the beings living on the land shall be approximated by measurements of their respiration rates.

Assumptions/rationale:

Respiration rate is one of the most important indicators of health.

Parent(s): M3. The measurement of entropy removed from a land parcel shall be approximated by measurements of the health of the beings living on that parcel.

M5 (T3) The measurements of the respiration rates of the beings living on a land parcel shall be approximated by measurements of the oxygen produced by that parcel.

Assumptions/rationale:

The respiration of plants and animals exists in a feedback loop in which oxygen molecules flow from plants to animals and carbon dioxide molecules flow from animals to plants. Therefore, a measurement of either yields an approximation of the respiration of all the living beings on the land.[4]

Parent(s): M4. The measurements of the health of the beings living on the land shall be approximated by measurements of their respiration rates.

M6 (T3) The measurements of oxygen production shall be scaled such that the parcel's synergistic contribution to planetary health is maximized.

Assumptions/rationale:

A measurement of entropy removal can be inaccurate if respiration only is considered. To ensure accurate measurement of entropy, land health measurements should consider multiple factors. For example, an owner of desert land could raze the living desert and irrigate with ground or river water to grow high-respiration plants, to the detriment of the "natural" ecosystem and thus to planetary health. Alternatively, an owner of forest land could raze the "natural" forest and plant a mono-crop, again to the detriment of planetary health, or a landowner could attempt to get credit for plant respiration on the same parcel with a fur farm where dogs and cats are skinned alive, in a crime against all living beings.

Parent(s): E18. The money shall consist of a fixed amount of entropy removed from the earth; M5. The measurements of the respiration rates of the beings living on a land parcel shall be approximated by measurements of the oxygen produced by that parcel.

---

[4]This requirement could be modified to use carbon dioxide sequestered rather than oxygen produced while continuing to satisfy all its parents. This would allow the new money to give us all a way to both pay people to help the living creatures on their land parcels *and* pay for other methods of capturing and sequestering or using CO_2. This could help those who are exploring the potential of the Samail Ophiolite in Oman, and other ophiolites around the world [559], along with minerals such as basalt and olivine-rich dunite [560], to absorb large amounts of carbon dioxide [561]. It is known, for example, that the magnesium and calcium in the Oman Ophiolite alone is capable of sequestering the entirety of human carbon dioxide production for hundreds of years [562]. On page 126 of *Symphony in C*, Hazen notes the rulers of Oman aren't yet interested in sequestering carbon dioxide because there's no money in it for them. Properly tuned entropy money solves this problem of our existing political world [232] by helping them get paid to sequester carbon dioxide. Companies measuring the carbon content of soil, such as Boomitra [563], could also provide carbon sequestration measurements.

M7 (T3) The money shall be scaled so 30 grams[5] of oxygen produced by a given land parcel is one US dollar.[6]

Assumptions/rationale:

If every 30 grams of oxygen produced by the national lands of We, the People, of the United States is a dollar, those national lands will produce enough oxygen US dollars to fund the entire federal government yearly budget.

Parent(s): E19. The money shall be scaled, upon initialization, to provide all of the USA national budget needs from national lands, with the scaling thereafter remaining at the initialization value; M5. The measurements of respiration of the beings living on the land shall be approximated by measurements of oxygen produced by that land.

---

[5]Educated guesses were used to produce this value (see Equation 12.3). A correct and up-to-date value must be computed immediately prior to the changeover from gold to oxygen.

[6]This requirement can be adjusted if requirement M5 is changed to C or CO_2.

D. CLASSICAL AND STATISTICAL THERMODYNAMICS ENTROPY

NTROPY is a measurable physical property most commonly associated with a state of disorder or randomness. In the Classical thermodynamics sense, the entropy of the matter and energy on a parcel can be thought of as the amount of energy on the parcel not available to do work. Using that meaning, a physical example of energy being used up and no longer available to do work is the potential energy stored in a lump of coal used to power an old-fashioned railway engine. If the coal gets turned into ash in the process of burning it to boil water and move the train, that energy, while still in existence, has done work and can't do any more. The potential energy available in the coal has been turned into the kinetic energy of the moving train, along with waste heat and sonic noise; the ash can't be burned again to move the train further.

Classical thermodynamics entropy has the dimensions of mass times length, times length, divided by time, divided by time, divided by temperature $\left(\frac{\text{mass} \cdot \text{length}^2}{\text{time}^2 \cdot \text{temperature}}\right)$, and is expressed in units of Joules per Kelvin in the SI, or International System of Units. Using the Clausius definition in the Classical thermodynamics paradigm, if an amount of heat Q flows into a large heat reservoir at temperature T above absolute zero, the entropy increase is $\Delta S = Q/T$. In the Classical thermodynamics sense of the second law of thermodynamics, sometimes called the entropy law, heat only moves from hotter objects to colder ones, never in reverse, at least not without supplying additional unused energy. This means the energy available to do work always decreases as temperatures everywhere tend to equalize, eliminating the possibility for work to be done. The second law of thermodynamics states a system is in a thermodynamic equilibrium if its free energy (the energy available to do work) is at an absolute minimum. As global entropy, meaning the entropy of the entire universe, is the amount of energy no longer available to do work, this is another way of saying global entropy always increases until thermodynamic equilibrium is reached—at this point, there is no more free energy. The ultimate result of this process is the temperature of everything is absolute zero, and no work can be done—often referred to as the heat death of the universe.[1]

The fact global entropy always increases is also the basis of the impossibility of a perpetual motion machine as some of the energy needed to move parts is always used up without contributing to their motion. For example, when a pendulum is pulled to one side and released, its maximum angle at the other side will be less than its starting angle on the first side—never greater than and never equal to. Even in a vacuum, with the lowest friction load-bearing surfaces ever, some of its kinetic energy will be used to heat the pivot joint and will therefore no longer be available to move the weight. As some have said, we're playing in the big casino of the universe, where you can't win, you can't break even, and you can't stop playing.

The perception of time itself could be one of the ways we humans have learned to sense the effects of the second law. We can see the world wearing out right in front of our eyes, especially in the mirror for those who've made it past twenty years old. In the Classical thermodynamics sense, the matter and energy in living beings on a parcel of living land is in a lower state of entropy than the matter and energy in a land of only rocks because the living beings themselves contain unused energy that can do work, whereas the rocks don't, at least not in the same magnitude.

The entropy of the matter and energy on a parcel can also be considered in the statistical thermodynamics sense in which the entropy is the same as the thermodynamic probability [p. 7 of 324], a concept introduced by Ludwig Boltzmann. Statistical thermodynamics provides a quantitative link between the properties of microscopic particles and their macroscopic behaviors. It provides a methodology to compute statistical properties of systems with very large numbers of particles

---

[1]Technically, global entropy increases once you get past the big bang, assuming that's how it all started. Terence McKenna reportedly pointed out we only need the one free miracle of the big bang, and then we can explain the rest. All we need do is get the matter and energy of the universe in a state of low entropy at the big bang—after that the second law holds.

moving in three dimensions, such as the air molecules in a room, the crystals in iron, or the molecules making up the reader. For example, it can be used to compute the average energy of the molecules of air in a room (temperature) or their average momentum (pressure). Statistical thermodynamics methods can be used to predict the temperature-dependent distribution of molecules in different energy levels in a closed system (the Boltzmann distribution). It allows for the solutions of problems intractable using Classical mechanics methods. For example, using Classical mechanics methods to predict the properties of air molecules in a room requires computation and tracking of the positions, velocities, and accelerations of on the order of 10^{24} particles. Statistical thermodynamics theory can use the properties of microscopic particles to predict macroscopic relationships, such as the ideal gas law, $PV = nRT$, whereas such relationships must be found experimentally using the theory of Classical thermodynamics. Using the statistical thermodynamics paradigm, the entropy, or thermodynamic probability, of an isolated gas of N molecules is $Entropy = S = ln\,W$, where $W = \dfrac{N!}{N_1!N_2!...N_s!}$, and N_i is the distribution of the gas molecules of state i [p. 7 of 324].

By thermodynamic probability we mean, for example, the chance one could put all the material elements making up you, meaning such-and-such ounces of carbon, so many ounces of hydrogen, that many of oxygen, and so on, in a stirred vat, and by pure random luck have you step out. That chance is small, while the chance of creating some uniform mix of gases, liquids, and solids from those elements is large. If the thermodynamic probability is the entropy, the entropy of the uniform mix is higher than the entropy of the same matter and energy if it is arranged as you. The fundamental reasoning behind the statistical thermodynamic paradigm is there are very many ways to arrange the atoms of you into a uniform mix, but very few ways to arrange them in the form of you. For an everyday example, the thermodynamic probability of the intact glass in your hand is lower than that of the same glass after you dropped it on the floor and it broke into a million shards of glass. While no laws of the physics of moving objects prevent the shards from randomly forming back into a glass, in the statistical thermodynamics sense such an event is so unlikely it is never seen. Statistically, there are more ways to arrange the atoms of the glass into broken shards than into a glass. In a not-so-everyday example of thermodynamic probability sometimes joked about among science nerds, according to the principles of statistical thermodynamics all the randomly moving molecules of air in the room you're in could randomly end up in the corner of the room, causing you to suffocate. Boltzmann's disciples claim if you wait around long enough this will actually happen, but in the meantime the thermodynamic probability of the air molecules when they're not all in the corner is much higher than when they're in the corner, and thus the molecules are usually scattered fairly evenly in the room so we can breathe. Again statistically, there are more ways to arrange the air molecules in the volume of the room than in the volume of the corner.

Figure D.1. *Higher entropy on Mars (left) or the earth's moon (center) than on the earth (right). (Images courtesy of WikiImages and Joshua Woroniecki from Pixabay.)*

As for a parcel of land that has been razed for raw materials, the probability of the arrangement of the materials on that parcel is higher than the probability of the arrangement of the materials on a healthy parcel. For example, there are a certain number of ways to arrange a collection of silicon, oxygen, iron, aluminum, and the other atoms rocks are made of into rocks on a razed parcel, but far fewer ways to arrange the atoms that make up plants and animals into plants and animals.[2] In general, the number of ways to arrange the matter and energy of a healthy parcel of land while keeping it healthy is lower than the number of ways to arrange the matter and energy of a less healthy parcel of land while keeping it less healthy.

---

[2]With some of us humans, it seems there may be only a very few ways of arranging the matter and energy in our bodies when we think amazing and sublime thoughts. For example, when Wolfgang Mozart would compose complex and beautiful musical pieces in his head [p. 423 of 564], or when the logician Kurt Gödel worked through the infinite regression of the liar's paradox on his way to discovering a proof of his incompleteness theorem, the probability of the arrangements of the matter and energy constituting those individuals had to have been vanishingly small.

Pictures of the surfaces of Mars and the earth's moon juxtaposed with the surface of the earth offer a graphic illustration of lower and higher entropy land (Figure D.1). The matter and energy on an acre of the earth's surface is in a lower entropy arrangement than the matter and energy on an acre of the surface of the moon or Mars. If enough entropy were removed from an acre on the surface of Mars or the moon, it could end up looking more like an acre on the earth.

E. UNIVERSAL BASIC INCOME

Figure E.1. *Spaceship Earth, our only home. Let's buy her a good future. (Photograph courtesy of NASA on Unsplash.)*

WHEN we propose our cities, counties, states, provinces, prefectures, and nation-states be paid for the breathable air produced by their parks, what we're really proposing is each of us in those geographic territories be paid, meaning we're all getting a type of universal basic income (UBI). Those are our parks—We, the People, of each city, county, state, prefecture, province, nation-state, etc., could choose to distribute our entropy money to the individuals of the groups as a UBI, if We were to become so inclined. The way We, the People, take specific actions is the group of us, or the committee, hires employees to do work for us. Distributing the new revenue stream from those parks to us individuals is one of the actions we could have our government employees take.

We, the People, of every polity could also choose to spend less and/or plant more trees and distribute even more revenue to us individuals, in an even bigger UBI. As noted previously, if We, the People, of these fifty states choose to let our federal government revenuers go, we could also choose to pay out the resulting savings to us individuals, too, in a national-level UBI. Entropy money gives citizens options for distributing their new financial windfalls, and motivation to direct their government employees to plant more trees, cut down fewer, and spend less money (Figure E.1).

Works Cited

[1]   Stanford University Libraries (2025). *What is Spaceship Earth?* Stanford University. URL: https://exhibits.stanford.edu/bucky/feature/what-is-spaceship-earth (visited on 04/20/2025) (cit. on p. xiv).

[2]   Kowalski, K. (2025). *What is Spaceship Earth? & Why It's Time Humanity Gets "On Board"*. SLOWW. URL: https://www.sloww.co/spaceship-earth/ (visited on 05/12/2025) (cit. on pp. xiv, 49).

[3]   73rd Congress (Jan. 1934). *Gold Reserve Act of 1934*. United States of America Federal Government. URL: https://fraser.stlouisfed.org/files/docs/historical/congressional/goldreserveact1934.pdf (visited on 02/03/2025) (cit. on pp. xv, 70, 138, 198, 231).

[4]   Parsson, J. O. (2011). *Dying of Money*. Indianapolis, IN: Dogear Publishing (cit. on pp. 3, 45, 49).

[5]   Fergusson, A. (2010). *When Money Dies*. First Edition. New York: PublicAffairs (cit. on pp. 3, 45, 49).

[6]   Stansberry, P. (2017). *The American Jubilee*. Ed. by Gwynallen, F. Baltimore, Maryland: Stansberry Research (cit. on pp. 3, 7).

[7]   Wolff, E. N. (Nov. 2017). "Has Middle Class Wealth Recovered?" In: *ASSA Meetings*. URL: https://www.nber.org/papers/w24085 (visited on 02/03/2025) (cit. on p. 3).

[8]   Martin, E. (Jan. 2018). *Only 39% of Americans have enough savings to cover a $1,000 emergency*. CNBC. URL: https://www.cnbc.com/2018/01/18/few-americans-have-enough-savings-to-cover-a-1000-emergency.html (visited on 02/03/2025) (cit. on p. 3).

[9]   Carmody, M. (Feb. 2019). *What caused hyperinflation in Venezuela: a rare blend of public ineptitude and private enterprise*. TheConversation.com. URL: https://theconversation.com/what-caused-hyperinflation-in-venezuela-a-rare-blend-of-public-ineptitude-and-private-enterprise-102483 (visited on 02/03/2025) (cit. on p. 3).

[10]   Smith, C. H. (May 2018a). *Burrito Index Update: Burrito Cost Triples, Official Inflation Up 43% from 2001*. Of Two Minds. URL: https://www.oftwominds.com/blogmay18/burrito-update5-18.html (visited on 02/03/2025) (cit. on p. 3).

[11]   —   (Apr. 2019). *America's Forced Financial Flight: Fleeing Unaffordable and Dysfunctional Cities*. Of Two Minds. URL: https://www.oftwominds.com/blogapr19/forced-flight4-19.html (visited on 02/03/2025) (cit. on p. 3).

[12]   Taggart, D. (July 2019). *Most Americans Can't Afford to Pay Rent, Eat Food, Buy Stuff, or Get Sick (And It's Just Going to Get WORSE)*. The Organic Prepper. URL: https://www.theorganicprepper.com/americans-cant-pay-rent-eat-food-buy-stuff-or-get-sick/ (visited on 02/03/2025) (cit. on p. 3).

[13]   Hickel, J. (Jan. 2019). *Bill Gates says poverty is decreasing. He couldn't be more wrong*. The Guardian. URL: https://www.theguardian.com/commentisfree/2019

/jan/29/bill-gates-davos-global-poverty-infographic-neoliberal/ (visited on 02/03/2025) (cit. on p. 3).

[14] Dickler, J. (Feb. 2023). *60% of Americans live paycheck to paycheck — 'inflation is part of their everyday lives,' expert says.* CNBC. URL: https://www.cnbc.com /2023/02/28/amid-stubborn-inflation-60percent-of-americans-live-paycheck-to -paycheck.html (visited on 02/03/2025) (cit. on p. 3).

[15] Mish (Apr. 2023). *70 Percent of Americans are Financially Stressed, 58 Percent Live Paycheck to Paycheck.* The Arena Group. URL: https://mishtalk.com/econo mics/70-percent-of-americans-are-financially-stressed-58-percent-live-payche ck-to-paycheck (visited on 02/03/2025) (cit. on p. 3).

[16] Snyder, M. (Nov. 2023a). *The Bottom 80% Has Gotten Significantly Poorer Since The Pandemic Began, And This Is Creating A "Robin Hood Mentality" All Over America.* The Economic Collapse. URL: https://theeconomiccollapseblog.com /the-bottom-80-has-gotten-significantly-poorer-since-the-pandemic-began- and-this-is-creating-a-robin-hood-mentality-all-over-america/ (visited on 02/03/2025) (cit. on p. 3).

[17] Nickson, E. (Jan. 2024a). *Our Enemies Walk Among Us.* Substack. URL: https://el izabethnickson.substack.com/p/our-enemies-walk-among-us-225 (visited on 02/03/2025) (cit. on p. 3).

[18] Feeney, M. (June 2024). *The rise of California's vanlords.* URL: https://unherd.c om/2024/06/the-rise-of-californias-vanlords/ (visited on 02/03/2025) (cit. on p. 3).

[19] Aguirre, F. (2009). *Surviving the Economic Collapse.* Buenos Aires: Fernando Acquirre. ISBN: 978-987-05-6345-7 (cit. on pp. 3, 5, 45).

[20] Kendall, M. (Feb. 2024). *It's now significantly more deadly to be homeless. Why are so many people dying?* Cal Matters. URL: https://calmatters.org/housing/ho melessness/2024/02/homeless-mortality-report/ (visited on 02/03/2025) (cit. on pp. 3, 7).

[21] Polanski, R. (1968). *Rosemary's Baby.* Motion picture. Horror drama film, 136 minutes, released June 12, 1968. Based on the novel "Rosemary's Baby" by Ira Levin. Score by Krzysztof Komeda. Hollywood, California. URL: https://www.i mdb.com/title/tt0063522/ (visited on 07/06/2025) (cit. on p. 4).

[22] Birnbaum, D. (July 2024). *Don't Think Hyperinflation Can Happen In The U.S.? Not So Fast.* Forbes. URL: https://www.forbes.com/sites/davidbirnbaum/2024/0 7/12/dont-think-hyperinflation-can-happen-in-the-us-not-so-fast/ (visited on 02/03/2025) (cit. on p. 4).

[23] Toscano, P. (Feb. 2011). *The Worst Hyperinflation Situations of All Time.* CNBC. URL: https://www.cnbc.com/2011/02/14/The-Worst-Hyperinflation-Situations- of-All-Time.html (visited on 02/03/2025) (cit. on p. 4).

[24] Eicholz, H. (Dec. 2014). *The Currency of Destruction.* Law & Liberty. URL: https: //lawliberty.org/the-currency-of-destruction/ (visited on 02/03/2025) (cit. on pp. 4, 5).

[25] Taylor, F. (2013). *The Downfall of Money: Germany's Hyperinflation and the Destruction of the Middle Class.* New York: Bloomsbury Press. ISBN: 978-1-62040- 236-8 (cit. on pp. 4, 49).

[26] Keim, B. (Oct. 2019). *Never Underestimate the Intelligence of Trees. Plants com- municate, nurture their seedlings, and get stressed.* NautilusNext Inc. URL: https:

//nautil.us/never-underestimate-the-intelligence-of-trees-237595/ (visited on 03/04/2025) (cit. on p. 5).

[27] Brown Jr., T. (1996). *Grandfather*. New York, New York: Berkley Books. ISBN: 0-425-15593-5 (cit. on p. 5).

[28] Smith, C. H. (Jan. 2025a). *I Quit! The Tsunami of Burnout Few See*. Of Two Minds. URL: https://www.oftwominds.com/blogjan25/quit-burnout1-25.html (visited on 02/03/2025) (cit. on p. 5).

[29] Read, L. E. (1958). *I, Pencil: My Family Tree as Told to Leonard E. Read*. Foundation for Economic Education (cit. on pp. 5, 65, 74, 125).

[30] Mullen, T. (Aug. 2018). *I, Interest Rate*. Foundation for Economic Freedom. URL: https://fee.org/articles/i-interest-rate/ (visited on 03/07/2025) (cit. on pp. 5, 17, 19).

[31] Boyce, J. K. (Nov. 2018). "The Environmental Cost of Inequality." In: *Sci. Am.* 319.5, p. 72. ISSN: 0036-8733. DOI: 10.1038/scientificamerican1118-72 (cit. on p. 6).

[32] Duraiappah, A. K. (Dec. 1998). "Poverty and Environmental Degradation: A Review and Analysis of the Nexus." In: *World Development* 26.12, pp. 2169–79. ISSN: 0305-750X. DOI: 10.1016/S0305-750X(98)00100-4 (cit. on p. 6).

[33] Carrington, D. (Sept. 2014). *Earth has lost half of its wildlife in the past 40 years, says WWF*. The Guardian. URL: https://www.theguardian.com/environment /2014/sep/29/earth-lost-50-wildlife-in-40-years-wwf (visited on 02/04/2025) (cit. on p. 6).

[34] MacDonald, J. (Jan. 2019). *When Endangered Wildlife Gets Inbred*. JSTOR Daily. URL: https://daily.jstor.org/when-endangered-wildlife-gets-inbred/ (visited on 02/04/2025) (cit. on p. 6).

[35] Watling, E. (Jan. 2019). *Monarch Butterflies are in danger and it's worse than most people realize*. Newsweek. URL: https://www.newsweek.com/monarch-bu tterflies-extinct-1302838 (visited on 02/04/2025) (cit. on p. 6).

[36] Lepawsky, J. (2019). *Our Tech Addiction Is Creating a 'Toxic Soup'*. Memorial University. URL: https://onezero.medium.com/our-tech-addiction-is-creating-a-toxic-soup-fdeb36bdcc51 (visited on 02/04/2025) (cit. on p. 6).

[37] Monroe, M. (2015). *Racing Extinction*. Motion picture. Documentary film, 90 minutes, released September 18, 2015. Screenplay by Mark Monroe. Distributed by Lionsgate and Discovery Channel. Nominated for Academy Award for Best Original Song. Boulder, Colorado. URL: https://www.imdb.com/title/tt1618448/ (visited on 07/06/2025) (cit. on p. 6).

[38] Ceballos, G., P. R. Ehrlich, and R. Dirzo (2017). "Biological annihilation via the ongoing sixth mass extinction signaled by vertebrate population losses and declines." In: *Proc. Natl. Acad. Sci. U.S.A.* 114.30, E6089–E6096. ISSN: 0027-8424. DOI: 10.1073/pnas.1704949114 (cit. on p. 6).

[39] Guarino, B. (Oct. 2018). *Hyperalarming study shows massive insect loss*. URL: https://www.washingtonpost.com/science/2018/10/15/hyperalarming-study-s hows-massive-insect-loss (visited on 02/04/2025) (cit. on p. 6).

[40] Bee Informed Team (June 2021). *United States Honey Bee Colony Losses 2020-2021*. Bee Informed. URL: https://beeinformed.org/2021/06/21/united-states-ho ney-bee-colony-losses-2020-2021-preliminary-results/ (visited on 02/04/2025) (cit. on p. 6).

[41] Stevenson, M. (Apr. 2019). *Sad News: Mexico Says Only 22 Vaquita Porpoises Remain.* NBC Los Angeles. URL: https://www.nbclosangeles.com/news/local/v aquita-endangered-mammal-dying-off-506797251.html (visited on 02/04/2025) (cit. on p. 6).

[42] Taub, B. (May 2022). *There Are Just 10 Vaquitas Left – But They Can Still Recover, Scientists Say.* IFLScience. URL: https://www.iflscience.com/there-are-just-1 0-vaquitas-left-but-they-can-still-recover-scientists-say-63569/ (visited on 02/04/2025) (cit. on p. 6).

[43] Funes, Y. (Mar. 2019). *World's Smallest Porpoise Down to About 10 Individuals Thanks to Illegal Fishing, Alarming Report Says.* Gizmodo USA, LLC. URL: https: //gizmodo.com/worlds-smallest-porpoise-down-to-about-10-individuals-t-183 3385068 (visited on 02/04/2025) (cit. on p. 6).

[44] Brown, P. (Jan. 2003). *One generation to save world, report warns.* The Guardian. URL: https://www.theguardian.com/environment/2003/jan/09/globalisation.fa mine (visited on 02/04/2025) (cit. on p. 6).

[45] Carrington, D. (Mar. 2019a). *Widespread losses of pollinating insects revealed across Britain.* The Guardian. URL: https://www.theguardian.com/environment /2019/mar/26/widespread-losses-of-pollinating-insects-revealed-across-britain (visited on 02/04/2025) (cit. on p. 6).

[46] Simon, M. (Mar. 2019a). *The fungi decimating amphibians is worse than we thought.* Wired Magazine. URL: https://www.wired.com/story/chytrid-fungi-a mphibian-decline/ (visited on 02/04/2025) (cit. on p. 6).

[47] Tangley, L. (Apr. 2019). "Bloom or Bust." In: *Natl. Wild.* 57.3, pp. 22–9 (cit. on p. 6).

[48] Crowther, T. W. et al. (Sept. 2015). "Mapping tree density at a global scale." In: *Nature* 525, pp. 201–5. DOI: 10.1038/nature14967 (cit. on p. 6).

[49] Holland, J. S. (Feb. 2019). "Under The Weather." In: *Natl. Wild.* 57.2 (cit. on p. 6).

[50] Snaith, E. (Apr. 2019). *Frogs, salamanders and toads suffering 'catastrophic population decline', scientists say.* Independent. URL: https://www.independent.co.u k/environment/frog-salamanders-toads-amphibians-extinction-population-fu ngal-disease-a8879581.html (visited on 02/04/2025) (cit. on p. 6).

[51] Leahy, S. (May 2019a). *One million species at risk of extinction, UN report warns.* National Geographic Society. URL: https://www.nationalgeographic.com/envir onment/article/ipbes-un-biodiversity-report-warns-one-million-species-at-ris k (visited on 03/06/2025) (cit. on p. 6).

[52] Clynes, T. (2018). "Finding True North." In: *Audubon* 120.4, pp. 20–9 (cit. on p. 6).

[53] McCauley, D. J. et al. (2015). "Marine defaunation: Animal loss in the global ocean." In: *Science* 347.6219, pp. 247–54. DOI: 10.1126/science.1255641 (cit. on p. 6).

[54] Jacobsen, R. (Oct. 2016). *Obituary: Great Barrier Reef (25 Million BC-...)* Frontline News. URL: https://www.all-creatures.org/articles/env-obituary-great-barrier- reef.html (visited on 02/04/2025) (cit. on p. 6).

[55] Scully, R. P. (July 2019). *Butterfly numbers fell by one third in the US over last two decades.* New Scientist Ltd. URL: https://www.newscientist.com/article/220 9171-butterfly-numbers-fell-by-one-third-in-the-us-over-last-two-decades/ (visited on 02/04/2025) (cit. on p. 6).

[56]   Snyder, M. (Feb. 2019). *Insect Apocalypse: The Global Food Chain Is Experiencing A Major Extinction Event And Scientists Don't Know Why.* The Economic Collapse Blog. URL: http://theeconomiccollapseblog.com/insect-apocalypse-the-global-food-chain-is-experiencing-a-major-extinction-event-and-scientists-dont-know-why/ (visited on 02/04/2025) (cit. on p. 6).

[57]   Adey, J. (Dec. 2019). *Building blocks of ocean food web in rapid decline as plankton productivity plunges.* CBC News. URL: https://www.cbc.ca/news/canada/newfoundland-labrador/ocean-phytoplankton-zooplankton-food-web-1.4927884 (visited on 03/05/2025) (cit. on p. 6).

[58]   Carrington, D. (Oct. 2018a). *Humanity has wiped out 60% of animal populations since 1970, report finds.* The Guardian. URL: https://www.theguardian.com/environment/2018/oct/30/humanity-wiped-out-animals-since-1970-major-report-finds (visited on 02/04/2025) (cit. on p. 6).

[59]   Rosenberg, K. V. et al. (Oct. 2019). "Decline of the North American Avifauna." In: *Science* 366.6461, pp. 120–4. DOI: 10.1126/science.aaw1313 (cit. on p. 6).

[60]   Axelson, G. (Sept. 2019). *Vanishing: More Than 1 in 4 Birds Has Disappeared in the Last 50 Years.* The Cornell Lab of Ornithology. URL: https://www.allaboutbirds.org/news/vanishing-1-in-4-birds-gone/ (visited on 02/04/2025) (cit. on p. 6).

[61]   Bosker, B. (Nov. 2019). *Why Everything Is Getting Louder.* The Atlantic. URL: https://www.theatlantic.com/magazine/archive/2019/11/the-end-of-silence/598366/ (visited on 02/04/2025) (cit. on p. 6).

[62]   Voynova, E. (Oct. 2018). *Elephants are not the only giants at risk from illegal wildlife trade).* World Wildlife Fund. URL: https://medium.com/@WWF/elephants-are-not-the-only-giants-at-risk-from-illegal-wildlife-trade-6e85c3432681 (visited on 02/04/2025) (cit. on p. 6).

[63]   Pyne, S. J. (Nov. 2019). *The planet is burning.* Aeon. URL: https://aeon.co/essays/the-planet-is-burning-around-us-is-it-time-to-declare-the-pyrocene (visited on 02/04/2025) (cit. on p. 6).

[64]   Simon, M. (Nov. 2019b). *Our Planet May Be Barreling Toward a Tipping Point.* Wired Magazine. URL: https://www.wired.com/story/climate-tipping-point/ (visited on 02/04/2025) (cit. on p. 6).

[65]   Hylton, W. S. (Jan. 2020). *History's Largest Mining Operation Is About to Begin.* The Atlantic. URL: https://www.theatlantic.com/magazine/archive/2020/01/20000-feet-under-the-sea/603040/ (visited on 02/04/2025) (cit. on p. 6).

[66]   Paddison, L. (Dec. 2019). *2019 Was The Year The World Burned.* Huffington Post. URL: https://www.huffpost.com/entry/wildfires-california-amazon-indonesia-climate-change_n_5dcd3f4ee4b0d43931d01baf (visited on 02/04/2025) (cit. on p. 6).

[67]   Mandel, K. (Dec. 2019). *Plastic Pollution Is A Global Problem We Can't Ignore.* Huffington Post. URL: https://www.huffpost.com/entry/plastic-waste-pollution-ocean_n_5dcc2afae4b0d43931cddd52 (visited on 02/04/2025) (cit. on p. 6).

[68]   Johnson, J. (Jan. 2020a). *'Entire Species Are Being Wiped Out': Ecologists Say Half a Billion Animals May Have Been Killed by Australia Wildfires.* Common Dreams. URL: https://www.commondreams.org/news/2020/01/02/entire-species-are-being-wiped-out-ecologists-say-half-billion-animals-may-have-been (visited on 02/04/2025) (cit. on p. 6).

[69] Davidson, J. (Nov. 2019). *'Functionally Extinct' Koalas Have Now Lost 80% of Habitat Following Recent Fires, Experts Say.* EcoWatch. URL: https://www.ec owatch.com/koalas-functionally-extinct-fires-2641450078.html (visited on 02/04/2025) (cit. on p. 6).

[70] Main, D. (Jan. 2020). *The Chinese paddlefish, one of the world's largest fish, has gone extinct.* National Geographic Society. URL: https://www.nationalgeogr aphic.com/animals/2020/01/chinese-paddlefish-one-of-largest-fish-extinct/ (visited on 02/04/2025) (cit. on p. 6).

[71] Rice, D. (Jan. 2020). *Over 1 billion animals feared dead in Australian wildfires, experts say.* USA Today. URL: https://www.usatoday.com/story/news/world/20 20/01/08/australian-fires-over-1-billion-animals-feared-dead-experts-say/2845 084001/ (visited on 02/04/2025) (cit. on p. 6).

[72] Qui, J. (Jan. 2020). "A Legend Among The Masses." In: *Audubon* 121.4, pp. 26–35. ISSN: 0097-7136 (cit. on p. 6).

[73] Langham, T. (Jan. 2019). *Running out of Time | Documentary on Holistic Management.* Fig Multimedia Tech. URL: https://environoego.com/running-out-of-t ime-documentary-on-holistic-management/ (visited on 02/04/2025) (cit. on p. 6).

[74] Nuwer, R. (Jan. 2020). *The Freshwater Giants Are Dying.* The New York Times Company. URL: https://www.nytimes.com/2020/01/21/science/freshwater-meg afauna-endangered.html (visited on 02/04/2025) (cit. on p. 6).

[75] França, F. M. et al. (Jan. 2020). "Climatic and local stressor interactions threaten tropical forests and coral reefs." In: *Philos. Trans. R. Soc. Lond., B, Biol. Sci.* 375.1794. ISSN: 0962-8436. DOI: 10.1098/rstb.2019.0116 (cit. on p. 6).

[76] National Oceanic and Atmospheric Administration (2025). *Beluga Whale.* U.S. Department of Commerce. URL: https://www.fisheries.noaa.gov/species/belug a-whale (visited on 02/04/2025) (cit. on p. 6).

[77] Joling, D. (Jan. 2020). *Alaska's Cook Inlet beluga whales continue population decline.* Associated Press. URL: https://www.pbs.org/newshour/world/alaskas-c ook-inlet-beluga-whales-continue-decline (visited on 02/04/2025) (cit. on p. 6).

[78] Zeldovich, L. (Jan. 2020). *We Consume a Spoonful of Plastic a Week.* JSTOR Daily. URL: https://daily.jstor.org/we-consume-a-spoonful-of-plastic-a-week/ (visited on 02/04/2025) (cit. on p. 6).

[79] Galloway, T. S. and C. N. Lewis (Mar. 2016). "Marine microplastics spell big problems for future generations." In: *Proc. Natl. Acad. Sci. U.S.A.* 113.9, pp. 2331–3. ISSN: 0027-8424. DOI: 10.1073/pnas.1600715113 (cit. on p. 6).

[80] Katsnelson, A. (May 2015). "Microplastics present pollution puzzle." In: *Proc. Natl. Acad. Sci. U.S.A.* 112.18, pp. 5547–9. ISSN: 0027-8424. DOI: 10.1073/pnas.15 04135112 (cit. on p. 6).

[81] Yeoman, B. (June 2019). "A Plague of Plastics." In: *Natl. Wild.* 57.4, pp. 22–9. ISSN: 0028-0402. URL: https://www.nwf.org/Home/Magazines/National-Wildlif e/2019/June-July/Conservation/Ocean-Plastic (visited on 02/04/2025) (cit. on p. 6).

[82] Tolmé, P. (June 2019). "Running the Gauntlet." In: *Natl. Wild.* 57.4, pp. 38–43. ISSN: 0028-0402. URL: https://www.nwf.org/Magazines/National-Wildlife/201 9/June-July/Conservation/Habitat-Corridors (visited on 02/04/2025) (cit. on p. 6).

[83]   Banham, P. (Mar. 2019). "Tigers Under Threat." In: *Animal Issues Digest*, pp. 6–7 (cit. on p. 6).

[84]   Safina, C. (Apr. 2020). *The secret call of the wild: how animals teach each other to survive*. The Guardian. URL: https://www.theguardian.com/environment/20 20/apr/09/the-secret-call-of-the-wild-how-animals-teach-each-other-to-surviv e-aoe (visited on 02/04/2025) (cit. on pp. 6, 58).

[85]   McGrath, M. (May 2019). *Nature crisis: Humans 'threaten 1m species with extinction'*. BBC News. URL: https://www.bbc.com/news/science-environment-48 169783 (visited on 02/04/2025) (cit. on p. 6).

[86]   Klink, R. van et al. (Apr. 2020). "Meta-analysis reveals declines in terrestrial but increases in freshwater insect abundances." In: *Science* 368.6489, pp. 417–20. DOI: 10.1126/science.aax9931 (cit. on p. 6).

[87]   Bar-On, Y. M., R. Phillips, and R. Milo (June 2018). "The biomass distribution on Earth." In: *Proc. Natl. Acad. Sci. U.S.A.* 115.25, pp. 6506–11. ISSN: 0027-8424. DOI: 10.1073/pnas.1711842115 (cit. on p. 6).

[88]   Srinivasan, A. (Aug. 2020). "What Have We Done to the Whale?" In: *The New Yorker*. URL: https://www.newyorker.com/magazine/2020/08/24/what-have-we -done-to-the-whale (visited on 02/04/2025) (cit. on p. 6).

[89]   WWF (2020). *Living Planet Report 2020*. Gland, Switzerland: World Wildlife Fund. URL: https://f.hubspotusercontent20.net/hubfs/4783129/LPR/PDFs /ENGLISH-FULL.pdf (visited on 02/04/2025) (cit. on p. 6).

[90]   Secretariat of the Convention on Biological Diversity (Sept. 2020). *Global Biodiversity Outlook 5*. Montreal: Oxford University Press. URL: https://www.c bd.int/gbo/gbo5/publication/gbo-5-en.pdf (visited on 02/04/2025) (cit. on p. 6).

[91]   Ward, M. et al. (Sept. 2020). "Just ten percent of the global terrestrial protected area network is structurally connected via intact land." In: *Nat. Commun.* 11.4563. DOI: 10.1038/s41467-020-18457-x (cit. on p. 6).

[92]   Schneider, J. (Oct. 2017). "Farewell to the World's Smallest Tarantula?" In: *Natl. Wild.* 55.6, pp. 10–12. ISSN: 0028-0402 (cit. on p. 6).

[93]   Warren, L. (Oct. 2017). "Out of Time?" In: *Natl. Wild.* 55.6, pp. 40–3. ISSN: 0028-0402 (cit. on p. 6).

[94]   Shah-Patel, B. (Mar. 2018). "The Slow Extinction of the "Gentle Giants" we know as Giraffes." In: *Animal Issues Digest* 48.3, p. 17 (cit. on p. 6).

[95]   Humane Society Wildlife Land Trust (Sept. 2018). "Fighting the biggest threat to wildlife's survival." In: *Wildlife Update* 17, p. 1 (cit. on p. 6).

[96]   Schlyer, K. (2018). "Borderlands Refuge." In: *American Forests* 124.2, pp. 24–31 (cit. on p. 6).

[97]   Hughes, K. (2021). *The World's Forgotten Fishes*. Switzerland: World Wildlife Fund. URL: https://wwfint.awsassets.panda.org/downloads/world_s_forgotten _fishes__report_final__1.pdf (visited on 02/04/2025) (cit. on p. 6).

[98]   Bergstrom, D. M. et al. (May 2021). "Combating ecosystem collapse from the tropics to the Antarctic." In: *Glob Change Biol.* 27.9, pp. 1692–1703. DOI: 10.111 1/gcb.15539 (cit. on p. 6).

[99]   gerryha (Feb. 2021). *Our Dying Planet*. URL: https://gerryha.gonevis.com/our-d ying-planet/ (visited on 02/04/2025) (cit. on p. 6).

[100] IPBES (May 2019). *Nature's Dangerous Decline 'Unprecedented'; Species Extinction Rates 'Accelerating'*. Intergovernmental Science-Policy Platform on Biodiversity and Ecosystem Services. URL: https://www.ipbes.net/news/Media-

Release-Global-Assessment?mod=article_inline#_ftn1 (visited on 02/04/2025) (cit. on p. 6).

[101]   Specktor, B. (June 2019). *The World's Plants Are Going Extinct About 500 Times Faster Than They Should, Study Finds*. Live Science. URL: https://www.livescience.com/65696-the-plants-are-dying.html (visited on 02/04/2025) (cit. on p. 6).

[102]   Hunziker, R. (Mar. 2018). *Insect Decimation Upstages Global Warming*. CounterPunch. URL: https://www.counterpunch.org/2018/03/27/insect-decimation-upstages-global-warming/ (visited on 02/04/2025) (cit. on p. 6).

[103]   Poppick, L. (Feb. 2019). *The Ocean Is Running Out of Breath, Scientists Warn*. Scientific American. URL: https://www.scientificamerican.com/article/the-ocean-is-running-out-of-breath-scientists-warn/ (visited on 02/04/2025) (cit. on p. 6).

[104]   Watts, J. (Mar. 2018). *Land degradation threatens human wellbeing, major report warns*. The Guardian. URL: https://www.theguardian.com/environment/2018/mar/26/land-degradation-is-undermining-human-wellbeing-un-report-warns (visited on 02/04/2025) (cit. on p. 6).

[105]   Ghosh, S. (May 2020). *Erosion, an important cause of mangrove loss in the Sundarbans*. Mongabay. URL: https://india.mongabay.com/2020/05/erosion-an-important-cause-of-mangrove-loss-in-the-sundarbans/ (visited on 02/04/2025) (cit. on p. 6).

[106]   Gosh, L. (July 2016). *Global Fish Stocks Depleted to 'Alarming' Levels*. EcoWatch. URL: https://www.ecowatch.com/one-third-of-commercial-fish-stocks-fished-at-unsustainable-levels-1910593830.html/ (visited on 02/04/2025) (cit. on p. 6).

[107]   Ripple, W. J. et al. (Dec. 2017). "World Scientists' Warning to Humanity: A Second Notice." In: *BioScience* 67.12, pp. 1026–8. ISSN: 1525-3244. DOI: 10.1093/biosci/bix125 (cit. on p. 6).

[108]   Monbiot, G. (Feb. 2022). "Lost at sea: How dumped fishing gear is killing marine life." In: *Cold Type* 231, pp. 5–6. URL: http://coldtype.net/Assets22/PDFs/ColdType231.February2022.pdf (visited on 02/04/2025) (cit. on p. 6).

[109]   Fan, W. et al. (Dec. 2022). "Evidence and Mass Quantification of Atmospheric Microplastics in a Coastal New Zealand City." In: *Environ. Sci. Technol.* 56.24, pp. 17556–68. ISSN: 0013-936X. DOI: 10.1021/acs.est.2c05850 (cit. on p. 6).

[110]   Gavrilovic, M. (Jan. 2023). *Earth currently experiencing a sixth mass extinction, according to scientists*. 60 Minutes. URL: https://www.youtube.com/watch?v=6TqhcZsxrPA (visited on 02/04/2025) (cit. on pp. 6, 57, 63, 200).

[111]   Nater, O. (June 2023a). "The disappearing "Lungs of Africa"." In: *Population Connection* 55.2, pp. 12–20. ISSN: 2331-0529 (cit. on p. 6).

[112]   Keefe, A. (Sept. 2017). *Heart-Wrenching Photos Show Rhinos Fighting to Survive*. National Geographic Society. URL: https://www.nationalgeographic.com/photography/article/rhino-day-gallery (visited on 02/04/2025) (cit. on p. 6).

[113]   Save The Children Federation (2023). *10 Humanitarian Crises That Demand Our Attention Now*. URL: https://www.savethechildren.org/us/charity-stories/humanitarian-crises-you-need-to-know-about (visited on 02/04/2025) (cit. on p. 6).

[114]   Godbold, D. L., E. Fritz, and A. Hüttermann (June 1988). "Aluminum toxicity and forest decline." In: *Ecology* 85.11, pp. 3888–92. ISSN: 00129658. DOI: 10.1073/pnas.85.11.3888 (cit. on p. 6).

[115] Effiong, U. and R. L. Neitzel (Jan. 2016). "Assessing the direct occupational and public health impacts of solar radiation management with stratospheric aerosols." In: *Environ Health* 15.7. ISSN: 1476-069X. DOI: 10.1186/s12940-016-00 89-0 (cit. on p. 6).

[116] Nickson, E. (Sept. 2023a). *Megadeath: the global conspiracy to kill every living thing until we submit.* Welcome to Absurdistan. URL: https://elizabethnickson.s ubstack.com/p/megadeath-the-global-conspiracy-to (visited on 02/04/2025) (cit. on pp. 6, 34).

[117] — (Sept. 2023b). *Burn Back Better; It's Not Climate Change, it's Psychopathy.* Substack. URL: https://elizabethnickson.substack.com/p/burn-back-better-its-n ot-climate (visited on 02/04/2025) (cit. on pp. 6, 34).

[118] Nater, O. (Sept. 2023b). "Deforestation increased in 2022." In: *Population Connection* 55.3, p. 8. ISSN: 2331-0529 (cit. on p. 6).

[119] Green, A. et al. (Oct. 2018). *Facts about our ecological crisis are incontrovertible. We must take action.* The Guardian. URL: https://www.theguardian.com/enviro nment/2018/oct/26/facts-about-our-ecological-crisis-are-incontrovertible-we-must-take-action (visited on 02/05/2025) (cit. on p. 6).

[120] Securities and Exchange Commission (Sept. 2023). *Self-Regulatory Organizations; New York Stock Exchange LLC; Notice of Filing of Proposed Rule Change To Amend the NYSE Listed Company Manual To Adopt Listing Standards for Natural Asset Companies.* National Archives - Federal Register. URL: https://www.feder alregister.gov/documents/2023/10/04/2023-22041/self-regulatory-organizatio ns-new-york-stock-exchange-llc-notice-of-filing-of-proposed-rule-change (visited on 02/05/2025) (cit. on pp. 6, 57, 61, 70, 82, 200).

[121] Nijhuis, M. (Mar. 2021). *Beloved Beasts.* New York: W. W. Norton & Company, Inc. ISBN: 978-1-324-00168-3 (cit. on pp. 6, 7, 128).

[122] Morningstar, C. (Nov. 2020). *The Great Reset: The Final Assault on the Living Planet [It's Not a Social Dilemma – It's the Calculated Destruction of the Social, Part III].* Wrong Kind of Green. URL: https://www.wrongkindofgreen.org/2020 /11/28/the-great-reset-the-final-assault-on-the-living-planet-its-not-a-soci al-dilemma-its-the-calculated-destruction-of-the-social-part-iii/ (visited on 02/05/2025) (cit. on pp. 6, 8).

[123] Smith, C. H. (Jan. 2025b). *The System's Self-Destruct Sequence Cannot Be Turned Off.* Of Two Minds. URL: https://www.oftwominds.com/blogjan25/self-destruct 1-25.html (visited on 02/05/2025) (cit. on p. 6).

[124] Jacobsen, R. (July 2022). *What I Saw When I Came Eye to Eye with a Whale.* Outside Interactive, Inc. URL: https://www.outsideonline.com/2415069/sperm-whales-research-dominica (visited on 03/03/2025) (cit. on p. 6).

[125] Valentine, S. (Mar. 2025). *Rockets Are Blasting the Environment. At launch sites, rockets are leaving a trail of damage to wildlife, vegetation, and water.* NautilusNext Inc. URL: https://nautil.us/rockets-are-blasting-the-environment-1195186/ (visited on 03/04/2025) (cit. on p. 6).

[126] Edwards, G. (Oct. 2019). *Scary issues facing our planet today.* World Wildlife Fund. URL: https://wwf.medium.com/scary-issues-facing-our-planet-today-f1e f392b248e (visited on 03/04/2025) (cit. on p. 6).

[127] Krehbiel, R. (Feb. 2019). *Defending Wildlife, No Matter How Small.* Defenders of Wildlife. URL: https://medium.com/wild-without-end/defending-wildlife-no-m atter-how-small-86ec871bd872 (visited on 03/07/2025) (cit. on pp. 6, 57).

[128] Muruven, D. (Nov. 2018). *We'd be as mad as hatters not to tackle the mercury poisoning the Amazon.* World Wildlife Fund. URL: https://wwf.medium.com/we d-be-as-mad-as-hatters-not-to-tackle-the-mercury-poisoning-the-amazon-c6a 6bbb9dd62 (visited on 03/09/2025) (cit. on p. 6).

[129] Hunt, C. (Nov. 2018). *The Third Great American Extinction Event (Present Day).* Defenders of Wildlife. URL: https://medium.com/wild-without-end/the-thi rd-great-american-extinction-event-present-day-3538b7a595b4 (visited on 03/09/2025) (cit. on p. 6).

[130] Carrington, D. (Nov. 2018b). *What is biodiversity and why does it matter to us?* The Guardian. URL: https://www.theguardian.com/news/2018/mar/12/what-i s-biodiversity-and-why-does-it-matter-to-us (visited on 03/10/2025) (cit. on pp. 6, 61, 110, 196).

[131] Chiang, T. (2014). *The Great Silence.* Video installation. London, United Kingdom. URL: https://vimeo.com/195588827 (visited on 10/06/2025) (cit. on p. 6).

[132] Tudge, C. (2005). *The Secret Life of Trees.* London, England: Penguin Books. ISBN: 978-0-141-01293-3 (cit. on pp. 6, 99, 121, 154, 197).

[133] Marino, L. (May 2019). *Eating someone.* Aeon. URL: https://aeon.co/essays/face-it-a-farmed-animal-is-someone-not-something (visited on 03/06/2025) (cit. on pp. 6, 125).

[134] Meijer, E. (May 2025). *The Woman Who Saw Birds as Individuals.* NautilusNext Inc. URL: https://nautil.us/the-woman-who-saw-birds-as-individuals-1207714/ (visited on 05/07/2025) (cit. on p. 6).

[135] Jones-Engel, L. (2023). "The Monkey Who Held My Face in Her Hands and Opened My Eyes." In: *PETA Global* (2), pp. 16–17. ISSN: 0899-9708 (cit. on p. 6).

[136] Quinn, D. (1992). *Ishmael.* New York, New York: Bantam Books. ISBN: 0-553-37540-7 (cit. on pp. 6, 121).

[137] Hazlitt, H. (1946). *Economics In One Lesson.* New York and London: Harper & Brothers Publishers (cit. on pp. 6, 25, 219).

[138] Anonymous (2025). *What Happened in 1971?* Unknown. URL: https://wtfhappe nedin1971.com/ (visited on 02/05/2025) (cit. on pp. 6, 37).

[139] Reinhart, C. M. and K. S. Rogoff (May 2009). "The Aftermath of Financial Crises." In: *Am. Econ. Rev.* 99.2, pp. 466–72. ISSN: 28282. DOI: 10.1257/aer.99.2.466 (cit. on p. 6).

[140] Woolf, S. H. et al. (Aug. 2018). "Changes in midlife death rates across racial and ethnic groups in the United States: systematic analysis of vital statistics." In: *BMJ* 362, k3096. ISSN: 0959-8138. DOI: 10.1136/bmj.k3096 (cit. on p. 7).

[141] Dalio, R. (Oct. 2017). *Our Biggest Economic, Social, and Political Issue).* LinkedIn. URL: https://www.linkedin.com/pulse/our-biggest-economic-social-political-is sue-two-economies-ray-dalio/ (visited on 03/09/2025) (cit. on pp. 7, 37).

[142] Snyder, M. (Dec. 2023b). *This Year, Americans Have Become Hungrier, Lonelier And More Desperate.* The Economic Collapse Blog. URL: https://theeconomiccol lapseblog.com/this-year-americans-have-become-hungrier-lonelier-and-more-desperate/ (visited on 02/05/2025) (cit. on p. 7).

[143] US Forest Service (2014). *U.S. Forest Resource Facts and Historical Trends.* report. United States Department of Agriculture (cit. on pp. 7, 57, 200).

[144] Thompson, E. P. (1991). *Customs in Common.* New York: The New Press. ISBN: 978-1-56584-074-4 (cit. on pp. 7, 124, 127, 128).

[145]   Hogue, A. R. (1985). *Origins Of The Common Law*. Indianapolis, IN: LibertyPress. ISBN: 978-0-86597-053-3 (cit. on pp. 7, 127).

[146]   Savory Institute (2025). *Regenerating the World's Grasslands*. URL: https://savor y.global/ (visited on 02/05/2025) (cit. on p. 7).

[147]   Nickson, E. (June 2024b). *Restoring the Soil to Make the Deserts Bloom*. Substack. URL: https://elizabethnickson.substack.com/p/restoring-the-soil-to-make-the-deserts (visited on 02/05/2025) (cit. on pp. 7, 197).

[148]   American Forests (2025). *The future for forests is full of promise*. URL: https://w ww.americanforests.org/ (visited on 02/05/2025) (cit. on p. 7).

[149]   Arbor Day Foundation (2025). *Plant a brighter future*. URL: https://www.arbord ay.org/ (visited on 02/05/2025) (cit. on p. 7).

[150]   Johnstone, C. (Mar. 2019a). *Your Plans For Revolution Don't Work. Nothing We've Tried Works*. Caitlin Johnstone, Rogue Journalist. URL: https://caitlinjohnstone .com/2019/03/28/your-plans-for-revolution-dont-work-nothing-weve-tried-w orks/ (visited on 02/05/2025) (cit. on pp. 8, 176).

[151]   Aggarwal, S. and M. O'Boyle (June 2020). *Rewiring the U.S. for economic recovery*. Tech. rep. Energy Innovation Policy & Technology, LLC (cit. on p. 8).

[152]   Mills, M. P. (Mar. 2019a). *The "New Energy Economy". An Exercise in Magical Thinking*. report. New York, NY. URL: https://www.manhattan-institute.org/gr een-energy-revolution-near-impossible/ (visited on 02/05/2025) (cit. on p. 8).

[153]   Eidson, J. (Jan. 2020). *Progressive Eco-Group Admits It: Renewable Energy is a Hoax that Benefits its Greenie Elmer Gantries like Al Gore*. American Thinker. URL: https://www.americanthinker.com/articles/2020/01/progressive_ecogrou p_admits_it_renewable_energy_is_a_hoax_that_benefits_its_greenie_elmer _gantries_like_al_gore.html (visited on 02/05/2025) (cit. on p. 8).

[154]   Tennenbaum, J. (Jan. 2020a). *Don't like CO_2? Advanced nuclear power is the answer*. Asia Times. URL: https://www.asiatimes.com/2020/01/article/carbon-di oxides-scourge-advanced-nuclear-power/ (visited on 02/05/2025) (cit. on p. 8).

[155]   —   (Jan. 2020b). *Germany's overdose of renewable energy*. Asia Times. URL: https://www.asiatimes.com/2020/01/article/germanys-overdose-of-renewable-energy/ (visited on 02/05/2025) (cit. on p. 8).

[156]   IER (Apr. 2015). *License to Kill: Wind and Solar Decimate Birds and Bats*. Institute For Energy Research. URL: https://www.instituteforenergyresearch.org/renew able/wind/license-to-kill-wind-and-solar-decimate-birds-and-bats/ (visited on 02/05/2025) (cit. on p. 8).

[157]   Wiegand, J. (July 2014). *Wind Power Slaughter: ex-USFWS Agent Speaks Out on Shiloh IV (California)*. MasterResource. URL: https://www.masterresource.org /cuisinarts-of-the-air/windpower-slaughter-shiloh-1/ (visited on 02/05/2025) (cit. on p. 8).

[158]   Elbein, S. (Mar. 2019). *Europe's renewable energy policy is built on burning American trees*. Vox. URL: https://www.vox.com/science-and-health/2019/3 /4/18216045/renewable-energy-wood-pellets-biomass (visited on 02/05/2025) (cit. on p. 8).

[159]   Wirtz, B. (Nov. 2019). *Solar Panels Produce Tons of Toxic Waste—Literally*. Foundation for Economic Education. URL: https://fee.org/articles/solar-panels-prod uce-tons-of-toxic-waste-literally/ (visited on 02/05/2025) (cit. on p. 8).

[160]   Mills, M. P. (July 2019b). *Inconvenient Energy Realities*. New York, NY: Manhattan Institute for Policy Research, Inc. URL: https://economics21.org/inconvenient-realities-new-energy-economy/ (visited on 02/05/2025) (cit. on p. 8).

[161]   Stop These Things (Sept. 2022). *Toxic Blade Time Bomb: New Study Exposes Scale of Wind Industry's Poisonous Plastics Legacy*. URL: https://stopthesethings.com/2022/09/03/toxic-blade-time-bomb-new-study-exposes-scale-of-wind-industrys-poisonous-plastics-legacy/ (visited on 02/05/2025) (cit. on p. 8).

[162]   Atasu, A., S. Duran, and L. N. V. Wassenhove (June 2021). *The Dark Side of Solar Power*. Harvard Business Publishing. URL: https://hbr.org/2021/06/the-dark-side-of-solar-power (visited on 02/05/2025) (cit. on p. 8).

[163]   Manion, M. et al. (2023). *Growing Solar, Protecting Nature*. Mass Audubon and Harvard Forest. URL: https://storymaps.arcgis.com/stories/932be293f1af43c8b776fdad24d9f071 (visited on 02/05/2025) (cit. on p. 8).

[164]   Merriman, J. (Jan. 2021). *How Many Birds Are Killed by Wind Turbines?* American Bird Conservancy. URL: https://abcbirds.org/blog21/wind-turbine-mortality/ (visited on 02/05/2025) (cit. on p. 8).

[165]   Kennedy Jr., R. F. (Oct. 2024). *Another Captive Agency Weaponized Against White House Critics*. URL: https://robertfkennedyjr.substack.com/p/rfk-jr-kennedy-whale-investigation (visited on 02/05/2025) (cit. on p. 8).

[166]   Shedlock, M. (Feb. 2025). *How Many More Ridiculous Green Energy Projects Will Fail?* Mish Talk. URL: https://mishtalk.com/economics/how-many-more-ridiculous-green-energy-projects-will-fail/ (visited on 02/14/2025) (cit. on p. 8).

[167]   Impelli, M. (Dec. 2023). *Golden Eagle's Death Sparks Shutdown of Wind Farm*. Newsweek. URL: https://www.newsweek.com/france-renewable-energy-wind-farm-golden-eagle-killed-shutdown-1855080 (visited on 02/14/2025) (cit. on p. 8).

[168]   Denholm, M. (Aug. 2023). *'Cutting-edge' wind farm still an eagle killer*. National Wind Watch, Inc. URL: https://www.wind-watch.org/news/2023/08/17/cutting-edge-wind-farm-still-an-eagle-killer/ (visited on 02/14/2025) (cit. on p. 8).

[169]   Brown, M. and C. Fassett (May 2023). *Criminal cases for killing eagles decline as wind turbine dangers grow*. The Associated Press. URL: https://apnews.com/article/dead-eagles-wind-turbines-enforcement-biden-53ce35355433e18a27324f9254a2475a (visited on 02/14/2025) (cit. on p. 8).

[170]   The Associated Press (Apr. 2022). *Wind energy company pleads guilty after at least 150 eagles killed in U.S.* URL: https://www.nbcnews.com/news/us-news/wind-energy-company-pleads-guilty-least-150-eagles-killed-us-rcna23360 (visited on 02/14/2025) (cit. on p. 8).

[171]   Wilson, R. (Mar. 2026). *Wyoming: A thorough assessment of the threat wind turbines pose to eagles needs to be done*. The Expose. URL: https://expose-news.com/2026/03/25/assessment-of-the-threat-wind-turbines-pose/ (visited on 04/28/2026) (cit. on p. 8).

[172]   McGlinchey, B. (Feb. 2025). *"Recycling" Makes Plastic Pollution Worse*. Stark Realities with Brian McGlinchey. URL: https://starkrealities.substack.com/p/recycling-makes-plastic-pollution-worse (visited on 02/12/2025) (cit. on p. 8).

[173]   Enck, J. and J. Dell (May 2022). *Plastic Recycling Doesn't Work and Will Never Work*. The Atlantic. URL: https://www.theatlantic.com/ideas/archive/2022/05/single-use-plastic-chemical-recycling-disposal/661141/ (visited on 02/12/2025) (cit. on p. 8).

[174] Macleod, A. (June 2023). *Updating Say's law for modern times*. Goldmoney. URL: https://www.goldmoney.com/research/updating-say-s-law-for-modern-times (visited on 02/05/2025) (cit. on p. 9).

[175] Mullen, T. (Aug. 2024). *The Fed's Fiat Money Is the Real Cause of Price Inflation*. Mises Institute. URL: https://mises.org/mises-wire/feds-fiat-money-real-cause-price-inflation (visited on 02/05/2025) (cit. on p. 9).

[176] Bernholz, P. (2003). *Monetary Regimes and Inflation: History, Economic and Political Relationships*. William Pratt House, Massachusetts: Edward Elgar Publishing, Inc. ISBN: 978-1-78471-762-9. DOI: 10.4337/9781784717636. URL: https://www.researchgate.net/publication/227378839_Monetary_Regimes_and_Inflation_History_Economic_and_Political_Relationships_-_Peter_Bernholz (visited on 05/07/2025) (cit. on p. 9).

[177] Polleit, T. (Feb. 2020). *Fed-Driven Asset Price Inflation Means You Can Now Buy Less House Than You Could Before*. Mises Institute. URL: https://mises.org/wire/fed-driven-asset-price-inflation-means-you-can-now-buy-less-house-you-could/ (visited on 02/05/2025) (cit. on p. 9).

[178] 94th Congress (Oct. 1976). *H.R. 13955 (94th): An Act to provide for amendment of the Bretton Woods Agreements Act, and for other purposes*. United States of America Federal Government. URL: https://www.congress.gov/94/statute/STATUTE-90/STATUTE-90-Pg2660.pdf (visited on 02/05/2025) (cit. on p. 10).

[179] 92nd Congress (Mar. 1972). *Par Value Modification Act*. United States of America Federal Government. URL: https://www.congress.gov/92/statute/STATUTE-86/STATUTE-86-Pg116-3.pdf (visited on 02/05/2025) (cit. on pp. 10, 70, 138, 198).

[180] 93rd Congress (Sept. 1973). *Par Value Modification Act reenactment*. United States of America Federal Government. URL: https://www.congress.gov/93/statute/STATUTE-87/STATUTE-87-Pg352-2.pdf (visited on 02/05/2025) (cit. on pp. 10, 47, 63, 70, 138, 198).

[181] U.S. Department of the Treasury (2025). *U.S. Treasury-Owned Gold*. URL: https://fiscaldata.treasury.gov/datasets/status-report-government-gold-reserve/u-s-treasury-owned-gold (visited on 09/03/2025) (cit. on pp. 10, 11, 13, 47, 63, 70, 101, 156, 198, 237).

[182] Dale Jr., E. L. (Feb. 1973). *GOLD TO BE $42,22*. New York Times. URL: https://www.nytimes.com/1973/02/13/archives/gold-to-be-4222-controls-on-lending-abroad-also-will-be-phased-out.html (visited on 02/05/2025) (cit. on pp. 10, 47, 48, 63, 198).

[183] Wilson, L. (May 2010). *Beware: Official U.S. Government Price for Gold is Only $42.22/oz*. Mining.com. URL: https://www.mining.com/beware-official-us-government-price-for-gold-is-only-4222oz/ (visited on 02/05/2025) (cit. on pp. 10, 47, 48, 63, 198, 231).

[184] Macleod, A. (Feb. 2024). *It Is Vital To Understand the Legal and Practical Role of Gold*. LewRockwell. URL: https://www.lewrockwell.com/2024/02/alasdair-macleod/it-is-vital-to-understand-the-legal-and-practical-role-of-gold/ (visited on 02/05/2025) (cit. on pp. 10, 12, 42, 47, 63, 198).

[185] Hülsmann, J. G. (1995). *The Ethics of Money Production*. Auburn, Alabama: Mises Institute. URL: https://mises.org/library/ethics-money-production (visited on 02/03/2025) (cit. on pp. 11–13, 19, 45, 69, 138, 198, 206, 227, 230).

[186]   Lips, F. (2001). *Gold Wars*. New York, New York: The Foundation for the Advancement of Monetary Education. ISBN: 978-0-9710380-0-4 (cit. on pp. 11, 14, 19, 39, 48, 232, 233, 236).

[187]   Second Congress of the United States (Apr. 1792). *Acts of the Second Congress of the United States, from the twenty-fourth day of October, 1791, to the ninth day of May, 1792*. Washington: Government Printing Office. URL: https://tile.lo c.gov/storage-services/service/ll/llsl//llsl-c2/llsl-c2.pdf (visited on 05/27/2025) (cit. on pp. 11, 69, 138, 198, 230).

[188]   Twenty-Third Congress of the United States (June 1834). *Acts of the Twenty Third Congress of the United States, from the second day of December, 1833, to the thirtieth day of June, 1834*. Washington: Government Printing Office. URL: https://tile.loc.gov/storage-services/service/ll/llsl//llsl-c23/llsl-c23.pdf (visited on 05/27/2025) (cit. on pp. 11, 69, 138, 198, 230).

[189]   Woudenberg, A. V. (June 2005). *The Curse of Gold*. Human Rights Watch. URL: https://www.hrw.org/report/2005/06/01/curse-gold (visited on 05/13/2025) (cit. on p. 11).

[190]   Şengör, A. M. C. (2023). *Is it "the earth" or Earth?* The Geological Society of America. URL: https://rock.geosociety.org/net/gsatoday/archive/27/3/pdf/i1052 -5173-27-3-19.pdf (visited on 09/20/2023) (cit. on p. 11).

[191]   Cantelon, W. (1973). *The Day the Dollar Dies*. Plainfield, New Jersey: Logos International. ISBN: 0-88270-013-8 (cit. on pp. 11, 12, 14, 69, 201, 221, 226, 227, 232, 235–237).

[192]   Alden, L. (2023). *Broken Money. Why Our Financial System is Failing Us and How We Can Make It Better*. New York, New York: Timestamp Press. ISBN: 9-798-98866-632-5 (cit. on pp. 12, 13, 15, 16, 25, 27, 28, 31, 38, 47, 58, 69, 72, 141, 149, 195–197, 203, 206, 224, 225, 237).

[193]   Griffin, G. E. (2010). *The Creature From Jekyll Island*. Fifth Edition. Westlake Village, California: American Media (cit. on pp. 12, 13, 16, 25, 31, 41, 43, 69, 215, 226, 227).

[194]   FOFOA (2025). *Friend Of Friend Of Another*. URL: http://fofoa.blogspot.com/ (visited on 02/05/2025) (cit. on pp. 12, 237).

[195]   Goodrich, F. et al. (1946). *It's a Wonderful Life*. Motion picture. Drama film, 130 minutes, released December 20, 1946. Screenplay by Frances Goodrich, Albert Hackett, and Jo Swerling. Based on the short story "The Greatest Gift" by Philip Van Doren Stern. Score by Dimitri Tiomkin. Hollywood, California. URL: https://www.imdb.com/title/tt0038650/ (visited on 07/06/2025) (cit. on p. 13).

[196]   mrspaz (2016). *The bank run from It's A Wonderful Life*. Reddit. URL: https://w ww.reddit.com/r/explainlikeimfive/comments/3xfovq/eli5_the_bank_run_fro m_its_a_wonderful_life/ (visited on 02/05/2025) (cit. on p. 13).

[197]   Jamilov, R. et al. (Dec. 2024). *Two centuries of systemic bank runs*. Centre For Economic Policy Research. URL: https://cepr.org/voxeu/columns/two-centurie s-systemic-bank-runs (visited on 02/05/2025) (cit. on p. 13).

[198]   Schmidtz, D. (1991). *The Limits of Government*. Boulder, Colorado: Westview Press, Inc. ISBN: 0-8133-0870-4 (cit. on p. 15).

[199]   Fairlie, S. (2009). "A Short History of Enclosure in Britain." In: *The Land Magazine* 7. URL: https://www.thelandmagazine.org.uk/articles/short-history-enclos ure-britain (visited on 02/05/2025) (cit. on pp. 15, 128, 129).

[200] Office of Management and Budget (2023). *Budget of the U.S. Government.* Washington, D.C.: The White House. URL: https://www.govinfo.gov/content/pkg/BUDGET-2023-BUD/pdf/BUDGET-2023-BUD.pdf (visited on 02/05/2025) (cit. on p. 16).

[201] Glennon, M. J. (2014). "National Security and Double Government." In: *Harvard Law School NSJ* 5.1 (cit. on p. 16).

[202] Hartung, W. D. and M. Smithberger (May 2019). *Boondoggle, Inc.* TomDispatch.com. URL: http://www.tomdispatch.com/post/176561/ (visited on 02/05/2025) (cit. on p. 16).

[203] Sachs, J. D. (Dec. 2023). *US Foreign Policy Is a Scam Built on Corruption.* Common Dreams. URL: https://www.commondreams.org/opinion/corruption-of-us-foreign-policy (visited on 02/05/2025) (cit. on p. 16).

[204] Lindorff, D. (Apr. 2010). *Your Tax Dollars at War: More Than 53% of Your Tax Payment Goes to the Military.* URL: https://www.commondreams.org/views/2010/04/13/your-tax-dollars-war-more-53-your-tax-payment-goes-military/ (visited on 02/05/2025) (cit. on p. 16).

[205] Rothbard, M. N. (Feb. 1950). *Not Worth a Continental.* Mises Institute. URL: https://mises.org/library/not-worth-continental (visited on 02/05/2025) (cit. on p. 16).

[206] Coogan, G. M. (1935). *Money Creators.* Newport Beach, California: Noontide Press. ISBN: 978-1-2583-5168-7 (cit. on pp. 16, 19, 25, 43, 69, 230).

[207] Rothbard, M. N. (2019). *Conceived in Liberty, Volume 5: The New Republic: 1784 - 1791.* Auburn, Alabama: Mises Institute. ISBN: 978-1-61016-708-6. URL: https://mises.org/library/conceived-liberty-volume-5-new-republic-1784-1791 (visited on 02/05/2025) (cit. on pp. 16, 34, 118, 157, 215, 228).

[208] Whalen, R. C. (2011). *Inflated. How Money and Debt Built the American Dream.* Hoboken, New Jersey: John Wiley & Sons, Inc. ISBN: 978-0-470-87514-8 (cit. on pp. 17, 27, 232, 235).

[209] BOG FRS (2025). *Federal Open Market Committee.* Board of Governors of the Federal Reserve System. URL: https://www.federalreserve.gov/monetarypolicy/fomc.htm (visited on 02/05/2025) (cit. on pp. 19, 29).

[210] Rothbard, M. N. (1963). *What Has Government Done to Our Money?* Auburn, Alabama: Mises Institute (cit. on pp. 19, 25, 43, 47).

[211] Fields, T. W. (2015). "Understanding the Inflation Tax." In: *Int. res. j. appl. financ.* 6.10, pp. 649–57 (cit. on pp. 19, 22, 43, 91, 216).

[212] Sanchez, D. (June 2018a). *The Federal Reserve's Shell Game.* Foundation for Economic Education. URL: https://fee.org/articles/the-federal-reserve-s-shell-game/ (visited on 02/05/2025) (cit. on p. 19).

[213] McCarthy, J. P. (2012). *The Money Spiders.* Palm Coast, Florida: Michael Ray King LLC. ISBN: 978-1-935795-04-9. URL: https://www.goodreads.com/work/quotes/21811966-the-money-spiders-the-ruin-nation-of-the-united-states-by-the-federal-r (visited on 02/05/2025) (cit. on p. 20).

[214] McFadden, L. T. (1978). *Congressman McFadden on the Federal Reserve Corporation Remarks in Congress, 1934.* Arizona Caucus Club. URL: https://famguardian.org/Subjects/MoneyBanking/Articles/mcfadden.htm (visited on 02/05/2025) (cit. on p. 20).

[215] Koning, J. P. (Oct. 2018). *Gold's Official Price is $42, and maybe that's a Good Thing.* Bullionstar. URL: https://www.bullionstar.com/blogs/jp-koning/golds

-official-price-is-42-and-maybe-thats-a-good-thing/ (visited on 02/05/2025) (cit. on pp. 22, 216).

[216]   LOC (2025). *The Federal Reserve System*. Library of Congress. URL: https://www.loc.gov/item/today-in-history/december-23 (visited on 02/05/2025) (cit. on pp. 22, 215, 216).

[217]   Kelton, S. (2020). *The Deficit Myth*. New York, New York: Public Affairs. ISBN: 978-1-5417-3618-4 (cit. on pp. 22, 216).

[218]   Keynes, J. M. (1919). *The Economic Consequences of the Peace*. New York, Evanston, San Francisco, London: Harper Torchbooks Harper & Row. ISBN: 978-3-030-04759-7 (cit. on p. 23).

[219]   Goodkind, T. (Apr. 2003). *Wizard's First Rule*. New York, New York: Tor Books. ISBN: 978-0-7653-7589-6 (cit. on p. 23).

[220]   Woods Jr., T. E. (2019). *Our Enemy The Fed*. Thomas Woods (cit. on pp. 25, 27–29, 39, 43, 91).

[221]   Sanchez, D. (June 2018b). *How Inflation Drinks Your Milkshake*. Foundation for Economic Education. URL: https://fee.org/articles/how-inflation-drinks-your-milkshake/ (visited on 02/05/2025) (cit. on p. 25).

[222]   Stoller, M. (Apr. 2020). *The Cantillon Effect: Why Wall Street Gets a Bailout and You Don't*. BIG by Matt Stoller. URL: https://mattstoller.substack.com/p/the-cantillon-effect-why-wall-street (visited on 02/05/2025) (cit. on pp. 26, 27, 91, 147).

[223]   Brown, E. (Nov. 2012). *It's the Interest, Stupid! Why Bankers Rule the World*. The Web of Debt Blog. URL: https://ellenbrown.com/2012/11/08/its-the-interest-stupid-why-bankers-rule-the-world/ (visited on 03/09/2025) (cit. on pp. 27, 38, 150).

[224]   Schmid, V. (2017a). *Inflation, the Hidden Tax*. The Epoch Times. URL: https://www.theepochtimes.com/inflation-the-hidden-tax-2_2351198.html (visited on 02/05/2025) (cit. on pp. 27, 47, 91).

[225]   von Mises, L. (1954). *The Theory of Money and Credit*. Auburn, Alabama: Mises Institute. ISBN: 978-1-933550-55-8 (cit. on pp. 29, 43).

[226]   Young, J. (2019). *Too Big to Fail: Definition, History, and Reforms*. investopedia. URL: https://www.investopedia.com/terms/t/too-big-to-fail.asp (visited on 02/05/2025) (cit. on p. 33).

[227]   Egan, M. (Mar. 2020). *Fed revives 2008-era program to unfreeze $1 trillion borrowing market*. CNN Business. URL: https://www.cnn.com/2020/03/17/business/fed-commercial-paper/index.html (visited on 02/05/2025) (cit. on p. 33).

[228]   Cox, J. (Mar. 2020). *The Federal Reserve just pledged asset purchases with no limit to support markets*. CNBC. URL: https://www.cnbc.com/2020/03/23/fed-announces-a-slew-of-new-programs-to-help-markets-including-open-ended-asset-purchases.html (visited on 02/05/2025) (cit. on p. 33).

[229]   Fujikawa, M. and S. Bhattacharya (2018). *Bank of Japan's $50 Billion Question: When to Stop Buying Stocks*. The Wall Street Journal. URL: https://www.wsj.com/articles/bank-of-japans-50-billion-question-when-to-stop-buying-stocks-1515973533 (visited on 02/05/2025) (cit. on p. 34).

[230]   Goldman, D. (Mar. 2020). *European Central Bank throws 750 billion euros at the economy to fight the coronavirus crash*. CNN Business. URL: https://edition.cnn.com/2020/03/18/economy/ecb-bailout/index.html (visited on 02/05/2025) (cit. on p. 34).

[231] Napolitano, A. P. (2014). *Suicide Pact: The Radical Expansion of Presidential Powers and the Lethal Threat to American Liberty*. Nashville, Tennessee: Nelson Books (cit. on p. 34).

[232] Mesquita, B. B. de and A. Smith (2011). *The Dictator's Handbook: Why Bad Behavior is Almost Always Good Politics*. New York: PublicAffairs (cit. on pp. 34, 41, 249).

[233] Silver, T. M. (2015). *An Abridged History Of The United States Psychopathocracy*. URL: http://themillenniumreport.com/2015/12/an-abridged-history-of-the-united-states-psychopathocracy/ (visited on 02/05/2025) (cit. on pp. 34, 125).

[234] Whitehead, J. W. (2013). *A Government of Wolves: The Emerging American Police State*. New York: Selectbooks (cit. on p. 34).

[235] Yin, G. et al. (July 2018). *Transplant Abuse in China Continues Despite Claims of Reform*. China Organ Harvest Research Center. URL: https://www.chinaorganharvest.org/app/uploads/2018/06/COHRC-2018-Report.pdf (visited on 02/05/2025) (cit. on p. 34).

[236] Van Maren, J. (Mar. 2020). *The Ghosts of the Armenian Genocide Still Haunt Modern Turkey*. The European Conservative. URL: https://europeanconservative.com/articles/essay/the-ghosts-of-the-armenian-genocide-still-haunt-modern-turkey/ (visited on 02/05/2025) (cit. on p. 34).

[237] Martin, W. (Sept. 2019). *China is harvesting thousands of human organs from its Uighur Muslim minority, UN human-rights body hears*. Insider, Inc. URL: https://www.insider.com/china-harvesting-organs-of-uighur-muslims-china-tribunal-tells-un-2019-9 (visited on 02/05/2025) (cit. on p. 34).

[238] Evans, R. J. (2005). *The Third Reich In Power*. New York: The Penguin Press. ISBN: 1-59420-074-2 (cit. on p. 34).

[239] Montefiore, S. S. (2004). *Stalin*. New York: Alfred A. Knopf. ISBN: 1-4000-4230-5 (cit. on p. 34).

[240] Jekielek, J. (Mar. 2026). *Killed to Order. China's Organ Harvesting Industry and the True Nature of America's Biggest Adversary*. What if everything you need to understand about the Chinese Communist Party—and how the free world should respond to it—could be explained through this one issue? In this urgent and eye-opening book, journalist Jan Jekielek distills decades of investigations from reputable sources, combined with his own research and in-depth firsthand insight, into a compelling case for rethinking our approach to the CCP. Through the lens of grave human rights abuses—most disturbingly, the state-sanctioned harvesting of organs from prisoners of conscience—Jekielek exposes the inner workings of a regime built on deception, coercion, and control. Killed to Order: The Organ Harvesting Industry of China and the True Nature of America's Biggest Adversary reveals why continuing to misunderstand the CCP poses a growing threat to global freedom. Skyhorse. ISBN: 978-1510786509 (cit. on p. 34).

[241] Rummel, R. J. (1994). *Death By Government*. New York: Routledge (cit. on pp. 34, 58, 64, 101, 173).

[242] Dyadkin, I. G. (1983). *Unnatural Deaths in the USSR, 1928 - 1954*. New Brunswick, New Jersey: Transaction Books (cit. on pp. 34, 64, 173).

[243] Courtois, S. et al. (1999). *The Black Book of Communism*. Cambridge, Massachusetts and London, England: Harvard University Press (cit. on pp. 34, 64, 173).

[244] Brashear, M. D. (Nov. 2019). *Holodomor Memorial Day in Ukraine and Around the Globe.* Foundation *for* Economic Education. URL: https://fee.org/article s/holodomor-memorial-day-in-ukraine-and-around-the-globe/ (visited on 02/05/2025) (cit. on pp. 34, 173).

[245] Browning, C. R. (1998). *Ordinary Men.* New York: Harper Perennial. ISBN: 0-06-099506-8 (cit. on pp. 34, 173).

[246] Marrs, J. (2015). *Population Control.* New York, New York: HarperCollins Publishers Inc. ISBN: 978-0-06-235989-6 (cit. on p. 34).

[247] Olsen, B. C. (2021). *Beyond Esoteric: Escaping Prison Planet.* Consortium of Collective Consciousness Publishing™. ISBN: 978-1-888729-74-0 (cit. on p. 34).

[248] Hancock, J. et al. (1776). *The unanimous Declaration of the thirteen united States of America.* Philadelphia, Pennsylvania: The representatives of the united States of America (cit. on p. 34).

[249] Wade, R. A. (1995). *Documents of Soviet History, vol 3 Lenin's Heirs, 1923-1925.* Gulf Breeze, Fl: Academic International Press (cit. on p. 34).

[250] PR (2023). *Who Gives Most to Charity?* Philanthropy Roundtable. URL: https ://www.philanthropyroundtable.org/almanac/who-gives-most-to-charity/ (visited on 02/05/2025) (cit. on p. 35).

[251] Roche, C. (Aug. 2014). "Has the US Dollar Lost 99% of its Purchasing Power Since 1913?" In: *Pragmatic Capitalism: Practical Views on Money.* URL: https: //www.pragcap.com/has-the-dollar-lost-99-precent-of-purchasing-power/ (visited on 02/05/2025) (cit. on p. 37).

[252] Desilver, D. (Aug. 2018). *For most U.S. workers, real wages have barely budged in decades.* Pew Research Center. URL: https://www.pewresearch.org/fact-tank/20 18/08/07/for-most-us-workers-real-wages-have-barely-budged-for-decades/ (visited on 02/05/2025) (cit. on p. 37).

[253] Booth, J. (2020). *The Price Of Tomorrow.* 5 Booths Consulting Inc. ISBN: 978-1-9992574-0-8 (cit. on pp. 38, 209).

[254] Smith, C. H. (Jan. 2018b). *Why Are so Few Americans Able to Get Ahead?* Of Two Minds. URL: https://www.oftwominds.com/blognov18/getting-ahead11-1 8.html (visited on 03/09/2025) (cit. on p. 38).

[255] Fiscal Data (Mar. 2023). *Historical Debt Outstanding.* US department of the Treasury. URL: https://fiscaldata.treasury.gov/datasets/historical-debt-outstand ing/historical-debt-outstanding/ (visited on 02/05/2025) (cit. on p. 38).

[256] Frost, N. (Jan. 2020). *The 1997 merger that paved the way for the Boeing 737 Max crisis.* Yahoo Finance. URL: https://finance.yahoo.com/news/1997-merger-pave d-way-boeing-090042193.html (visited on 02/05/2025) (cit. on p. 39).

[257] Eban, K. (May 2019). *Bottle of Lies.* New York, NY: Ecco, an imprint of Harper-Collins Publishers. ISBN: 978-93-91165-32-1 (cit. on p. 39).

[258] Aird, C. (Sept. 2018). *Young Single People in Japan Aren't Having Sex And The Reason Is Proving Fatal.* SBS (Special Broadcasting Service). URL: https://www.s bs.com.au/news/the-feed/young-single-people-in-japan-aren-t-having-sex-an d-the-reason-is-proving-fatal (visited on 02/05/2025) (cit. on p. 39).

[259] Malo, E. G. (Feb. 2024). *federalism fixes this.* Substack. URL: https://boriquagato .substack.com/p/federalism-fixes-this (visited on 02/05/2025) (cit. on p. 39).

[260] Mansbridge, J. J. (1983). *Beyond Adversary Democracy.* Chicago and London: The University of Chicago Press. ISBN: 0-226-50355-0 (cit. on p. 40).

[261] John, M. and D. Ranasinghe (Sept. 2022). *Europe says goodbye to negative interest rates - or just 'au revoir'?* Reuters. URL: https://www.reuters.com/euro pe/europe-says-goodbye-negative-rates-or-just-au-revoir-2022-09-22/ (visited on 02/05/2025) (cit. on p. 42).

[262] Co, M. (Apr. 2019). *Negative Interest Rates, Cursed Cash, and Bitcoin.* Medium.com. URL: https://medium.com/@burningw0rds/negative-intere st-rates-cursed-cash-and-bitcoin-be195c0573c6 (visited on 02/05/2025) (cit. on p. 42).

[263] Staff News & Analysis (Aug. 2014). *Shock: CFR Suggests That Central Banks Print Money and Hand It Out Directly to Consumers.* The Daily Bell. URL: https://www.thedailybell.com/all-articles/gold-silver/shock-cfr-suggests-that-cent ral-banks-print-money-and-hand-it-out-directly-to-consumers/ (visited on 02/05/2025) (cit. on p. 42).

[264] Bruce, J. (2013). *Money For Nothing: Inside the Federal Reserve.* Motion picture. Documentary film, 104 minutes, released September 6, 2013. Written by Jim Bruce. Narrated by Liev Schreiber. Produced by Liberty Street Films. New York, New York. URL: https://www.imdb.com/title/tt2752724/ (visited on 07/06/2025) (cit. on p. 42).

[265] Bernanke, B. S. (Apr. 2016). *What tools does the Fed have left? Part 3: Helicopter money.* The Brookings Institution. URL: https://www.brookings.edu/article s/what-tools-does-the-fed-have-left-part-3-helicopter-money/ (visited on 02/05/2025) (cit. on p. 42).

[266] Friedman, M. (1969). *The Optimum Quantity of Money.* Chicago, Illinois: Aldine Publishing Company (cit. on p. 43).

[267] Mitchell, D. J. (Oct. 2018). *Keynesian Monetary Policy: A Recipe for False Booms and Real Busts.* URL: https://danieljmitchell.wordpress.com/2018/10/13/keyne sian-monetary-policy-a-recipe-for-false-booms-and-real-busts/ (visited on 02/05/2025) (cit. on p. 43).

[268] Ebeling, R. M. (Sept. 2015). *Monetary Central Planning and the State.* ASIN: B01608MZ1M. Fairfax, Virginia: Future of Freedom Foundation (cit. on p. 43).

[269] Eisenhower, D. D. (Apr. 1953). *The Chance for Peace.* American Society of Newspaper Editors. URL: https://www.eisenhowerlibrary.gov/sites/default/file s/file/chance_for_peace.pdf (visited on 02/05/2025) (cit. on pp. 44, 127, 219).

[270] Johnson, J. L. (Feb. 2024). *The Federal Mega-Debt is Here to Stay.* Mises Institute. URL: https://mises.org/mises-wire/federal-mega-debt-here-stay (visited on 02/05/2025) (cit. on p. 45).

[271] Snyder, M. (Jan. 2025). *11 Reasons Why The Federal Reserve Is Bad.* The Economic Collapse Blog. URL: https://theeconomiccollapseblog.com/11-reasons-why-the-federal-reserve-is-bad-2/ (visited on 02/05/2025) (cit. on p. 45).

[272] Salerno, J. T. (May 2024). *Hyperinflation and the Destruction of Human Person-ality.* Mises Institute. URL: https://mises.org/misesian/hyperinflation-and-destr uction-human-personality/ (visited on 02/05/2025) (cit. on p. 45).

[273] Agorist, M. (Jan. 2022). *80% OF All US Dollars In Existence Have Been Printed In Just The Past Two Years.* The Washington Standard. URL: https://thewashingto nstandard.com/80-of-all-us-dollars-in-existence-have-been-printed-in-just-the -past-two-years/ (visited on 02/05/2025) (cit. on p. 45).

[274] Siripurapu, A. and N. Berman (July 2023). *The Dollar: The World's Reserve Currency*. Council on Foreign Relations. URL: https://www.cfr.org/background er/dollar-worlds-reserve-currency (visited on 02/05/2025) (cit. on p. 45).

[275] Lioudis, N. (Oct. 2024). *What Is the Gold Standard? History and Collapse*. Investo-pedia. URL: https://www.investopedia.com/ask/answers/09/gold-standard.asp (visited on 02/05/2025) (cit. on p. 45).

[276] Smith, B. (Feb. 2024). *Global Economic War – Where the Dollar Stands in the Chaos*. Birch Gold Group. URL: https://www.birchgold.com/blog/news/global-e conomic-war/ (visited on 02/05/2025) (cit. on p. 46).

[277] Schmid, V. (June 2017b). *Bank Money: 'The Root of All Evil'*. The Epoch Times. URL: https://www.theepochtimes.com/bank-money-the-root-of-all-evil_22517 83.html (visited on 02/05/2025) (cit. on p. 47).

[278] admin (Oct. 2023). *SEC Poised to Authorize "Natural Asset Companies"*. American Stewards of Liberty. URL: https://americanstewards.us/sec-poised-to-authorize-natural-asset-companies/ (visited on 02/05/2025) (cit. on pp. 57, 200).

[279] von Hayek, F. A. (1945). *The Use of Knowledge in Society*. New York: Dell Publishing. ISBN: 0-385-31428-0 (cit. on pp. 58, 124).

[280] Carden, A. (2013). "Economic Calculation in the Environmentalist Common-wealth." In: *Quart. J. Austrian. Econ.* 16.1, pp. 27–44 (cit. on pp. 58, 125).

[281] von Mises, L. (1920). *Economic Calculation in the Socialist Commonwealth*. Auburn, Alabama: Mises Institute (cit. on p. 58).

[282] O'Mara, C. (Oct. 2018). "Troubling urban tree declines." In: *Natl. Wild.* 56.6 (cit. on p. 60).

[283] Nassar, D. and M. M. Barbour (Oct. 2019). *Rooted*. Aeon. URL: https://aeon.co/e ssays/what-can-an-embodied-history-of-trees-teach-us-about-life (visited on 03/04/2025) (cit. on p. 60).

[284] Marinelli, J. (Apr. 2019). "A Plea for Trees." In: *Natl. Wild.* 57.3 (cit. on p. 60).

[285] Zeldovich, L. (May 2019). *How Trees Can Save Lakes From Algae Blooms*. JSTOR Daily. URL: https://daily.jstor.org/how-trees-can-save-lakes-from-algae-bloom s/ (visited on 02/05/2025) (cit. on p. 60).

[286] Daley, J. (Mar. 2020). *We can build new climate consensus out of wood*. The Hill. URL: https://thehill.com/blogs/congress-blog/energy-environment/487694-we-can-build-new-climate-consensus-out-of-wood (visited on 02/05/2025) (cit. on pp. 60, 197).

[287] Climate Forests (2025). *Let Trees Grow, Protect The Climate*. Climate Forests. URL: https://www.climate-forests.org/ (visited on 02/05/2025) (cit. on p. 61).

[288] Griscom, B. W. et al. (Oct. 2017). "Natural climate solutions." In: *Proc. Natl. Acad. Sci.* 114.44, pp. 11645–50. ISSN: 0027-8424. DOI: 10.1073/pnas.1710465114 (cit. on pp. 61, 85, 197).

[289] WWF (2018). *Living Planet Report 2018*. Gland, Switzerland: World Wildlife Fund. URL: https://c402277.ssl.cf1.rackcdn.com/publications/1187/files/original /LPR2018_Full_Report_Spreads.pdf (visited on 02/05/2025) (cit. on pp. 61, 104).

[290] Popkin, G. (2018). "Eyes in the Sky." In: *American Forests* 124.3, pp. 24–31 (cit. on pp. 61, 154).

[291] REACCH PNA (May 2013). *Monitoring - Eddy Covariance Flux Towers*. URL: https://www.youtube.com/watch?v=ighAqUtUq3g (visited on 02/05/2025) (cit. on pp. 61, 154).

[292] Figuerola-Ferrando, L. et al. (May 2023). "Global patterns and drivers of genetic diversity among marine habitat-forming species." In: *Glob. Ecol. Biogeogr.* 32.7, pp. 1031–1240. DOI: 10.1111/geb.13685 (cit. on p. 61).

[293] Vaughan, A. (May 2019). *Free-floating DNA to reveal the health of river and lake ecosystems.* New Scientist. URL: https://www.newscientist.com/article/2203112-free-floating-dna-to-reveal-the-health-of-river-and-lake-ecosystems/ (visited on 02/05/2025) (cit. on p. 61).

[294] Mohammed, G. H. et al. (2019). "Remote sensing of solar-induced chlorophyll fluorescence (SIF) in vegetation." In: *Remote Sens. Environ.* 231, p. 111177. ISSN: 0034-4257. DOI: 10.1016/j.rse.2019.04.030 (cit. on pp. 62, 154).

[295] ESA (2025). *FLEX Objectives.* The European Space Agency. URL: https://earth.esa.int/eogateway/missions/flex/objectives (visited on 02/05/2025) (cit. on p. 62).

[296] Miller, J. R. et al. (July 2003). "Progress on the development of an integrated canopy fluorescence model." In: Geoscience and Remote Sensing Symposium, 2003. Toulouse, France: IEEE International, pp. 601–3. ISBN: 0-7803-7929-2. DOI: 10.1109/IGARSS.2003.1293855 (cit. on pp. 62, 154).

[297] Zarco-Tejada, P. J., J. R. Miller, and G. H. Mohammed (2002). "Remote Sensing of Solar-Induced Chlorophyll Fluorescence from Vegetation Hyperspectral Reflectance and Radiative Transfer Simulation." In: *From Laboratory Spectroscopy to Remotely Sensed Spectra of Terrestrial Ecosystems.* Ed. by Muttiah, R. S. Amsterdam, The Netherlands: Springer Science+Business Media Dordrecht, pp. 233–69. ISBN: 978-90-481-6076-1. DOI: 10.1007/978-94-017-1620-8 (cit. on pp. 62, 154).

[298] Wagle, P. et al. (June 2016). "Comparison of solar-induced chlorophyll fluorescence, light-use efficiency, and process-based GPP models in maize." In: *Ecol. Appl.* 26.4, pp. 1211–22. ISSN: 1051-0761. DOI: 10.1890/15-1434 (cit. on pp. 62, 154).

[299] ESA (Dec. 2014). *Glowing plants a sign of health.* European Space Agency. URL: http://www.esa.int/Applications/Observing_the_Earth/Glowing_plants_a_sign_of_health (visited on 02/05/2025) (cit. on pp. 62, 154).

[300] Pinto, F. et al. (Apr. 2017). "Multiangular Observation of Canopy Sun-Induced Chlorophyll Fluorescence by Combining Imaging Spectroscopy and Stereoscopy." In: *Remote Sens.* 9.5, p. 415. DOI: 10.3390/rs9050415 (cit. on pp. 62, 154).

[301] Carter, G., A. F. Theisen, and R. J. Mitchell (Jan. 1990). "Chlorophyll fluorescence measured using the Fraunhofer line-depth principle and relationship to photosynthetic rate in the field." In: *Plant Cell Environ.* 13.1, pp. 79–83. DOI: 10.1111/j.1365-3040.1990.tb01302.x (cit. on pp. 62, 154).

[302] Damm, A. et al. (Mar. 2010). "Deriving Sun-Induced Chlorophyll Fluorescence from Airborne Based Spectrometer Data." In: Hyperspectral 2010 Workshop. Frascati, Italy: ESA, p. 683 (cit. on p. 62).

[303] Alonso, L. et al. (Oct. 2008). "Improved Fraunhofer Line Discrimination Method for Vegetation Fluorescence Quantification." In: *IEEE Geosci. Remote. Sens. Lett.* 5.4, pp. 620–4. DOI: 10.1109/LGRS.2008.2001180 (cit. on p. 62).

[304] Moreno, J. et al. (Oct. 2006). "FLuorescence EXplorer (FLEX): an optimised payload to map vegetation photosynthesis from space." In: 57th International Astronautical Congress. Valencia, Spain: American Institute of Astronautical Congress. DOI: 10.2514/6.IAC-06-B1.3.04 (cit. on pp. 62, 193).

[305] Key, R. et al. (Mar. 2012). "The Geostationary Carbon Process Mapper." In: *2012 IEEE Aerospace Conference.* Big Sky, MT: IEEE, pp. 1–16. ISBN: 978-1-4577-0556-4. DOI: 10.1109/AERO.2012.6187029 (cit. on p. 62).

[306] Frankenberg, C. et al. (May 2014). "Prospects for chlorophyll fluorescence remote sensing from the Orbiting Carbon Observatory-2." In: *Remote Sens Environ* 147, pp. 1–12. ISSN: 0034-4257. DOI: 10.1016/j.rse.2014.02.007 (cit. on p. 62).

[307] Ni, Z. et al. (July 2019). "Estimation of Chlorophyll Fluorescence at Different Scales: A Review." In: *Sensors* 19.13, p. 3000. ISSN: 1424-8220. DOI: 10.3390/s191 33000 (cit. on p. 62).

[308] Joiner, J. et al. (Mar. 2011). "First observations of global and seasonal terrestrial chlorophyll fluorescence from space." In: *Biogeosciences* 8.3, pp. 637–51. DOI: 10.5194/bg-8-637-2011 (cit. on pp. 62, 154).

[309] Selding, P. B. de (Sept. 2015). *Panel Endorses Vegetation Fluorescence Mapper for ESA's Earth Explorer Program.* Space News. URL: https://spacenews.com/panel-endorses-vegetation-fluorescence-mapper-for-esas-earth-explorer-program/ (visited on 02/05/2025) (cit. on p. 62).

[310] Buis, A. and P. Lynch (Dec. 2016). "NASA Releases New Eye-Popping View of Carbon Dioxide." In: *Jet Propulsion Laboratory* (cit. on p. 62).

[311] Moon (Sept. 2023). *The Metaverse situation gets much worse.* Youtube. URL: https://www.youtube.com/watch?v=2w4GS7ZR20Y (visited on 02/05/2025) (cit. on p. 62).

[312] Lang, D. (July 2017). *Towards an Internet of Living Things.* Medium. URL: https://davidtlang.medium.com/towards-an-internet-of-living-things-f1aada3f9a17 (visited on 03/10/2025) (cit. on p. 62).

[313] Conniff, R. (2012). *What's Wrong with Putting a Price on Nature?* URL: https://e 360.yale.edu/features/ecosystem_services_whats_wrong_with_putting_a_pric e_on_nature (visited on 02/05/2025) (cit. on pp. 64, 200).

[314] Shaw, G. B. (1921). *Back to Methuselah.* The serpent speaks these words to Eve. London, England: Constable and Company, Ltd. (cit. on p. 67).

[315] Messy Nessy Chic (Mar. 2019). *When Seashells Were Money.* URL: https://www .messynessychic.com/2019/03/18/when-seashells-were-money/ (visited on 02/05/2025) (cit. on p. 69).

[316] Tréguer, P. (2025). *Meaning and Origin of the Phrasal Verb 'shell out'.* word histories. URL: https://wordhistories.net/2016/09/21/shell-out/ (visited on 02/05/2025) (cit. on p. 69).

[317] Radford, R. A. (Nov. 1945). "The Economic Organization of a P.O.W. Camp." In: *Economica* 12.48, pp. 189–201. ISSN: 0013-0427 (cit. on p. 69).

[318] Shrem, C. (Aug. 2018). *A Geek in Prison — Part 13 — MackerelCoin & My Socioeconomic Observations of Prison.* Medium. URL: https://medium.com/@csh rem/a-geek-in-prison-part-13-mackerelcoin-my-socioeconomic-observations-of-prison-ebc057a83e1d (visited on 02/05/2025) (cit. on p. 69).

[319] Wadhwa, T. (Dec. 2016). *A 26-year old Bitcoin entrepreneur was handed prison time, and the experience only confirmed his belief in the cryptocurrency.* Business Insider. URL: https://www.businessinsider.nl/bitcoin-entrepreneur-charlie-shr em-gives-first-interview-out-of-prison-to-wall-and-broadcast-2016-11/?jwsou rce=cl (visited on 02/05/2025) (cit. on p. 69).

[320]   56th Congress of the United States (Mar. 1901). *The Statutes At Large Of The United States Of America, from December, 1899, to March, 1901.* Washington: Government Printing Office. URL: https://tile.loc.gov/storage-services/service/l l/llsl//llsl-c56/llsl-c56.pdf (visited on 02/05/2025) (cit. on pp. 69, 138, 156, 198, 227, 230).

[321]   Ghizoni, S. K. (Nov. 2013a). *Creation of the Bretton Woods System.* Federal Reserve History. URL: https://www.federalreservehistory.org/essays/bretton-w oods-created (visited on 02/05/2025) (cit. on pp. 70, 202, 232).

[322]   Office of the Historian (2025). *Bretton Woods-GATT, 1941–1947.* United States Department of State. URL: https://history.state.gov/milestones/1937-1945/brett on-woods (visited on 02/05/2025) (cit. on pp. 70, 202, 232).

[323]   Chen, J. (Feb. 2024). *Bretton Woods Agreement and the Institutions It Created Explained.* URL: https://www.investopedia.com/terms/b/brettonwoodsagreeme nt.asp (visited on 02/05/2025) (cit. on pp. 70, 202, 232).

[324]   Georgescu-Roegen, N. (1971). *The Entropy Law and the Economic Process.* Cambridge, Massachusetts: Harvard University Press. ISBN: 0-674-25780-4 (cit. on pp. 70, 81, 116, 252, 253).

[325]   Anderson, J. (June 2019). *How much Silver and Gold is there in the World?* SD Bullion. URL: https://sdbullion.com/blog/how-much-silver-gold-is-there (visited on 02/05/2025) (cit. on p. 71).

[326]   Garret, O. (June 2018). *The 3 Biggest Trends That Will Drive Gold In The Next 30 Years.* Forbes. URL: https://www.forbes.com/sites/oliviergarret/2018/06/20 /the-3-biggest-trends-that-will-drive-gold-in-the-next-30-years/ (visited on 02/05/2025) (cit. on p. 71).

[327]   King, H. M. (2025). *The Many Uses of Gold.* Geoscience News and Information. URL: https://geology.com/minerals/gold/uses-of-gold.shtml (visited on 05/17/2025) (cit. on p. 71).

[328]   Eliseo, J. (July 2016). *Stock to flow and why gold is not a commodity.* Gold Industry Group. URL: https://www.goldindustrygroup.com.au/news/2016/7/7 /gold-investor-series-stock-to-flow-why-gold-is-not-a-commodity (visited on 02/05/2025) (cit. on pp. 71, 72).

[329]   Barton, P. (July 2011). *Stock to Flow Ratio – A Primer.* Gold Standard Institute International. URL: https://goldstandardinstitute.net/2011/07/16/stock-to-flow-ratio-a-primer/ (visited on 02/05/2025) (cit. on p. 72).

[330]   Phillips, T. and F. Milhorance (May 2021). *Brazil aerial photos show miners' devastation of indigenous people's land.* The Guardian. URL: https://www.thegu ardian.com/global-development/2021/may/27/brazil-aerial-photos-reveal-dev astation-by-goldminers-on-indigenous-land (visited on 02/05/2025) (cit. on p. 73).

[331]   Gertner, J. (2019). "Reverse Engineering the Climate Crisis Is Not Only Possible – It's Necessary." In: *Audubon* 121.3, pp. 66–8. ISSN: 0097-7136. URL: https://www .audubon.org/magazine/fall-2019/reverse-engineering-climate-crisis-not-only (visited on 02/05/2025) (cit. on p. 84).

[332]   Jenkins, M. (Sept. 2018). "Carbon Capture." In: *Nature Conservancy Magazine,* pp. 28–36. ISSN: 1540-2428 (cit. on p. 85).

[333]   Paton, I. M. (Sept. 2023). *Man-Made Climate Change is a Hoax.* Substack. URL: https://ivanmpaton.substack.com/p/man-made-climate-change-is-a-hoax (visited on 02/05/2025) (cit. on p. 85).

[334] Butler, B. J. et al. (Mar. 2021). *Family Forest Ownerships of the United States, 2018: Results from the USDA Forest Service, National Woodland Owner Survey. A Technical Document Supporting the USDA Forest Service 2020 RPA Assessment.* report. United States Department of Agriculture, Forest Service, Northern Research Station. DOI: 10.2737/nrs-gtr-199. (Visited on 02/05/2025) (cit. on pp. 85, 87, 90, 92, 103).

[335] Hodge, S. A. (2016). *The Compliance Costs of IRS Regulations.* report. The Tax Foundation (cit. on pp. 89, 245).

[336] Williams, W. E. (Oct. 2017). *Who Pays What in Taxes?* LewRockwell. URL: https ://www.lewrockwell.com/2017/10/walter-e-williams/who-pays-what-in-taxes/ (visited on 03/10/2025) (cit. on p. 89).

[337] US Forest Service (May 2008). *Who Owns America's Forests?* report. United States Department of Agriculture (cit. on p. 93).

[338] Propagate Ventures (2025). *Do You Want to Plant Trees?* URL: https://www.pro pagateventures.com/ (visited on 02/05/2025) (cit. on p. 93).

[339] Rodale Institute (2025). *The Future is Organic.* URL: https://rodaleinstitute.org/ (visited on 02/05/2025) (cit. on p. 93).

[340] Bates, A. (2010). *The Biochar Solution.* Gabriola Island, British Columbia: New Society Publishers. ISBN: 978-0-86571-677-3 (cit. on pp. 93, 197).

[341] Putol, R. (Sept. 2024). *Organic farming practices boost soil carbon storage.* Earth.com, Inc. URL: https://www.earth.com/news/organic-farming-pra ctices-boost-soil-carbon-storage/ (visited on 02/05/2025) (cit. on pp. 93, 197).

[342] Scheub, U. et al. (2016). *Terra Preta. How the World's Most Fertile Soil Can Help Reverse Climate Change and Reduce World Hunger.* Vancouver, British Columbia: Greystone Books Ltd. ISBN: 978-1-77164-110-4 (cit. on pp. 93, 197).

[343] NWF (2025). *National Wildlife Federation.* URL: https://www.nwf.org/ (visited on 02/05/2025) (cit. on p. 94).

[344] Macleod, A. (Nov. 2018). *Prices When Gold Is Money.* Goldmoney. URL: https: //www.goldmoney.com/research/goldmoney-insights/prices-when-gold-is-mo ney (visited on 02/05/2025) (cit. on p. 96).

[345] Stefano Boeri Architetti (July 2017). "Liuzhou Forest City." In: *Architect.* URL: https://www.architectmagazine.com/project-gallery/liuzhou-forest-city_o (visited on 02/05/2025) (cit. on p. 96).

[346] Kintisch, E. (Dec. 2015). "Born to rewild. A father and son's quixotic quest to bring back a lost ecosystem—and save the world." In: *Science* 350 (6265), pp. 1148–51. ISSN: 1095-9203. DOI: 10.1126/science.350.6265.1148 (cit. on p. 96).

[347] Phelan, R. (2025). *Revive & Restore.* Genetic Rescue of Endangered and Extinct Species. URL: https://reviverestore.org/ (visited on 10/26/2025) (cit. on p. 96).

[348] Zimmer, C. (Apr. 2013). "Bringing Them Back to Life." In: *National Geographic Magazine* 223.4, pp. 28–43 (cit. on p. 96).

[349] Kluger, J. (Apr. 2025). *The Return of the Dire Wolf.* Time USA, LLC. URL: https: //time.com/7274542/colossal-dire-wolf/ (visited on 04/07/2025) (cit. on p. 96).

[350] Kazamia, E. (Apr. 2025). *The Last of Their Kind.* Nautilus: Science Connected. URL: https://nautil.us/the-last-of-their-kind-1204387/ (visited on 04/24/2025) (cit. on p. 96).

[351] Bruch, K. (2021). *The Last Old Growth Sawyer.* Kalispell, Montana: Scott Publishing Company. ISBN: 978-1-954463-01-1 (cit. on pp. 96, 111, 118, 197).

[352]   Gentile, G., J. Gentile, and A. J. Gentile (2023a). *Solar storms: more dangerous than you think. Can we survive another Carrington Event?* The Why Files. URL: https://www.youtube.com/watch?v=ftrbdFGTQO4 (visited on 02/05/2025) (cit. on pp. 97, 130).

[353]   Guest, C. et al. (1984). *This Is Spinal Tap.* Motion picture. Mockumentary comedy film, 82 minutes, released March 2, 1984. Screenplay by Christopher Guest, Michael McKean, Harry Shearer, and Rob Reiner. Score by Christopher Guest, Michael McKean, Harry Shearer, and Rob Reiner. Los Angeles, California. URL: https://www.imdb.com/title/tt0088258/ (visited on 07/06/2025) (cit. on p. 98).

[354]   Kinsella, N. S. (2001). "Against Intellectual Property." In: *J. Libert. Stud.* 15.2, pp. 1–53. ISSN: 0363-2873 (cit. on p. 98).

[355]   Barnett, J. M. (June 2021). *How IP Rights Keep Markets Free.* Washington, D.C.: The Hudson Institute. URL: https://s3.amazonaws.com/media.hudson.org /Barnett_How%20IP%20Rights%20Keep%20Markets%20Free.pdf (visited on 02/05/2025) (cit. on p. 98).

[356]   Levine, D. K. and M. Boldrin (2008). *Against Intellectual Monopoly.* New York, New York: Cambridge University Press (cit. on pp. 98, 99).

[357]   Meyer, A. (2024). *Why the U.S. Patent System is literally a Scam!* FD Finance. URL: https://www.youtube.com/watch?v=c4NIFzG8NcU (visited on 02/05/2025) (cit. on p. 99).

[358]   Ghizoni, S. K. (Nov. 2013b). *Nixon Ends Convertibility of U.S. Dollars to Gold and Announces Wage/Price Controls.* Federal Reserve Bank of St. Louis. URL: https://www.federalreservehistory.org/essays/gold-convertibility-ends/ (visited on 02/05/2025) (cit. on p. 101).

[359]   Hooper, R. (Apr. 2021). *Suzanne Simard interview: How I uncovered the hidden language of trees.* New Scientist. URL: https://www.newscientist.com/article/m g25033320-900-suzanne-simard-interview-how-i-uncovered-the-hidden-langu age-of-trees/ (visited on 02/05/2025) (cit. on p. 110).

[360]   Himanen, S. J. et al. (Mar. 2010). "Birch (Betula spp.) leaves adsorb and re-release volatiles specific to neighbouring plants — a mechanism for associational herbivore resistance?" In: *New Phytol.* 186.3, pp. 722–32. ISSN: 1469-8137. DOI: 10.1111/j.1469-8137.2010.03220.x (cit. on p. 110).

[361]   Hall, S. S. (May 2013). "On Beyond 100." In: *National Geographic Magazine* 223.5, pp. 28–49 (cit. on p. 115).

[362]   Ullekh N. P. (Dec. 2018). *The Quest for Immortality.* Open Media Network Pvt. Ltd. URL: https://openthemagazine.com/cover-stories/new-year-2019-issue/the -quest-for-immortality/ (visited on 02/05/2025) (cit. on p. 115).

[363]   Errico, J. P. (Sept. 2024). *From Controversy to Cutting-Edge: The Fountain of Youth.* RealClearHealth. URL: https://realclearwire.com/articles/2024/09/30 /from_controversy_to_cutting-edge_the_fountain_of_youth_1061910.html (visited on 02/05/2025) (cit. on p. 115).

[364]   SENS (2024). *Strategies for Engineered Negligible Senescence.* SENS research foundation. URL: http://www.sens.org/ (visited on 05/28/2024) (cit. on pp. 115, 181).

[365]   Dunn, J. (Sept. 2020). *Is Aging a Disease You Can Reverse? A Look at the Science Behind the Longevity Movement.* Vogue. URL: https://www.vogue.com/article/h ow-to-live-longer-longevity (visited on 02/05/2025) (cit. on p. 115).

[366] Grey, A. de and M. Rae (Oct. 2008). *Ending Aging*. Stuttgart, Germany: St. Martin's Griffin. ISBN: 978-0-312-36706-0 (cit. on p. 115).

[367] Sinclair, D. (2026). *Live Your Longest, Healthiest Life. Join the Longevity Revolution*. Lifespan Podcast, LLC. URL: https://www.lifespan.com/ (visited on 04/28/2026) (cit. on p. 115).

[368] Muneoka, K., M. Han, and D. M. Gardiner (2008). "Regrowing Limbs: Can People Regenerate Body Parts?" In: *Sci. Am.* 298.4, pp. 56–63. ISSN: 0036-8733. URL: https://www.scientificamerican.com/article/regrowing-human-limbs/ (visited on 02/05/2025) (cit. on pp. 116, 128, 152, 205, 209).

[369] Marshall, P. (2010). *Demanding The Impossible*. Oakland, California: PM Press. ISBN: 978-1-60486-064-1 (cit. on pp. 118, 125).

[370] Peron, J. (Apr. 2018). *Why Capitalism Evolved*. URL: https://medium.com/the-radical-center/why-capitalism-evolved-2caa7402ecf0 (visited on 03/03/2025) (cit. on pp. 119, 125).

[371] Merriam-Webster (2025). *Posse comitatus*. Merriam-Webster, Incorporated. URL: https://www.merriam-webster.com/dictionary/posse%5C%20comitatus (visited on 02/05/2025) (cit. on p. 119).

[372] Bruce, V. (2025). *The Grim Reaper and the Tax Man*. The Blurred Line. URL: https://furrynuff.wordpress.com/2011/09/05/the-grim-reaper-and-the-tax-man/ (visited on 02/05/2025) (cit. on p. 120).

[373] Forest-Climate Working Group (2025). *America's only forest sector coalition working to advance climate change solutions*. American Forests. URL: http://www.forestclimateworkinggroup.org/ (visited on 02/05/2025) (cit. on pp. 121, 197).

[374] Pearce, F. (Sept. 2020). *Natural Debate: Do Forests Grow Better With Our Help or Without?* Yale School of the Environment. URL: https://e360.yale.edu/features/natural-debate-do-forests-grow-better-with-our-help-or-without (visited on 02/05/2025) (cit. on p. 121).

[375] Falge, E. et al. (2002). "Seasonality of ecosystem respiration and gross primary production as derived from FLUXNET measurements." In: *Agric. For. Meteorol.* 113, pp. 53–74 (cit. on pp. 121, 197).

[376] Barford, C. C. et al. (Nov. 2001). "Factors Controlling Long- and Short-Term Sequestration of Atmospheric CO_2 in a Mid-latitude Forest." In: *Science* 294.5547, pp. 1688–91. DOI: 10.1126/science.1062962 (cit. on pp. 121, 197).

[377] Biopact (Nov. 2006). *Idea that forests are 'carbon sinks' no longer holds*. URL: https://global.mongabay.com/news/bioenergy/2006/11/idea-that-forests-are-carbon-sinks-no.html (visited on 02/05/2025) (cit. on pp. 121, 197).

[378] Planet Snapshots (May 2024). *Issue 124: Church Forests*. Planet. URL: https://medium.com/@planetsnapshots/issue-124-church-forests-1f5164b05e8e (visited on 02/05/2025) (cit. on p. 121).

[379] Popova, M. (2025). *The Healing Power of Gardens*. Brain Pickings. URL: https://www.brainpickings.org/2019/05/27/oliver-sacks-gardens/ (visited on 02/05/2025) (cit. on p. 122).

[380] Arnold, C. (2020). "tree think." In: *American Forests* 126.2, pp. 36–43 (cit. on p. 122).

[381] Leahy, I. (2020). "Returning to a Land That Owns Us." In: *American Forests* 126.2, pp. 44–5 (cit. on p. 122).

[382] Brownstein, B. (Mar. 2019). *Why Long Lines at Motor Vehicle Departments Never Disappear*. Foundation for Economic Education. URL: https://fee.org/articles

/why-long-lines-at-motor-vehicle-departments-never-disappear/ (visited on 02/05/2025) (cit. on p. 123).

[383] Hoppe, H. (2003). "Government and the Private Production of Defense." In: *The Myth of National Defense*. Ed. by Hoppe, H. Auburn, Alabama: Mises Institute. ISBN: 978-0-945466-37-6 (cit. on p. 123).

[384] — (2009). *The Private Production of Defense*. Auburn, Alabama: Mises Institute (cit. on pp. 123, 129).

[385] Hasnas, J. (2005a). "Ethics and the Problem of White Collar Crime." In: *American University Law Review* 54, pp. 579–660 (cit. on p. 123).

[386] — (2006). *Trapped. When Acting Ethically is Against The Law*. Washington, D.C.: Cato Institute. ISBN: 978-1-930865-88-4 (cit. on p. 123).

[387] Benson, B. L. (1990). *The Enterprise of Law*. Oakland, California: Independent Institute. ISBN: 978-1-59813-044-7 (cit. on p. 124).

[388] Hasnas, J. (Sept. 2005b). "Hayek, The Common Law, and Fluid Drive." In: *New York University Journal of Law & Liberty* 1.0, pp. 79–110 (cit. on pp. 124, 129).

[389] — (2008). "The Obviousness of Anarchy." In: *Anarchism/Minarchism*. Ed. by Long, R. T. and Machan, T. R. London: Routledge. ISBN: 978-1-138-26546-2. DOI: 10.4324/9781315566955 (cit. on p. 124).

[390] — (1995). "The Myth of the Rule of Law." In: *Wisconsin Law Review* 199 (cit. on pp. 124, 128).

[391] Green, B. D. and R. G. Nix (Nov. 2006). *Geothermal — The Energy Under Our Feet. Geothermal Resource Estimates for the United States*. Golden, Colorado: National Renewable Energy Laboratory. URL: https://docs.nrel.gov/docs/fy07o sti/40665.pdf (visited on 04/28/2026) (cit. on p. 124).

[392] Cromwell, D. (July 2020). "Six months to avert climate crisis." In: *Cold Type* 209, pp. 46–50 (cit. on p. 125).

[393] Farr, W. K., R. A. Lord, and J. L. Wolfenbarger (1998). "Economic Freedom, Political Freedom, and Economic Well-Being." In: *Cato J.* 18.2, pp. 247–62. ISSN: 0273-3072 (cit. on p. 125).

[394] Dawson, J. W. (2002). "Causality in the freedom – growth relationship." In: *Eur. J. Polit. Econ.* 19.3, pp. 479–95. ISSN: 0176-2680. DOI: 10.1016/S0176-2680(03)000 09-0 (cit. on p. 125).

[395] Giavazzi, F. and G. Tabellini (2005). "Economic and political liberalizations." In: *J. Monet. Econ.* 52.7, pp. 1297–1330. ISSN: 0304-3932. DOI: 10.1016/j.jmoneco.20 05.05.002 (cit. on p. 125).

[396] Haan, J. de, S. Lundström, and J.-E. Sturm (Apr. 2006). "Market-Oriented Institutions and Policies and Economic Growth: A Critical Survey." In: *J. Econ. Surv.* 20.2, pp. 157–91. ISSN: 0950-0804. DOI: 10.1111/j.0950-0804.2006.00278.x (cit. on p. 125).

[397] Netter, J. M. and W. L. Megginson (June 2001). "From State to Market." In: *J Econ. Lit.* 39.2, pp. 321–89. ISSN: 0022-0515. DOI: 10.1257/jel.39.2.321 (cit. on p. 125).

[398] Gwartney, J. et al. (Sept. 2020). *Economic Freedom of the World. Annual Report 2020*. Vancouver, B.C.: Fraser Institute. URL: https://www.fraserinstitute.or g/sites/default/files/economic-freedom-of-the-world-2020.pdf (visited on 02/05/2025) (cit. on p. 125).

[399]   Sawyer, C. (June 2023). *A startling film about the evils of sex trafficking in America.* Youtube. URL: https://www.youtube.com/watch?v=KOB3kzXmMGQ (visited on 02/05/2025) (cit. on p. 125).

[400]   Andersen, R. (Mar. 2019). *A Journey Into the Animal Mind.* The Atlantic. URL: https://www.theatlantic.com/magazine/archive/2019/03/what-the-crow-knows/580726/ (visited on 02/05/2025) (cit. on p. 125).

[401]   Woodruff, M. (July 2020). *The face of the fish.* Aeon. URL: https://aeon.co/essays/fish-are-nothing-like-us-except-that-they-are-sentient-beings (visited on 02/05/2025) (cit. on p. 126).

[402]   Safina, C. (2015). *Beyond Words.* New York: Henry Holy and Company. ISBN: 978-1-250-09459-9 (cit. on p. 126).

[403]   Masson, J. M. and S. McCarthy (1995). *When Elephants Weep.* New York: Dell Publishing. ISBN: 0-385-31428-0 (cit. on p. 126).

[404]   Newkirk, I. (Apr. 2021). "Help Us Close the National Primate Torture Centers." In: *PETA Global* 2. ISSN: 0899-9708 (cit. on p. 126).

[405]   Kinder World (2025). *Hell on Earth: The Slaughterhouse Experience of 5 Animals.* URL: https://www.kinderworld.org/videos/meat-industry/slaughterhouse-what-hell-looks-like/ (visited on 02/05/2025) (cit. on p. 126).

[406]   IDAUSA (2025). *Fighting For Animals, People and the Environment Since 1983.* In Defense of Animals. URL: https://www.idausa.org/ (visited on 02/05/2025) (cit. on p. 126).

[407]   PETA (2025). *Animals Are Not Ours.* People for the Ethical Treatment of Animals. URL: https://www.peta.org/ (visited on 02/05/2025) (cit. on p. 126).

[408]   ALDF (June 2023). "Victory for Primates in Laboratories." In: *The Animals' Advocate* 42.3, pp. 3–4 (cit. on p. 126).

[409]   Gavin, H. (Sept. 2018). *Harrowing footage reveals 'HORRIFIC cruelty' of animal market where dogs are BURNED ALIVE.* Express Newspapers. URL: https://www.express.co.uk/news/world/1013575/tomohon-extreme-market-indonesia-sulawesi-dog-cat-meat-trade-rabies (visited on 02/05/2025) (cit. on p. 126).

[410]   Humane Ventures (2025). *Animal Clock.* URL: https://www.animalclock.org/ (visited on 02/05/2025) (cit. on p. 126).

[411]   Count Leo Tolstoi (1896). *Patriotism and Christianity.* Paternoster Square, London: Walter Scott, LTD. (cit. on p. 126).

[412]   Gilbert, G. M. (1961). *Nuremberg Diary.* New York: New American Library. ISBN: 978-0-306-80661-2 (cit. on p. 126).

[413]   Milius, J., F. F. Coppola, and M. Herr (1979). *Apocalypse Now.* Motion picture. Psychological epic war film, 153 minutes, released May 19, 1979. Loosely based on "Heart of Darkness" by Joseph Conrad. Score by Carmine Coppola and Francis Coppola. Culver City, California. URL: https://www.imdb.com/title/tt0078788/ (visited on 10/06/2025) (cit. on p. 127).

[414]   Rodat, R. (1998). *Saving Private Ryan.* Motion picture. Epic war film, 170 minutes, released July 24, 1998. Score by John Williams. Universal City, California. URL: https://www.imdb.com/title/tt0120815/ (visited on 10/06/2025) (cit. on p. 127).

[415]   McKenna, B. C. et al. (2010). *The Pacific.* TV Mini Series. War drama, 10 episodes, 47 - 61 minutes, released 2010. Score by Hans Zimmer, Geoff Zanelli, and Blake Neely. Universal City, California. URL: https://www.imdb.com/title/tt0374463/ (visited on 10/06/2025) (cit. on p. 127).

[416] Lowi Jr., A. and C. Holloway (Dec. 2019). *Thorium*. LewRockwell. URL: https://www.lewrockwell.com/2019/12/no_author/thorium/ (visited on 02/05/2025) (cit. on p. 128).

[417] Dawson, L. A. et al. (2016). "Digit Regeneration in Mammals." In: *Innovations in Molecular Mechanisms and Tissue Engineering*. Ed. by Wilson-Rawls, J. and Kusumi, K. Gewerbestrasse 11, 6330 Cham, Switzerland: Humana Press, an imprint of Springer Nature, pp. 79–99. ISBN: 978-3-319-44994-4. DOI: 10.1007/978-3-319-44996-8_5 (cit. on p. 128).

[418] Featherstone, A. W. (2016). *Restoring the ancient Caledonian Forest*. TEDx. URL: https://www.youtube.com/watch?v=nAGHUkby2Is (visited on 02/05/2025) (cit. on p. 128).

[419] Fennell, L. A. (2011). "Ostrom's Law: Property Rights in the Commons." In: *John M. Olin Program in Law and Economics Working Paper* 584. URL: https://chicagounbound.uchicago.edu/cgi/viewcontent.cgi?article=1356&context=law_and_economics (visited on 02/05/2025) (cit. on p. 128).

[420] Ostrom, E. (1990). *Governing the Commons*. Cambridge: Cambridge University Press. ISBN: 978-0-511-80776-3 (cit. on p. 128).

[421] Tannehill, M. and L. Tannehill (Oct. 1970). *The Market for Liberty*. Auburn, Alabama: Mises Institute (cit. on p. 129).

[422] Verma, V. (Sept. 2024). *Earth to Pass Through the Same Taurid Meteor Stream in 2032 That May Have Triggered a Mass Extinction 12,800 Years Ago*. How & Whys. URL: https://howandwhys.com/taurid-meteor-stream-in-2032-2/ (visited on 02/05/2025) (cit. on p. 129).

[423] Gentile, G., J. Gentile, and A. J. Gentile (Nov. 2023b). *Göbekli Tepe and the Prophecy of Pillar 43 | Apocalypse and the Vulture Stone*. The Why Files. URL: https://www.youtube.com/watch?v=r4xzFWW-FAA (visited on 02/05/2025) (cit. on p. 129).

[424] Cox, B. (Jan. 2025). *James Webb Insane Discovery Could Destroy The Universe*. Interstellar Insights. URL: https://www.youtube.com/watch?v=BoOGd5BhWQs (visited on 02/05/2025) (cit. on p. 129).

[425] Weber, D. (1992). *Mutineers' Moon*. New York: Baen Books (cit. on p. 131).

[426] Moffitt, D. (1986a). *The Genesis Quest*. New York: Ballantine Books (cit. on pp. 131, 205).

[427] — (1986b). *Second Genesis*. New York: Ballantine Books (cit. on pp. 131, 205).

[428] Dyson, F. J. (Nov. 1997a). *Warm-Blooded Plants and Freeze-Dried Fish*. The Atlantic online. URL: https://www.theatlantic.com/past/docs/issues/97nov/space.htm (visited on 02/05/2025) (cit. on p. 131).

[429] Semay, C. and B. Silvestre-Brac (Feb. 2007). "Equation of motion of an interstellar Bussard ramjet with radiation and mass loss." In: *Acta Astronaut.* 61.10, pp. 817–22. ISSN: 0094-5765. DOI: 10.1016/j.actaastro.2007.02.003 (cit. on p. 131).

[430] Brin, D. (1983). *Startide Rising*. New York: Bantam Books (cit. on p. 132).

[431] Kasdan, L. and G. Lucas (1983). *Return of the Jedi*. Motion picture. Science fiction film, 131 minutes, released May 25, 1983. Screenplay by Lawrence Kasdan and George Lucas, based on a story by George Lucas. Score by John Williams. Also known as "Star Wars: Episode VI—Return of the Jedi." San Francisco, California. URL: https://www.imdb.com/title/tt0086190/ (visited on 07/06/2025) (cit. on p. 133).

[432]   Deming, D. (Apr. 2022a). *Our Underground Future*. LewRockwell. URL: https:
         //www.lewrockwell.com/2022/04/david-deming/our-underground-future/
         (visited on 02/05/2025) (cit. on p. 133).

[433]   —   (Dec. 2022b). *Human Potential Is Illimitable*. LewRockwell. URL: https:
         //www.lewrockwell.com/2022/12/david-deming/human-potential-is-illimitabl
         e/ (visited on 02/05/2025) (cit. on p. 133).

[434]   Nakamoto, S. (2008). *Bitcoin: A Peer-to-Peer Electronic Cash System*. URL: https:
         //www.bitcoin.org/bitcoin.pdf (visited on 02/05/2025) (cit. on p. 140).

[435]   Johnson, A. B. (Oct. 2020b). *Usernames & Dash Platform Name Service (DPNS) |
         Dash Platform #4*. Dash Digital Cash. URL: https://www.youtube.com/watch?v
         =qQ4WikHu32E (visited on 02/05/2025) (cit. on pp. 140, 141).

[436]   —   (Feb. 2021). *General Usability | How Dash Fixed It*. Dash DAO. URL:
         https://www.youtube.com/watch?v=FW2euFrYqMM (visited on 02/05/2025)
         (cit. on p. 140).

[437]   Siradegyan, M. (July 2024). *Introducing Dash Evolution*. Dash Core Group. URL:
         https://www.dash.org/blog/introducing-dash-evolution-platform/ (visited on
         06/19/2025) (cit. on p. 140).

[438]   CryptoWorldReview (Nov. 2021). *Why Dash Wins as Digital Cash*. Medium.
         URL: https://medium.com/@CryptoWorldRev2/what-dash-digital-cash-is-do
         ing-better-than-anyone-else-in-crypto-9d5d9acb353 (visited on 02/05/2025)
         (cit. on p. 140).

[439]   Johnson, A. B. (Apr. 2023). *SEC Calls Dash "Unregistered Security": What Does
         This Mean?* Dash Incubator. URL: https://www.youtube.com/watch?v=erzdzts
         LyMU (visited on 02/05/2025) (cit. on p. 140).

[440]   Epiq (2025). *Yes, Blockchain Can Be Hacked: 3 Ways It Can Be Done*. URL: https://w
         ww.epiqglobal.com/en-us/resource-center/articles/blockchain-can-be-hacked
         (visited on 02/05/2025) (cit. on p. 141).

[441]   Johnson, A. B. (Sept. 2020c). *Dash is Becoming a Decentralized Cloud | Dash
         Platform #1*. Dash Digital Cash. URL: https://www.youtube.com/watch?v=9Wq
         UMrIN58Q (visited on 02/05/2025) (cit. on p. 141).

[442]   —   (Sept. 2020d). *What is Dash Drive? | Dash Platform #2*. Dash Digital
         Cash. URL: https://www.youtube.com/watch?v=14N5pnl5W0Y (visited on
         02/05/2025) (cit. on p. 141).

[443]   —   (Sept. 2020e). *What is Dash's Decentralized API? (DAPI) | Dash Platform
         #3*. Dash Digital Cash. URL: https://www.youtube.com/watch?v=S0pq-qOu9cQ
         (visited on 02/05/2025) (cit. on p. 141).

[444]   —   (Oct. 2020f). *What is Dash Platform Protocol? (DPP) | Dash Platform #5*.
         Dash Digital Cash. URL: https://www.youtube.com/watch?v=y8LDANH6Ggw
         (visited on 02/05/2025) (cit. on p. 141).

[445]   Smith, H. (Jan. 2021). *The GameStop Short Squeeze Accelerates*. The Motley Fool.
         URL: https://www.fool.com/investing/2021/01/25/the-gamestop-short-squeeze-
         continues/ (visited on 02/05/2025) (cit. on p. 143).

[446]   Editors of Wikipedia (2025). *GameStop short squeeze*. Wikipedia. URL: https://e
         n.wikipedia.org/wiki/GameStop_short_squeeze (visited on 02/05/2025) (cit. on
         p. 143).

[447]   Jones, C. (June 2021). *A Short Squeeze Could Save GameStop Investors A Third
         Time*. Forbes. URL: https://www.forbes.com/sites/chuckjones/2021/06/11

/a-short-squeeze-could-save-gamestop-investors-a-third-time/ (visited on 02/05/2025) (cit. on p. 143).

[448]   Jesse (Mar. 2010). *Brown's Bottom: Was This a Bailout of the Multinational Bullion Banks Involving the NY Fed?* Jesse's Café Américain. URL: https://jessescrossro adscafe.blogspot.com/2010/03/browns-bottom-is-enormous-issue-in-uk.html (visited on 02/08/2025) (cit. on p. 144).

[449]   Howe, R. H. (Dec. 2004). *Déjà Vu: Central Banks at the Abyss.* The Golden Sextant. URL: https://goldensextant.com/savingthemselves/ (visited on 02/05/2025) (cit. on p. 144).

[450]   Google for Developers (2025). *Earth Engine Data Catalog.* URL: https://develop ers.google.com/earth-engine/datasets/catalog/ (visited on 02/05/2025) (cit. on p. 154).

[451]   Freedman, A. (Oct. 2021). *New wildfire risk monitoring tool unveiled.* Axios. URL: https://www.axios.com/2021/10/22/wildfire-risk-monitoring-tool-terrafuse-ai/ (visited on 02/05/2025) (cit. on p. 154).

[452]   Jones, T. (July 2019). *What Are the Gold-Backed Stablecoins?* Airdrop Alert. URL: https://blogs.airdropalert.com/what-are-the-gold-backed-stablecoins/ (visited on 02/05/2025) (cit. on p. 154).

[453]   Mattereum (2025). *Just One World For Business With Mattereum.* MTRM Industries Limited. URL: https://mattereum.com/ (visited on 02/05/2025) (cit. on p. 154).

[454]   Grigg, I. (July 2004). *The Ricardian Contract.* Satoshi Nakamoto Institute. URL: https://nakamotoinstitute.org/the-ricardian-contract/ (visited on 02/05/2025) (cit. on p. 154).

[455]   CIVIC (2025). *Seamless user management.* Civic Technologies. URL: https://civi c.com/ (visited on 02/05/2025) (cit. on p. 155).

[456]   brightID (2025). *Proof of Uniqueness.* URL: https://www.brightid.org/ (visited on 02/05/2025) (cit. on p. 155).

[457]   Markham, J. W. (Nov. 2001). *Volumes 1-3 of A Financial History of the United States.* England: Routledge. ISBN: 978-0-7656-0730-0 (cit. on pp. 156, 198, 227, 230).

[458]   Giambruno, N. (2023). *The International Monetary System Is on the Verge of Collapse... Here's What Comes Next.* Doug Casey's International Man. URL: https://internationalman.com/articles/the-international-monetary-system-i s-on-the-verge-of-collapse-heres-what-comes-next/ (visited on 02/05/2025) (cit. on pp. 156, 237).

[459]   Ramis, H., D. Kenney, and C. Miller (1978). *Animal House.* Motion picture. Comedy film, 109 minutes, released July 28, 1978. Screenplay by Harold Ramis, Douglas C. Kenney, and Chris Miller. Score by Elmer Bernstein. Hollywood, California. URL: https://www.imdb.com/title/tt0077975/ (visited on 07/06/2025) (cit. on p. 157).

[460]   The Modex Team (Mar. 2018). *A brief history of blockchain, smart contracts and their implementation.* (From the link, search on: A brief history of blockchain). Medium.com. URL: https://medium.com/@modex_tech (visited on 02/05/2025) (cit. on p. 160).

[461]   Lenin, V. I. (1902). *What Is To Be Done? Burning Questions of Our Movement.* Pamphlet, first published March 1902. Stuttgart. URL: https://www.marxists.or g/archive/lenin/works/1901/witbd/ (visited on 06/19/2025) (cit. on p. 173).

[462]   Corballis, M. C. (Mar. 2000). "Phylogeny from apes to humans." In: *The Descent of Mind: Psychological Perspectives on Hominid Evolution*. Ed. by Corballis, M. C. and Lea, S. E. G. Oxford: Oxford University Press, pp. 40–70. ISBN: 978-0-19-263259-3. DOI: 10.1093/acprof:oso/9780192632593.003.0003 (cit. on p. 174).

[463]   Gintis, H., C. van Schaik, and C. Boehm (June 2015). "Zoon Politikon." In: *Current Anthropology* 56.3 (cit. on pp. 174, 175).

[464]   Turnbull, C. M. (1965). "The Mbuti Pygmies." In: *Anthropological Papers of the American Museum of Natural History*. Vol. 50. 3. New York: American Museum of Natural History (cit. on p. 174).

[465]   —   (1966). *Wayward Servants*. London: Eyre & Spottlswoode (cit. on p. 174).

[466]   Lee, R. B. (1979). *The !Kung San*. Cambridge: Cambridge University Press (cit. on p. 174).

[467]   Marshall, L. (1976). *The !Kung of Nyae Nyae*. Cambridge, MA: Harvard University Press (cit. on p. 174).

[468]   Lee, R. B. and I. Devore (1976). *Kalahari Hunter-Gatherers: Studies of the !Kung San and Their Neighbors*. Cambridge, MA: Harvard University Press (cit. on p. 174).

[469]   Wiessner, P. W. (1976). *Hxaro: a regional system of reciprocity for reducing risk among the !Kung San*. Ph. D. Thesis (cit. on p. 174).

[470]   Morris, B. (1975). *An Analysis of the Economy and Social Organisation of the Malapantaram, a South Indian hunting and gathering people*. Ph. D. Thesis (cit. on p. 174).

[471]   Gardner, P. M. (1972). "The Paliyans." In: *Hunters and Gatherers Today*. Ed. by Bicchieri, M. G. New York: Holt, Rinehart & Winston (cit. on p. 174).

[472]   Endicott, K. M. (1974). *Batek Negrito Economy and Social Organisation*. Ph. D. Thesis (cit. on p. 174).

[473]   —   (1979a). *Batek Negrito religion: the world-view and rituals of a hunting and gathering people of Peninsular Malaysia*. New York: Clarendon Press (cit. on p. 174).

[474]   Endicott, K. L. (1979b). *Batek Negrito sex roles*. Master's Thesis (cit. on p. 174).

[475]   Woodburn, J. C. (1968a). "An Introduction to Hadza Ecology." In: *Man the Hunter*. Ed. by Lee, R. B. and DeVore, I. Chicago: Aldine Publishing Company (cit. on p. 174).

[476]   —   (1968b). "Stability and Flexibility in Hadza Residential Groupings." In: *Man the Hunter*. Ed. by Lee, R. B. and DeVore, I. Chicago: Aldine Publishing Company (cit. on p. 174).

[477]   —   (1970). *Hunters and Gatherers*. London: The British Museum (cit. on p. 174).

[478]   —   (1972). "Ecology, Nomadic Movement and the Composition of the Local Group Among Hunters and Gatherers." In: *Man, Settlement and Urbanism*. Ed. by Ucko, P. J., Tringham, R., and Dimbleby, G. W. London: Duckworth (cit. on p. 174).

[479]   —   (Sept. 1982). "Egalitarian Societies." In: *Man (N.S.)* 17.3, pp. 431–51 (cit. on p. 174).

[480]   Gray, P. (2013). *Free To Learn*. New York: Basic Books (cit. on p. 174).

[481]   Boehm, C. (1993). "Egalitarian Behavior and Reverse Dominance Hierarchy." In: *Current Anthropology* 34.3, pp. 227–54 (cit. on p. 174).

[482] — (1999). *Hierarchy in the Forest: The Evolution of Egalitarian Behavior.* Cambridge, MA: Harvard University Press (cit. on pp. 174, 175).

[483] Graeber, D. and D. Wengrow (Mar. 2018). *How to change the course of human history.* Eurozine. URL: https://www.eurozine.com/change-course-human-hist ory/ (visited on 03/10/2025) (cit. on pp. 175, 176).

[484] Marshak, A. (1989). "Evolution of the human Capacity: The Symbolic Evidence." In: *Yearbook of Physical Anthropology* 32.S10, pp. 1–34. DOI: 10.1002/ajpa.13303 20503 (cit. on p. 175).

[485] — (1992). "The Origin of Language: An Anthropological Approach." In: *Language Origin: A Multidisciplinary Approach.* Ed. by Wind, J. et al. Dordrecht, Boston and London: Kluwer Academic Publishers, pp. 421–48. ISBN: 978-0-7923-1369-4 (cit. on p. 175).

[486] Lee, R. B. (Jan. 1988). "Reflections on Primitive Communism." In: *Hunters and Gatherers. History, Evolution and Social Change Volume I.* Ed. by Ingold, T., Riches, D., and Woodburn, J. C. Explorations in anthropology. Oxford: Berg Publishers, pp. 252–68. ISBN: 978-0-85496-734-6 (cit. on p. 175).

[487] Bregman, R. (May 2020). *The real Lord of the Flies: what happened when six boys were shipwrecked for 15 months.* The Guardian. URL: https://www.theguardian .com/books/2020/may/09/the-real-lord-of-the-flies-what-happened-when-six-boys-were-shipwrecked-for-15-months (visited on 03/03/2025) (cit. on p. 176).

[488] Venkataraman, V. V. (July 2024). *The Ju/'hoansi protocol. Hunter-gatherer societies are highly expert in group deliberation and decision-making which respects both difference and unity.* Aeon Media Group Ltd. URL: https://aeon.co/essay s/what-the-ju-hoansi-can-tell-us-about-group-decision-making (visited on 02/05/2025) (cit. on p. 176).

[489] Sheldrake, R. (2013). *The Sense of Being Stared At.* Rochester, Vermont: Park Street Press. ISBN: 978-1-62055-097-7 (cit. on pp. 185, 207).

[490] Horgan, J. (July 2014). *Scientific Heretic Rupert Sheldrake on Morphic Fields, Psychic Dogs and Other Mysteries.* Scientific American. URL: https://www.scien tificamerican.com/blog/cross-check/scientific-heretic-rupert-sheldrake-on-mo rphic-fields-psychic-dogs-and-other-mysteries/ (visited on 02/05/2025) (cit. on pp. 185, 207).

[491] Sheff, D. (Dec. 2000). *All We Are Saying: The Last Major Interview with John Lennon and Yoko Ono.* New York: St. Martin's Griffin, an Imprint of St. Martin's Press. ISBN: 978-1-250-62506-9 (cit. on p. 185).

[492] Bohm, D. (1994). *Thought as a System.* London, England: Routledge, an imprint of the Taylor & Francis Group. ISBN: 0-415-11030-0 (cit. on pp. 191, 203, 205).

[493] — (1998). *On Creativity.* London, England: Routledge, an imprint of the Taylor & Francis Group. ISBN: 0-415-17396-5 (cit. on pp. 191, 203, 205).

[494] Kean, S. (2017). *Caesar's Last Breath.* New York, Boston, London: Little, Brown and Company. ISBN: 978-0-316-38164-2 (cit. on p. 194).

[495] Carroll, L. (1871). *Through the Looking Glass.* London: Macmillan & Co. (cit. on p. 194).

[496] Johnstone, C. (Mar. 2019b). *America's Venezuela Strategy: Coup By Sheer Narrative Controls.* Caitlin Johnstone Rogue Journalist. URL: https://caitlinjohnstone.c om/2019/03/20/americas-venezuela-strategy-coup-by-sheer-narrative-control/ (visited on 02/05/2025) (cit. on p. 195).

[497] Freeman, K. D. (Sept. 2022). *According to Plan*. California: Liberty Hawk Publishing (cit. on p. 195).

[498] Cameron, J., D. Giler, and W. Hill (1986). *Aliens*. Motion picture. Science fiction action film, 137 minutes, released July 18, 1986. Screenplay by James Cameron, based on a story by James Cameron, David Giler, and Walter Hill. Score by James Horner. Los Angeles, California. URL: https://www.imdb.com/title/tt0090605/ (visited on 07/06/2025) (cit. on p. 195).

[499] Day, A. (Aug. 2024). *Fifty Shades of Central Bank Tyranny*. Brownstone Institute. URL: https://brownstone.org/articles/fifty-shades-of-central-bank-tyranny/ (visited on 02/05/2025) (cit. on p. 196).

[500] Burrowes, R. J. (Sept. 2024). *The Brave New World of 2030: 'You'll Own Nothing. And You'll be Happy.'* Center for Research on Globalization. URL: https://www.globalresearch.ca/brave-new-world-2030-own-nothing-happy/5864030 (visited on 02/05/2025) (cit. on p. 196).

[501] Edmond, C. (July 2017). *Yes, you really can plant trees all over a city to make it cleaner and better*. World Economic Forum. URL: https://www.weforum.org/agenda/2017/07/welcome-to-china-s-urban-forest/ (visited on 02/05/2025) (cit. on pp. 196, 197).

[502] Wigington, D. (2021). *The Dimming*. Geoengineering Watch. URL: https://geoengineeringwatch.org/the-dimming-full-length-climate-engineering-documentary/ (visited on 05/07/2025) (cit. on p. 196).

[503] Prashad, V. (June 2025). "Where hundreds of millions are dying of hunger." In: *Cold Type* 270, pp. 26–7. URL: https://www.coldtype.net/Assets23/PDFs/ColdType270June2025.pdf (visited on 06/02/2025) (cit. on pp. 196, 197).

[504] Engelhart, M. (Mar. 2025). *Why Are We Ignoring the Most Powerful Climate Solution?* Epoch Times. URL: https://www.theepochtimes.com/opinion/why-are-we-ignoring-the-most-powerful-climate-solution-5819166 (visited on 03/07/2025) (cit. on p. 197).

[505] Rebel Educator (Apr. 2023). *AI could be a grassroots revolution*. Substack. URL: https://rebeleducator.substack.com/p/ai-could-be-a-grassroots-revolution (visited on 02/05/2025) (cit. on p. 197).

[506] Pretty, J. (Feb. 2008). "Agricultural sustainability: concepts, principles and evidence." In: *Philos. Trans. R. Soc. B: Biol. Sci.* 363.491, pp. 447–65. ISSN: 09628436, 14712970. DOI: 10.1098/rstb.2007.2163 (cit. on p. 197).

[507] Carrington, D. (July 2019b). *Tree planting 'has mind-blowing potential' to tackle climate crisis*. The Guardian). URL: https://www.theguardian.com/environment/2019/jul/04/planting-billions-trees-best-tackle-climate-crisis-scientists-canopy-emissions (visited on 02/05/2025) (cit. on p. 197).

[508] Dyson, F. J. (Sept. 1997b). "Can we control the carbon dioxide in the atmosphere?" In: *Energy* 2.3, pp. 287–91. DOI: 10.1016/0360-5442(77)90033-0 (cit. on p. 197).

[509] Morris, C. (Apr. 2020). *Why We Need More Than a Trillion Trees*. Climate Xchange. URL: https://climate-xchange.org/2020/04/why-we-need-more-than-a-trillion-trees/ (visited on 03/03/2025) (cit. on p. 197).

[510] Pulgar-Vidal, M. (May 2019). *Natural ecosystems are key to tackling climate change*. Aeon. URL: https://medium.com/wwftogetherpossible/natural-ecosystems-are-key-to-tackling-climate-change-2d5daa01fec (visited on 03/06/2025) (cit. on p. 197).

[511]   Monument, A. (Jan. 2019). *Can we halt runaway climate change? Forests hold the key*. World Wildlife Fund. URL: https://wwf.medium.com/can-we-halt-runaway-climate-change-forests-hold-the-key-fb2f38c0d4d9 (visited on 03/07/2025) (cit. on p. 197).

[512]   TNC (Oct. 2017). *Nature's Make or Break Potential for Climate Change*. The Nature Conservancy. URL: https://www.nature.org/en-us/what-we-do/our-insights/perspectives/natures-make-or-break-potential-for-climate-change/ (visited on 03/10/2025) (cit. on p. 197).

[513]   Nikolov, N. and K. F. Zeller (Aug. 2024). "Roles of Earth's Albedo Variations and Top-of-the-Atmosphere Energy Imbalance in Recent Warming: New Insights from Satellite and Surface Observations." In: *Geomatics* 4.3, pp. 311–41. ISSN: 2673-7418. DOI: 10.3390/geomatics4030017 (cit. on p. 197).

[514]   Finley, R. (2004). *Poison Darts*. Russ Finley. ISBN: 0-9742938-1-4 (cit. on p. 197).

[515]   Iraji, A. (May 2024). *Overpopulation Reconsidered: A Decentralized Approach*. Mises Institute. URL: https://mises.org/mises-wire/overpopulation-reconsidered-decentralized-approach/ (visited on 02/05/2025) (cit. on p. 198).

[516]   Hornberger, J. G. (Dec. 2022). *The Fed's Destructive Guessing Game*. Future of Freedom Foundation. URL: https://www.fff.org/2022/12/15/the-feds-destructive-guessing-game/ (visited on 02/05/2025) (cit. on p. 198).

[517]   Peters, G. and J. T. Woolley (Jan. 1934). *Proclamation 2072 - Fixing the Weight of the Gold Dollar*. The American Presidency Project. URL: https://www.presidency.ucsb.edu/node/208125/ (visited on 02/05/2025) (cit. on pp. 198, 231).

[518]   Roosevelt, F. D. (Feb. 1934). *Proclamation 2072 - Fixing the Weight of the Gold Dollar*. Wikisource. URL: https://en.wikisource.org/wiki/Fixing_the_Weight_of_the_Gold_Dollar,_1934 (visited on 02/05/2025) (cit. on pp. 198, 231).

[519]   Snyder, M. (May 2024). *Our Deer In The Headlights Moment: The "Worst Market Crash Since 1929" Is Rapidly Approaching And The Fed Doesn't Know Which Way To Go*. The Economic Collapse Blog. URL: https://theeconomiccollapseblog.com/our-deer-in-the-headlights-moment-the-worst-market-crash-since-1929-is-rapidly-approaching-and-the-fed-doesnt-know-which-way-to-go/ (visited on 02/05/2025) (cit. on p. 199).

[520]   The Syndicate.Info (2013). *Arctic Death Spiral and the Methane Time Bomb*. Youtube. URL: https://www.youtube.com/watch?v=m6pFDu7lLV4 (visited on 02/05/2025) (cit. on p. 200).

[521]   Washington State (2018). *Initiative Measure No. 1631 concerns pollution*. Washington (cit. on p. 200).

[522]   Amadeo, K. (2019). *Why the US Dollar Is the Global Currency*. the balance. URL: https://www.thebalance.com/world-currency-3305931 (visited on 02/05/2025) (cit. on p. 202).

[523]   Kaplan, J. (Jan. 2020). *Peter Singer - ordinary people are evil*. Youtube. URL: https://www.youtube.com/watch?v=KVl5kMXz1vA/ (visited on 02/05/2025) (cit. on p. 202).

[524]   Singer, P. (1972). "Famine, Affluence, and Morality." In: *Philos. Public Aff.* 1.3, pp. 229–43. ISSN: 10884963, 00483915. URL: https://www.jstor.org/stable/2265052 (visited on 02/05/2025) (cit. on p. 202).

[525]   Weiser, S. and O. Stone (1987). *Wall Street*. Motion picture. Drama film, 126 minutes, released December 11, 1987. Screenplay by Stanley Weiser and Oliver

Stone. Score by Stewart Copeland. Los Angeles, California. URL: https://www.i mdb.com/title/tt0094291/ (visited on 07/06/2025) (cit. on p. 210).

[526]   Richardson, G. and J. Romero (Dec. 2015). *The Meeting at Jekyll Island*. Federal Reserve History. URL: https://www.federalreservehistory.org/essays/jekyll_isl and_conference (visited on 02/05/2025) (cit. on p. 215).

[527]   Richards, L. L. (2002). *Shays's Rebellion*. Philadelphia: University of Pennsylvania Press. ISBN: 0-8122-1870-1 (cit. on p. 215).

[528]   Stockman, D. (June 2019). *The 'Deficits Don't Matter' Folly*. LewRockwell. URL: https://www.lewrockwell.com/2019/06/david-stockman/the-deficits-dont-mat ter-folly/ (visited on 02/05/2025) (cit. on p. 219).

[529]   Drew, K. F., ed. (1991). *The Laws of the Salian Franks*. Philadelphia, PA: University of Pennsylvania Press. ISBN: 978-0-8122-1322-5 (cit. on p. 223).

[530]   Rivers, T. J., ed. (1977). *Laws of the Alamans and Bavarians*. Philadelphia, PA: University of Pennsylvania Press. ISBN: 978-0-8122-7731-9 (cit. on p. 223).

[531]   Wormald, P. (Oct. 1999). *The Making of English Law: King Alfred to the Twelfth Century. Vol. 1: Legislation and Its Limits*. Oxford, UK: Blackwell Publishers Ltd. ISBN: 978-0-631-13496-1 (cit. on p. 223).

[532]   Cronon, W. (2003). *Changes in the Land: Indians, Colonists, and the Ecology of New England*. Revised. New York: Hill and Wang. ISBN: 978-0-8090-1634-1 (cit. on p. 223).

[533]   Ceci, L. (1982). "The Value of Wampum among the New York Iroquois: A Case Study in Artifact Analysis." In: *J. Anthropol. Res.* 38.1, pp. 97–107. ISSN: 0091-7710. DOI: 10.1086/jar.38.1.3629847 (cit. on p. 223).

[534]   Fenton, W. N. (1998). *The Great Law and the Longhouse: A Political History of the Iroquois Confederacy*. Norman: University of Oklahoma Press. ISBN: 0-8061-3003-2 (cit. on p. 223).

[535]   Richter, D. K. (1992). *The Ordeal of the Longhouse: The Peoples of the Iroquois League in the Era of European Colonization*. Chapel Hill: University of North Carolina Press. ISBN: 978-0-8078-4394-9 (cit. on p. 223).

[536]   Hendy, M. F. (1985). *Studies in the Byzantine Monetary Economy c.300–1450*. Cambridge: Cambridge University Press. ISBN: 978-0-521-24715-3 (cit. on p. 223).

[537]   Banaji, J. (July 2001). *Agrarian Change in Late Antiquity: Gold, Labour, and Aristocratic Dominance*. Oxford: Oxford University Press. ISBN: 978-0-19-924440-9 (cit. on p. 223).

[538]   Pritchard, J. B., ed. (Dec. 1969). *Ancient Near Eastern Texts Relating to the Old Testament*. 3rd with Supplement. Princeton: Princeton University Press. ISBN: 978-0-691-03503-1 (cit. on p. 223).

[539]   Botterweck, G. J., H. Ringgren, and H.-J. Fabry, eds. (2006). *Theological Dictionary of the Old Testament*. Vol. 15. Grand Rapids: Wm. B. Eerdmans Publishing Co. ISBN: 978-0-8028-2339-7 (cit. on p. 223).

[540]   Kletter, R. (1998). *Economic Keystones: The Weight System of the Kingdom of Judah*. Journal for the Study of the Old Testament Supplement Series. Sheffield: Sheffield Academic Press. ISBN: 978-1-85075-920-1 (cit. on p. 223).

[541]   Grierson, P. (1979). *Dark Age Numismatics: Selected Studies*. London: Variorum Reprints. ISBN: 978-0-86078-041-0 (cit. on p. 224).

[542]   Wray, L. R. (2015). *Modern Money Theory. A Primer on Macroeconomics for Sovereign Monetary Systems*. 2nd ed. Explores the state's role in defining money

through its monetary system and tax policies, emphasizing money as a state monopoly. London: Palgrave Macmillan. ISBN: 978-1-137-53991-5 (cit. on p. 225).

[543] Schelling, T. C. (1960). *The Strategy of Conflict*. Cambridge: Harvard University Press. ISBN: 978-0-674-84031-7 (cit. on pp. 225, 245).

[544] Editors of Wiktionary (2025). *thaler*. Wiktionary. URL: https://en.wiktionary.or g/wiki/thaler (visited on 02/05/2025) (cit. on p. 226).

[545] Editors of Encyclopaedia Britannica (2025). *Jáchymov*. Encyclopaedia Britannica. URL: https://www.britannica.com/place/Jachymov (visited on 02/05/2025) (cit. on p. 226).

[546] Silver Coins (2025). *Silver Thaler Coin*. URL: https://www.silver-coins.org/articl es/coin-history/silver-thaler-coin.html (visited on 03/05/2025) (cit. on pp. 226, 227).

[547] Fraňková, R. (Jan. 2020). *Predecessor of US dollar minted 500 years ago in Jáchymov*. Radio Prague Int. URL: https://english.radio.cz/predecessor-us-dollar-min ted-500-years-ago-jachymov-8111166/ (visited on 02/05/2025) (cit. on pp. 226, 227).

[548] Owen, R. L. (1939). *National economy and the banking system of the United States: an exposition of the principles of modern monetary science in their relation to the national economy and the banking system of the United States*. Washington: United States Government Printing Office (cit. on p. 230).

[549] Kirchubel, M. A. (July 2009). *Vile Acts of Evil. Volume 1 Banking in America*. CreateSpace Independent Publishing Platform. ISBN: 978-1-4486-4225-0 (cit. on p. 230).

[550] Del Mar, A. (1899). *The History of Money In America. From the Earliest Times to the Establishment of the Constitution*. 62 Reade Street, New York: The Cambridge Encyclopedia Company (cit. on p. 230).

[551] Pense, A. W. (Sept. 1992). "The Decline and Fall of the Roman *Denarius*." In: *Mater. Charact.* 29.2, pp. 213–22. ISSN: 10445803. DOI: 10.1016/1044-5803(92)901 16-Y (cit. on p. 230).

[552] Angell, J. W. (1934). "Gold, Banks, and the New Deal." In: *Polit. Sci. Q.* 49.4, pp. 481–505. ISSN: 0032-3195 (cit. on p. 231).

[553] Richardson, G., A. Komai, and M. Gou (Nov. 2013). *Gold Reserve Act of 1934*. Federal Reserve History. URL: https://www.federalreservehistory.org/essays/g old-reserve-act (visited on 02/05/2025) (cit. on p. 231).

[554] Peters, G. and J. T. Woolley (Apr. 1933). *Executive Order 6102 — Forbidding the Hoarding of Gold Coin, Gold Bullion and Gold Certificates*. The American Presidency Project. URL: https://www.presidency.ucsb.edu/node/208042/ (visited on 02/05/2025) (cit. on p. 231).

[555] Hornberger, J. G. (June 2023). *What Debt Ceiling?* Future of Freedom Foundation. URL: https://www.fff.org/2023/06/01/what-debt-ceiling/ (visited on 02/05/2025) (cit. on p. 232).

[556] belangp (May 2020). *Gold The Truth Hidden in Plain Sight part 6 Not Fiat but not Fixed Gold Backing Either*. YouTube. URL: https://www.youtube.com/watch ?v=YMUtayfendY (visited on 02/05/2025) (cit. on p. 233).

[557] Wen, Y. and B. Reinbold (May 2020). *The Changing Relationship between Trade and America's Gold Reserves*. Federal Reserve Bank of St. Louis (Regional Economist). URL: https://www.stlouisfed.org/publications/regional-econom

ist/first-quarter-2020/changing-relationship-trade-americas-gold-reserves/ (visited on 02/05/2025) (cit. on p. 236).

[558] Board of Governors (Sept. 2023). *Federal Reserve Balance Sheet: Factors Affecting Reserve Balances - H.4.1.* URL: https://www.federalreserve.gov/releases/h41/202 30921/h41.pdf (visited on 02/05/2025) (cit. on p. 237).

[559] Carnevale, D. C. (2013). "Carbon Sequestration Potential of the Coast Range Ophiolite in California." MA thesis. Kingston, Rhode Island. DOI: 10.23860/thes is-carnevale-daniel-2013 (cit. on p. 249).

[560] Montserrat, F. et al. (2017). "Olivine Dissolution in Seawater: Implications for CO_2 Sequestration through Enhanced Weathering in Coastal Environments." In: *Environ. Sci. Technol.* 51.7, pp. 3960–72. ISSN: 0013-936X. DOI: 10.1021/acs.es t.6b05942 (cit. on p. 249).

[561] Leahy, S. (Oct. 2019b). *Earth's rocks can absorb a shocking amount of carbon: here's how.* National Geographic Society. URL: https://www.nationalgeographi c.com/science/2019/10/earth-rocks-can-absorb-shocking-amount-of-carbon/ (visited on 02/05/2025) (cit. on p. 249).

[562] Hazen, R. M. (2019). *Symphony in C.* New York, London: W. W. Norton & Company. ISBN: 978-0-393-60943-1 (cit. on p. 249).

[563] Boomitra (2025). *Unlocking Carbon Removal on a Gigaton Scale.* URL: https://bo omitra.com/ (visited on 02/05/2025) (cit. on p. 249).

[564] Penrose, R. (1989). *The Emperor's New Mind.* New York, New York: Penguin Books. ISBN: 0 14 01.4534 6 (cit. on p. 254).